Broken and Whole

D1524655

ESSAYS ON RELIGION AND THE BODY

BT
10
C62
1993

EDITED BY

Maureen A. Tilley and *Susan A. Ross*
The Florida State University   Loyola University, Chicago

THE ANNUAL PUBLICATION OF THE
COLLEGE THEOLOGY SOCIETY

1993

VOLUME 39

Regis College Library
15 ST. MARY STREET
TORONTO, ONTARIO, CANADA
M4Y 2R5

UNIVERSITY
PRESS OF
AMERICA

Lanham • New York • London

Copyright © 1995 by
The College Theology Society

University Press of America®, Inc.
4720 Boston Way
Lanham, Maryland 20706

3 Henrietta Street
London WC2E 8LU England

All rights reserved
Printed in the United States of America
British Cataloging in Publication Information Available

Copublished by arrangement with the
College Theology Society

Library of Congress Cataloging-in-Publication Data

Broken and whole: essays on religion and the body / edited by Maureen A. Tilley and
Susan A. Ross
p. cm. — (The Annual publication of the College
Theology Society ; v. 39)
1. Body, Human—Religious aspects—Christianity. I. Tilley, Maureen A. II. Ross,
Susan A. III. Series

| BT741.2.B75 1994 | 94-34566 |
| 233'.5—dc20 | CIP |

ISBN 0-8191-9746-7 (cloth: alk paper)
ISBN 0-8191-9747-5 (paper: alk paper)

⊖™ The paper used in this publication meets the minimum requirements of
American National Standard for Information Sciences—Permanence of
Paper for Printed Library Materials, ANSI Z39.48–1964.

CONTENTS

Introduction:

Embodied Religion

It was the perfect place for a conference, a college high in the hills above the San Francisco Bay. The summer sun glinted off the rocks jutting out of the fields of sun-bleached grass. The warm rays bathed the people who stood conversing on the hillside. They were warmed down to their bones. Their toes were toasted as they stood on the hard black asphalt of the parking lot next to the college dormitory. The lot had been recently paved and the sun kept the surface just a little soft under their feet. One man adjusted the visor of his cap, a woman put on her sunglasses, and another man shaded his squinting eyes with his hand. Still the brilliant orange of poppies and the intense blue of cornflowers assaulted their eyes. All was warm and bright.

Then as the day waned, cool breezes swept across the campus. The conference participants pulled their sweaters and jackets a little more snugly around them. A woman tightened her scarf against the wind. Little knots of people descended from the hills to shady verandas and shadowy passages which led to the darkened interior of the white-washed chapel of the college. There cool water was poured on their hands as songs and incense drifted across the pews and aisles and swirled around the polychrome statues. By the time the Eucharist had ended, all the senses had been stimulated.

One evening during the meeting, lightning from a summer storm caused a power outage. As the conference participants lit candles to illuminate a room, light and shadows sculpted the faces of old friends in new ways. Toward midnight they stumbled in the unfamiliar darkness of the dormitory rooms and the contours of their bodies met the immovable corners of desks and bed posts.

There in California, the origin of so many theories of the nature of the body, the home of countless body-oriented therapies, members of the College Theology Society met for their 1993 Annual Meeting at St. Mary's College of Moraga. The theme of the meeting was "Religion and the Body." Perhaps there could be no better place to think and speak of the body than this environment which invited a reacquaintance with one's own body in a strange spaces alternately warm and light, then cool and dark.

Why would a professional society of theologians gather to converse and debate about the body when issues of war and peace, justice, feminism, Bible and sacraments all called to them with urgent voices? Be assured, gentle reader, this was no flight from reality, no disengagement from the intellectual life, no retreat into sentiment and sensuality. The Society chose the theme "Religion and the Body" for its contemporary relevance to the work of the Society and to the challenges facing today's Church.

Why the body? Besides the fact that everybody has one, there were other reasons. Contemporary film and print advertising has testified to the power of images of the body. The proliferation of studies on mind/body, sacramentality, the body in antiquity, the history of sexuality, etc., still attest a lively interest in the topic within the scholarly world. Study of the body and embodied life has brought significant change to the theological, philosophical and historical disciplines which are home to the members of the Society. In addition, academics have been perennially challenged when they see that both the general society and popular religious praxis lack a consensus on the significance of the body despite credal professions about its value. The situation is no less so in the present. Today's controversial religious issues in Catholicism are all issues of embodiment: women's ordination, priestly celibacy, abortion. Authority is an issue primarily in relationship to body issues. By focusing on the body and the sacramental Church, members of the College Theology Society have the opportunity to develop strategies for the shaping of the Church of the future instead of merely recording and analyzing its history.

Broken and Whole: Essays on Religion and the Body contains some of the best presentations made by members of the College Theology Society at its 1993 conference at the sun-drenched campus of St. Mary's Moraga. Amidst the glory of the flowering fields and quiet darkness of the night, members of the Society reflected on religion and the body, exploring the implications of the human body for religious experience. They follow in the footsteps of Christians throughout history who have tried to make sense of embodied existence.

The writings of the earliest Christians were permeated with

language about the body, with language about the broken and the whole. This should be no surprise in a religion which professes the incarnation, the embodiment, of the Divine. In the Gospel of John, one finds a meditation on the mystery of embodied existence in the metaphorical saying attributed to Jesus: "Unless a grain of wheat falls into the earth and dies, it remains just a single grain; but if it dies, it bears much fruit" (Jn. 12.24 NRSV). Within a generation of the death of Jesus, Christians celebrated the death of their Lord in the broken and the whole. Paul wrote to his converts: "The bread that we break, is it not a sharing in the body of Christ?" (1 Cor. 10.16 NRSV). Other Christians reflected in a similar manner. One of the earliest liturgical texts which articulated the relationship between this being broken and whole as the Church, the body of Christ, is preserved in the *Didache*: "Just as the bread broken was first scattered on the hills, then was gathered and became one, so let your Church be gathered from the ends of the earth into your kingdom, for yours is glory and power through all ages."[1] The theme of the broken and the whole surfaces in this literature precisely at the point where the authors declare the unity of Christians with, in, and through Christ, i.e., in the body of Christ and the bodies of the Christians.

The authors of the essays in this volume challenge the readers to consider the body specifically in relation to religion. Part I: Historical Perspectives on Religion and the Body, contains selections which address issues of embodiment with very particular historical contexts. In the first essay, "Desire and Delight: A New Reading of Augustine's *Confessions*," Margaret Miles sounds a wake-up call for the consideration of religion and the body for all of the conference participants. As a plenary speaker she drew attention to the power and beauty of the *Confessions*. She spoke of its seductive qualities which induce an obedient reading of the text, obedience both to Augustine and to his interpreters over the last millennium and a half, especially in their construction of the body. She also rehearsed her own conversion to a new and gendered disobedient reading of the text.

In response to Professor Miles' plenary address, Morny Joy offers her "Incontinent Observations" which highlight the methodological foundations of Professor Miles' reading. She then proceeds with her own "disobedience" to ask irreverent and impertinent questions regarding the historical reading of gendered bodies. Her observations expose the cultural conditioning of the readings of texts and they challenge her readers to read with new eyes.

New eyes not only see the familiar as strangely new and revelatory but they probe the dark corners for the old which had been ignored. Imitating the householder who brings out of storeroom both what is new and what is old (Matt. 13.52), Frederick G. McLeod reaches into the treasure trove of Christianity and draws from its ancient shelf the insights of "The Antiochene Tradition Regarding the Role of the Body Within the 'Image of God'." If humanity was, according to classic anthropology, a whole of parts, an entity of body and soul, where would one find 'the image of God' in each human being? The dominant view of ancient Christianity was that under the influence of neo-platonic thought the image of God was found in the soul, the spiritual side of human beings, because it was most closely related to the spiritual Being of its creator. In an approach manifestly different from Augustine and the Alexandrians, the Antiochene answers were eminently biblical and often surprising. Their reply located the image of God in the human being but not in the soul alone. A variety of answers included the human being as a composite whole and, at least among the Edessenes, the body itself provides an image of God.

But the body shows more than the image of God. James Gaffney in "Body as Moral Metaphor in Dante's *Commedia*" describes how bodies reveal the totality of the person including the state of the soul. Their varied circumstances in the afterlife, their postures, and actions serve Dante as metaphors for the moral condition of the whole person. Gaffney's perceptive comments help everyone who had ever read the *Commedia* to see, hear, and feel in their own persons the poetry of the Italian master.

Finally, from the more modern shelf of the household of faith William Madges draws his insights on how the individualism of the Enlightenment made its mark in nineteenth-century Germany. In "Sex, Celibacy, and the Modern Self in Nineteenth-Century Germany," he describes the changes in sexual practices and a contemporary theological discussion of obligatory clerical celibacy. His article strikes a singularly modern note which brings us to the second part of the volume.

The essays in Part II: Critical Perspectives on Christianity and the Body, take a serious look at the ways in which metaphors of the body play out in Christian theology. From Polynesian religions to computers, from the rainforests to Freud, our essayists ask what difference it makes if we take the human body, as well as the entire body of creation, seriously. Often these answers are that Christianity has failed to nurture its own incarnational roots, or, worse, has sold this heritage for a mess of Gnostic pottage. Jill Raitt's keynote address, "Christianity, Inc.," plays on the multiple ways in which Christianity is a corporate entity: negatively, as an organization which engages in hostile take-overs of other religious traditions; positively, as a tradition in which membership means incorporation into the body of Christ. Her experience at the East-West Center and in the religious tradition of the Polynesian peoples impelled her to "re-own" her own tradition in seeing how in "the many faces of the people of God, the face of God becomes clearer" (p. 112).

In his response, "Inkblots and Authenticity," William Loewe suggests that Bernard Lonergan's ideas provide a helpful focus for the issues that Raitt has raised. The need for intellectual, moral and religious conversion that Lonergan outlines in his work may steer the thinking Christian through both the commitment to one's own tradition as *true* and the necessary critical attitude of its historical manifestations to a chastened "reappropriation" of the tradition.

Next, Gary Mann brings a very old idea--Gnosticism--to a consideration of some very new realities--the electronic age of information systems. In "Em-Bodied Spirit/In-Spired Matter: Against Tech-Gnosticism," Mann claims that, like the ancients, we have become dualists: we seek escape from the natural world to superior, unearthly cyber-space. But in the sciences, a new paradigm of reality is emerging: one that sees it as "staccatic" (broken, discontinuous), thematic, and alive. By revisioning the Christian idea of Spirit in terms of contemporary science and theology, a new paradigm of God's dynamic energy as embodied in the world emerges.

The next three essays were originally given as a panel response to Sallie McFague's book, *The Body of God*,[2] which had been published just prior to the convention. In "The World as God's Body: Theological Ethics and Panentheism," William C. French begins by giving a very helpful precis of the book's argument. In his critique, he suggests that the notion of sin that he finds implicit, but not fully developed by McFague, can be expanded by considering how ecological sin is embedded in social, not just individual, acts. Borrowing a page from the military, French offers the metaphor of nature as "superpower" in its capacity for retaliating against the evils of the ecological sin inflicted upon it. John P. McCarthy muses on the enormous difference between Sigmund Freud's consideration of nature in *The Future of an Illusion* and that of McFague. Rather than nature being the threat to humanity, the situation is now reversed. And this provokes McCarthy to question the seemingly inevitable anthropocentrism involved in thinking about the world as

God's body. If we are to take nature far more seriously than we ever have, does this mean that "humanity always has a ticket to the show?" (p. 149). Is it possible to de-center theology in such a way as to allow for nature itself to have a voice? Susan A. Ross offers a feminist response to McFague. Given the emphasis of much contemporary feminist thought on the social construction of gender and a critique of "natural" categories, how does a proposal like McFague's--which is, above all, to take nature seriously--respond to the issue of who defines nature? Along with this, she asks: if McFague's position is in fact the position of the wealthy, who constitute the main threat to nature, how does nature and the ecological crisis appear to the poor of the world? Might there be different questions and different responses?

Part III: Spirituality and the Body, extends the concern for the body. How does the body enhance the life of prayer, help to envision the world as a more just place, provide new ways of envisioning God? Pamela Smith's essay, "Chronic Pain and Creative Possibility," draws on her own experience with chronic illness as well as that of others who suffer with chronic physical problems. While taking issue with interpretations of suffering that see it as always redemptive and with conceptions of a God who willingly inflicts suffering on humanity, Smith nevertheless argues that physical suffering *can be*--although not necessarily is--an occasion for transformation. Envisioning God as "power with," Smith provides critical resources for understanding the complexities of illness, pain and suffering.

Joy Milos' essay, "Rosemary Haughton on Spirituality and Sexuality," draws out the English theologian's concern for the incarnate dimension of Christianity. Haughton's emphasis on the physicality of Christianity and its symbolic and mythic expression provide a substantial contribution to the tradition, one whose significance has been largely unnoticed. And finally, Sandra Schneiders's essay, "Spirituality as an Academic Discipline," considers the difficulties inherent in bringing together the rigors of intellectual pursuit with the living of a spiritual life. In sorting out the "research" and "formative" approaches to the study of spirituality, and the resources that interdisciplinary, cross-cultural and interreligious methods can bring to the discipline, Schneiders brings coherence to this body of knowledge and the bodies who study it.

The three parts of *Broken and Whole* then come full circle, from Margaret Miles' attempt to help us see the body and knowledge of the body anew to Sandra Schneider's reflections on a systematic approach to spirituality which includes embodied persons in their particular situations. We hope that our readers will join this circle. As editors, we would like to acknowledge the assistance of all the midwives of the birth of this volume. In particular we would like to express our thanks to Felicidad Oberholzer, local coordinator for Annual Meeting of the College Theology Society at Moraga. Without her efforts these papers would not have had their original audiences. We also acknowledge the graciousness of the plenary speakers, Jill Raitt and Margaret Miles, the care of the anonymous reviewers who helped us to select and refine the essays submitted by members of the Society, and the meticulous labors of Terrence Tilley who produced the camera-ready copy for our publishers.

Maureen A. Tilley

Susan A. Ross

July 25, 1994

NOTES

1. *The Didache*, in *Springtime of the Liturgy: Liturgical Texts of the First Four Centuries*, by Lucien Deiss, translated by Matthew J. O'Connell (Collegeville: Liturgical, 1979), p. 75.

2. Sallie McFague, *The Body of God: An Ecological Theology* (Minneapolis: Fortress Press, 1993).

HISTORICAL PERSPECTIVES

ON

RELIGION AND THE BODY

DESIRE AND DELIGHT:

A NEW READING OF

AUGUSTINE'S *CONFESSIONS*

Margaret R. Miles

Perhaps it should be acknowledged at the outset that my most recent reading of Augustine's *Confessions*--as a text on and about pleasure--was influenced by the *way* I read it. Let me explain. Two decades ago, as a doctoral student, I studied Augustine passionately. I wrote my dissertation on his idea of the meaning and value of the human body. Since then, however, I have reread Augustine's *Confessions* only in pieces, in pressured preparation for classes and seminars. These later readings produced an Augustine which, in his own words, was "a piece of difficult ground, not to be worked over without much sweat" (X.16). In the summer of 1989, however, I planned a markedly different reading experience. I went with three dear friends for a month to the blue-and-white Greek island of Paros, taking with me the *Confessions* in Latin. In the mornings I read Augustine excitedly, making copious notes, examining Augustine's language and grammar in detail. Afternoons, we went to a beach where I sat under a tree and pondered the morning's reading, sometimes writing pages of ideas I had about it, sometimes writing nothing, but letting ideas float in and out like the softly lapping Mediterranean--the same sea that touched Augustine's Ostia and Hippo Regius.

This experience reminded me of why I became an academic in the first place. It was for the pleasure of the kind of passionate engagement with books and ideas that I again experienced on the island of Paros. My own pleasure alerted me to an aspect of the

Confessions I had not noticed when I read it as an anxious doctoral student or, subsequently, as a harried teacher: namely that the *Confessions* is both a pleasurable text, and text that is centrally *about* pleasure. It is explicitly about desire, longing, passion--physical and spiritual--constantly both, and both most evidently when Augustine most intends to distinguish spiritual from physical. It is an erotic text, a book preoccupied with bodies, pleasures, and pains. It narrates Augustine's desperate attempt to get--and to keep--the greatest degree of pleasure.

The *Confessions* deserves to be called a great piece of literature in that it repays an almost infinite number of readings. In Augustine's colorful Latin, the *Confessions* is overwhelming; as generations of readers have testified, it is next to impossible to maintain a stance of critical detachment. Even in translation, the beauty and richness of Augustine's language, his passion and honesty, and the powerful resolution of his search for "God and the self" are evident. The reader is quickly seduced into a passionate relationship, which sometimes takes the form of violent disagreement, sometimes frustration, sometimes amazement that a North African who lived over fifteen hundred years ago could express so accurately an idea or emotion one recognizes so intimately. Reading the *Confessions* is a pleasure; this is perhaps the most straightforward meaning of my claim that it is a text of pleasure. I will assume that you have read the *Confessions* attentively; I will not reiterate Augustine's narrative, but will explore several of the "pleasures of the text," both pleasures discussed in the *Confessions*, and those belonging to the reader and interpreter of this difficult, complex, and fascinating book.

I.

Let me begin with some observations on interpretation. Reading Augustine's *Confessions* requires that one must somehow manage to see simultaneously the problems and dangers of Augustine's thought --the authoritarianism, the exclusionary strategies--*and* its extraordinary power and beauty. To insist on seeing only the problems is to imagine generation after generation of credulous readers who permitted themselves to be bullied by the text, maneuvered into positions of helpless and passive voyeurism and acquiescence to its conclusions. One must imagine readers who were willing to sacrifice their critical faculties for the mild titillation of Augustine's lifestory --cheap thrills, indeed! This interpretive stance fails to respect the myriad readers who found the *Confessions* a poignant, gripping, and even a transformative text.

On the other hand, if one reads in the *Confessions* only its powerful beauty, one is susceptible to its many seductions, its prohibitions, its silences, its politics and institutional allegiances. A text--any text, but especially a powerful text--not only reflects but also inevitably contributes to the reproduction of the social arrangements it assumes, supports, or advocates. Its values and loyalties, then, must be examined and their social and institutional effects noticed. And few would deny that the *Confessions* has played a role in forming powerful Western institutions--like monasticism, church, and marriage. Is it quite accidental that what is subordinated in the *Confessions* has largely been undervalued also in Western culture--for example, women and the natural world of bodies and senses? It cannot, of course, be claimed that the *Confessions caused* such marginalizations, but neither can it be doubted that the *Confessions* contributed to the shaping of Western values, social arrangements, and institutions.

An adequate reading of the *Confessions*, then, must demonstrate both its strong beauty and its politics because both speak simultaneously. Roland Barthes once said that you get the cultural message in the same instant that you get the pleasure. The pleasure carries and coats the message; the greater the pleasure, the more effectively and directly is the message transported. While we are entranced, we are not usually critical. And so a sort of interpretive cyclic oscillation must occur in which strands of the *Confessions* which are separated for close examination are subsequently gathered and rewoven. Although they are necessarily discussed seriatim, text, context, and subtext must subsequently be mixed, as the separate instruments on different soundtracks are mixed, if the powerful music of the text is to be heard in its full strength and beauty.

My interpretation of the *Confessions* is necessarily and inevitably directed by the specificity of my own social location as a late-twentieth century academic Anglo Saxon woman. It is, therefore, in some important sense, a disobedient reading, in that in addition to endeavoring to grasp Augustine's agenda, I notice features of the text that --although *there*--would, perhaps, not have popped into the eye of an ancient reader, or even a modern male reader. In acknowledging my perspectival reading, then, I admit only what any honest reader must "confess," namely that human beings lack a universal, transcendent, or God's-eye perspective from which to interpret, and must inevitably entail, in our interpretations, the complex sensitivities, blindnesses, and insights to which our particular experience and training has led.

One strange discovery I made in my most recent rereading of the *Confessions* is that, in my former readings, I had obediently assumed the position of the sympathetic male colleague for whom Augustine wrote. The *Confessions* was not written to be read by a woman; to read it with what is recognized as "understanding" is to read it as a man--an educated skill. As the song says: "it's second nature to me now, like breathing out and breathing in." The difficult and interesting task, then, was to notice not only Augustine's actual and authorial treatment of women, but also--and more importantly --to notice that the metaphor that dominates his construction of pleasure is male sexuality. For Augustine's sexual experience was not accidental or incidental to the primary concerns of the *Confessions*. In spite of his loud and frequent disclaimers, I suspect that Augustine learned more than he acknowledged from his sexual experience; that he learned from it what Audre Lorde has called "the deep and irreplaceable knowledge of the capacity for joy."[1]

II.

Pleasure, as Augustine knew, is one of the most puzzlingly elusive and variable of human experiences. Why, in the midst of professional achievement, friendships, and sexual relationships, did Augustine describe himself as pleasureless? In his *Confessions*, Augustine narrates his own desire from infancy forward as a compulsive grasping at every object that crossed his path in the fear that something would be missed--his word for his anxiety-ridden rapaciousness is concupiscence. In stealing pears from a neighbor's tree, in achieving professional success as a teacher of rhetoric, as in sexual activity, Augustine energetically pursued the objects of his desire until he exhausted himself to the point of intellectual and emotional collapse.

The "pear tree incident" provides a good example of Augustine's skill in engaging his readers. The 40-year-old Augustine who wrote the *Confessions* was a master of the textual "tease." In Book II, narrating his sexual maturation, he engages the reader's prurient interest by describing his father's delight in observing his sexual maturity--and his mother's apprehension. He says that he was "allowed to dissipate myself in all kinds of ways." The reader anticipates some juicy stories, but Augustine proceeds to relate in detail an incident in which he and some companions stole pears they neither wanted nor enjoyed from a neighbor's tree. Augustine analyzes this deed minutely as an instance of gratuitous evil-doing. The theft of pears takes the place of any concrete example of his sexual activity. Having identified the structure of all concupiscence as pleasureless "enjoyment" of compulsively acquired objects, Augustines uses the incident of the pear theft to illustrate his point, rather than a story of sexual misbehavior.

Twentieth-century readers frequently express scorn for the "pear tree incident," calling it a trivial and uninteresting example of evil, nothing more than a demonstration of Augustine's neurotic self-flagellation. Our irritation is, I think, at least partly to be explained by the fact that our anticipation of a good story about sex has been deliberately cultivated--and disappointed. Augustine has engaged erotic interest, thereby strengthening the reader's interest, but failed to deliver what the text seems to promise. He repeatedly uses this textual strategy; each time he evokes the "torrent of pitch which boils and swells with the high tides of foul lust" (II.2), it is quickly followed either by philosophical or theological reflection, or by the story of another kind of experience, rather than by a description of sex.

Provocatively, Augustine characterizes the Carthaginian society of his young adulthood as a "hissing cauldron of unholy loves."

My soul was in poor health; it burst out into feverish spots which brought the wretched longing to be scratched by contact with the objects of sense . . . . It was a sweet thing to me both to love and to be loved, and more sweet still when I was able to enjoy the body of my lover (III.1).

Documenting his frantic pursuit of strong feeling, tormented by "rods of red-hot iron--the rods of jealousies and suspicions, fears, angers, and quarrels," Augustine insists in retrospect that he got no pleasure from erotic experience. He compares his erotic experience to stage plays, in which one participates briefly, but unsatisfyingly, in the sufferings of the characters in the play.

Certainly, an obedient reader finds ample textual justification for this flattening of the complexity and richness of sexual relationship. Augustine insists that sex, for him, was pleasureless because it was compulsive, and acting out compulsions never produces pleasure. Yet the negative rhetoric he uses to describe sexuality--"chains," "hard slavery," "scratching the itching scab of concupiscence"--is oddly contradicted by the conventional language of sexual pleasure he is forced to use to designate what he refers to:

It was a sweet thing to me both to love and to be loved, and
more sweet still when I was able to enjoy the body of my lover.
And so I muddied the clear spring of friendship with the dirt of
physical desire and clouded over its brightness with the dark hell
of lust (III.1).

Yet he also mentions without giving details: sweetness, delights,
desires, voluptuousness. Evidence of sexual delight thus slips through
the textual defenses against it, confusing the reader.

Several aspects of Augustine's bleak account of sexual relationship ring false: first, his highly selective description of his feelings as
they occurred. His memories are dangerous both to author and
reader and must be heavily controlled if they are to be represented
at all. They are dangerous to Augustine because he has a healthy
respect for the durability of compulsive habits, a sense of the fragility of a resolution that is a gift, and therefore not within his control.
In a different way, Augustine is aware that his memories are also
dangerous to readers: if he presents sexual experience as attractive,
he will encourage imitation. And it is clear that Augustine hopes the
reader will learn from his experience, *not* that she will duplicate his
experience in order to come to the place of experiential knowledge
to which Augustine has come. As pastor, bishop, and spiritual authority, he commits the perennial mistake of parents: he forgets that
his present vantage point is the direct and cumulative result of the
long process by which he achieved it. He refuses to be aware of the
continuity and subjective integrity of his journey, to acknowledge
that it was, in fact, by following with the utmost passion a destructive and treacherous path that he came to the emotional bankruptcy
which led to a breakthrough. He wants his readers to accept his
conclusions without the experience of a similar learning process.

Secondly, Augustine's interpretation of sex does not acknowledge the perspective of his sexual partners. For sexual relationship
is marked precisely by the impossibility of a unilateral interpretation.
Two subjectivities are inevitably involved, making erotic experience
permanently ambiguous. One of the partners--one lover, one author
--cannot define what that experience *was*. One's partner--one's read-
er--feels, thinks, hears, and reads differently, and Augustine has
apparently neither elicited, nor attempted to imagine, nor even
acknowledged his partner's experience.

Moreover, Augustine did not recount the destructive effects of
his aggressive lust on other people--only on himself. My curiosity
about the woman with whom he lived for thirteen years and who

bore their son--a woman whose name he never mentions--is not satisfied in the *Confessions*. He does give a more ample account of his mother; he describes her as focused single-mindedly on himself, his happiness, and his salvation to Catholic Christianity. Though Monica had a husband and other children, her son pictures her as completely and passionately attached to himself, following him from North Africa to Milan, praying continually for him with tears "which fell streaming and watered the ground beneath her eyes in every place where she prayed." Monica was, according to Augustine's report, a passionate woman, but her passion was consumed in her relationship with God and Augustine. Augustine places her on a pedestal, a model of selfless female desire: "I cannot express how she loved me and how she labored with much greater pain to give me birth in the spirit than she had labored when giving birth to me in the flesh." We learn little of her own subjectivity or of any woman's subjectivity from Augustine's heroic epic. The women of the tale are there at all because they are crucial to Augustine's support system. None of the women who appear in Augustine's autobiography stands in her own light, the subject of her own experience; all are evaluated according to their role in Augustine's heroic epic.

The central moment in Augustine's autobiography, the moment for which the book is famous, is that of his conversion. Curiously, it was not a moment of intellectual insight; nor was it a moment of religious ecstasy or a moment of belief. Augustine narrates this experience quite explicitly as a conversion from compulsive sexual activity to continence.

Prefiguring and mirroring his conversion account, Augustine juxtaposed images of himself as alternatively distracted or dispersed among pleasures or gathered and collected in a disciplined "return" to himself and to God throughout the *Confessions*. His model of the spiritual life as re-collection has become the dominant model of Western Christian subjectivity and spirituality and has, in the twentieth century passed into secular culture in the form of numerous varieties of psychotherapy and secular spirituality. The model is one of centering, of arresting the hemorrhage of energy and attention that flows out of the self onto other human beings and objects of all sorts, and pulling that energy within, collecting, focusing, centering. This is Augustine's model; it is based, I will claim in a minute, on Augustine's sexual experience, and I will question it as a useful and usable model for women in particular and for late twentieth-century people in general. Augustine's clearest definition of the model occurs in the following passage:

> I have been spilled and scattered among times whose order I do not know; my thoughts, the innermost bowels of my soul, are torn apart with the crowding tumults of variety, and so it will be until all together I can flow into you [God], purified and molten by the fire of your love.

Generations of readers have managed not to notice Augustine's pervasive sexual imagery by insisting that the *Confessions* is a *spiritual* classic. Re-collection, continence was, for Augustine, both a literal practice, a renunciation of sexual activity, and his model of the spiritual life. His images of sin as "turning away from you, God, toward lower things--casting away, as it were, its own insides, and swelling with desire for what is outside," and being "spilled and scattered" are direct and literal allusions to male orgasm. Continence, on the other hand was, for Augustine, the pivotal point of change. Again, his model is concrete and explicit, based on retention of "precious bodily fluids":

> The Word calls you to come back . . . you will lose nothing. What is withered in you will flower again, and all your illnesses will be made well, and all that was flowing and wasting from you will regain shape and substance and will form part of you again (XI.29).

Continence, as we have seen, was the key to changing not only the course of Augustine's life but also the direction of his longing and passion. As a practice it was, for Augustine, I emphasize, not an inactivity, a *not* doing. Continence was, quite literally, a *practice*, simultaneously a gathering and centering of the self and an energetic resistance. But continence was more than a practice for Augustine. It was also symbolic of a unified and unifying affection and attention, and thus continence defined the form and dynamic of the spiritual life for Augustine and, as a result of the strength and beauty of his description, for Western Christianity.

It is time to ask: what *did* Augustine *recognize* as pleasurable? Two prominent features of his notion of pleasure are permanence and intensity. Defining pleasure in this way, however, creates a problem. Either permanence or intensity, in isolation from the other, would perhaps be achievable. One can take immense pleasure in elegant ideas, in beautiful and unchanging principles of mathematics, or even in a changeless God. But surely such abstractions fail to produce the intense delight of a single spring morning. And it is difficult, on the basis of sensory experience, to imagine pleasure that is both intense and permanent. The senses fatigue; they cannot sustain a receptive sensitivity to any stimulus for very long. But what Augustine wants is sensual experience that remains--or is continuously renewed at optimal excitment.

Augustine was a demanding lover of pleasure, and he claimed, in fact, to have found an object that stimulates like this, that produces a synesthesia that floods the body's senses as it does the "eye of the mind" (VII.1), and the "ear of the heart" (IV.5):

> What do I love when I love you? [he asks, addressing God] Not the beauty of the body nor the glory of time, not the brightness of light shining so friendly to the eye, not the sweet and various melodies of singing, not the fragrance of flowers and ointments and spices, not manna and honey, not limbs welcome to the embraces of the flesh; it is not these that I love when I love my God. And yet I do love a kind of light, melody, fragrance, food, embracement when I love my God; for he is the light, the melody, the fragrance, the food, the embracement of my inner self --there where is a brilliance that space cannot contain, a sound that time cannot carry away, a perfume that no breeze disperses, a taste undiminished by eating, a clinging together that no satiety will sunder (X.6).

Augustine's model of pleasure was one in which rest, peace, and equilibrium are held together with emotional intensity and permanence. His ideal was not to sacrifice some pleasures so that others could be cultivated. It was the ordering of all the pleasures of a human life so that those associated with enjoyment of objects in the sensible world would not usurp all of a person's attention and affection. When pleasures are constellated around a single object of love, he said, they can be enjoyed without fear of distraction. All the pleasurable beauty of the world can then be recognized as evidence of the consummate goodness of its creator.

Augustine was well aware of the potential danger of his construction of spirituality; he knew that he must *keep* insisting that no disparagement of objects--good in themselves, the good creation of a good Creator--was intended. Yet it was the dynamic of temptation and resistance he described so forcefully that has captured the attention of generations of Christians rather than his affirmation of sensual objects.[2] Augustine's formulation of the spiritual life as a firm and cautious management of the world of senses and objects has played a role in forming the values of the Christian West, values that have contributed to the present condition of the earth, a planet in ecological and nuclear crisis.

Augustine's theory of how to get, and to keep, the greatest amount of pleasure was somewhat at odds with his practice, for what had been his most fascinating "pleasure" is conspicuously missing from the ordered pleasures he described. For Augustine, sex was consuming, totalitarian; he felt that it was not possible for him to enjoy a sexual relationship in freedom. And so his conversion revolved around the resolution of this problem area in his life. He sacrificed sexual activity in order to achieve two "goods" he could not manage while he was sexually active--choice and control. He did not, it should be noted, in the *Confessions* or in his other works, press his own resolution on anyone else or describe celibacy as the norm for "serious" Christians. Nevertheless, his rhetorical power ensured that his description of his own resolution was powerfully affecting, contributing to the subsequent glorification of the sexless life in Catholic Christianity.

As we have seen, some of the objects Augustine had written about as false pleasures--good in themselves, but failing to produce happiness for their grasping lovers--reappear in the closing books of the *Confessions* as real, re-formed pleasures. At least one pleasure, however, is conspicuously missing: Augustine did not integrate sexuality into his reconstruction of true pleasure as he did, for example, the pleasures of the senses. Yet, significantly, poignantly, his understanding of the spiritual life itself depends for its structure on the sexual activity he has known. The spiritual life is defined by collecting and retaining, rather than spilling and scattering, the precious, dangerously fluid and slippery "self." Augustine's sexuality "returns" as form rather than content of his reformed life.

To recognize Augustine's conception of spirituality as based on his own most intimate physical experience is not to discount it, but rather to reveal its touching poignancy, its fragility, and its contingency. It is also to urge that other models of spirituality be imagined, fleshed out, and bodied forth. Alternative models are desperately needed, models that respond to the crises of our own day by emphasizing attention to, and affection for, the vulnerable and threatened earth, by energizing committed labor for peace and justice, and by illuminating the spiritual discipline of loving relationship and community.

My reading of Augustine's interpretation of sex is informed by my society's acceptance of sex as a positive, valuable, and pleasurable activity when it occurs in relationships of mutuality and equality. Seen through this lens, Augustine's sexual "lust" seems "normal" and his failure to appreciate and enjoy it seems overscrupulous and ungrateful. However, I am also keenly aware that there is, as far as can be detected, no unsocialized sexuality, no sexuality which is innocent and individual until it is forced to serve society's economic and reproductive needs. Sexualization is a central feature of the socialization of every individual. Moreover, sexuality is gendered: women and men in all known societies are expected and trained, in myriad ways, to think, respond, and behave differently from each other. Men's and women's roles in societies are also different; their access to power is gendered, as well as governed by class and race. In Western societies, designed and administered by men, most men have more power than most women, so that heterosexual "relationships of mutuality and equality" seldom exist between a man and a woman in anything but--at best--an artificially secluded private sphere.

This begins to suggest the possibility of a hermeneutic of generosity: First, it is understandable that a very sensitive and responsible person like Augustine might choose not to participate in an arena of human life so burdened with socialized responses, so culturally overdetermined, so, in Augustine's term, "unfree." Second, Augustine represents himself as suffering from addiction to sex; he called it "slavery." Augustine despaired of his own ability to live an integrated sexuality. He claimed that the sacrifice of sexual activity was necessary in order to achieve an integrated life, a life in which his commitments were chosen and realistically consonant with his capacity to remain faithful to them.

III.

But I have recognized *since* completing *Desire and Delight* that interpreting Augustine as a sexual addict is reading him too obediently. It is certainly his way of presenting his pre-conversion experience. And it is easy for twentieth-century North Americans, living in a society in which addictions of many kinds have reached epidemic levels, to understand that there are good things that the addict cannot permit her/himself, though others who do not find them so consuming can enjoy them. Yet to accept Augustine's self-presentation as a sexual addict also conceals something--*someone*--important. It masks the inevitable influence on Augustine of a thirteen-year-

long, intimate realtionship, entered when he was eighteen years old.
The reduction of Augustine's relationship with his partner to a
sexual addiction neglects--as Augustine neglected--to acknowledge
the woman who shared his life, who bore their son, a woman whose
strength, integrity, and commitment was revealed in her decision to
live a permanently celibate life after her life with Augustine. She
was a "one-man woman," a socially recognized and much-valued--by
men!--category. Augustine admired her without being able to emu-
late her. Perhaps, if one took Augustine's partner seriously, one
could even begin to detect, in his mature thought, images and metaphors, values, understandings of relationship that could have come
to him in this relationship, and remained with him long after the
relationship had ended.

As a "great text of the Western world," the *Confessions* has
played a role in the social construction of desire. This powerful
statement of desire and fulfillment has formed and informed Western people's amorphous, polymorphous, multiple and inarticulate
longings. But what we have thought of as "human" desire is always
marked by the particularities of individual lives, by socially constructed gender assumptions, expectations, and roles, by social location, institutional affiliation, class, and race. If the claim that desire
is socially constructed and differentiated according to these factors
seems farfetched, attempt to imagine a female protagonist of the
Confessions. Could Augustine's demanding, energetic, aggressive
passion have occurred--much less been admired and become a classic
formulation of physical and spiritual desire--in a woman, in his time
or in ours?

I am envious of the social construction and support of Augustine's passion, both his relentless pursuit of worldly satisfaction and
his latter passionate love of God, combined with institutional authority. To search frantically, desperately; to long restlessly, lustfully,
feverishly; to embody the kind of consuming and complex desire that
knows its object when it touches it . . . Few women have sustained
such uncompromising desire, at least partly because women have had
few literary paradigms, few images, few models. Rather, in the societies of the Christian West, women's desire has been constructed
to serve male desire as its mirror and counterpart.

The lack of female models does not mean, of course, that no
women have managed to formulate and pursue a distinctive desire;
it does mean that it is immensely more difficult for women to do
so in societies that have no female epic heroes, no models but male
models for passionately seeking women. Many--though not most--

women have learned to use male models, to adopt, adapt, or rebel against these models of heroic hunger. Educated women have learned to read as men, blind to the biology and socialization, the institutions, and the legal and social arrangements that have *authorized* the author.

A gendered reading of the *Confessions* is attentive to who speaks and who listens; it reveals the myriad ways that the male author's experience informs and gives body to his text. It is certainly significant that Augustine critiqued his society's construction of male sexuality, equating tumescence and the myth of male helplessness in the face of sexual urges with pride and sin. He experienced, he says, a vast relief and freedom in the practice of continence. Later in his career he formulated a model of sexuality based on principles of complementarity and responsibility. It was not a model he had ever lived, and it did not go as far as to imagine equality and mutuality, but it became an enormously influential model. Without the institutional and personal authority of an Augustine, no alternative model could hope to produce the social effects of Augustine's formulation of heterosexual relationship.

Clearly, Augustine failed to address the gender socialization planted deeply in his society and in his own psyche. Rather, the *effect*, even if not the intention, of his authorship was to reinforce rather than to alter Western gender constructions by giving theological validation to beliefs about women's and men's "natures." A female-gendered reading of Augustine is often, then, a ravaging-- rather than a ravishing--experience. In my "reading" of the *Confessions* I have endeavored to acknowledge and describe both its dangers and its delights. It is, I repeat, necessary to see both in full strength in order to understand either. Having seen both with clarity and vividness, we can take up Augustine's task of strenuous critique and reconstruction rather than his conclusions. We can learn from his longing to *have it all* rather than from his own resolution. And we can relish the strength and beauty and richness of his repertoire of metaphors and images without relinquishing our questions, our sensitivities, our reservations, and our images. And we can allow Augustine's intense vision of the Great Beauty to alert us to its presence--a presence Augustine himself saw as above the vicissitudes of human life--but which we can see as *within* the sensuous sensible world, in human relationships, and in passionate longing in its myriad beautiful and unbeautiful forms.

NOTES

1. Audre Lorde, *Sister Outsider* (Freedom, California: The Crossing Press, 1989), 57.

2. Geoffrey Galt Harpham named and discussed the dynamic of temptation and resistance in a remarkable book, *The Ascetic Imperative in Culture and Criticism* (Chicago: University of Chicago Press, 1987).

INCONTINENT OBSERVATIONS:

A RESPONSE TO MARGARET MILES

Morny Joy

I would like to thank Margaret Miles for an address that is eloquent, honest and thoroughly engaging (in the different senses of that word). Her work on Augustine provides a contemporary perspective of his work--at once respectful and measured, yet demanding in evaluating the relevance of Augustine's itinerary for contemporary readers. In particular, I found her stance as a woman one that resonates very much with my own concerns. In fact, one thought kept recurring as I read Margaret's Miles' paper: "What would he make of us?" For we are a species that he did not anticipate. Two educated women, neither protected by, nor dependent upon the patronage of men for subsistence, who dare to question not so much the integrity of his motives, as the universal validity of his claims and the strategy of his rhetoric. As such, I am (as is Margaret Miles) on many levels a suspicious reader. These levels mirror my own diverse loyalties which, listening to Margaret Miles, have been brought into full play in my consciousness. Her presentation has also made me profoundly sensitive to the many resources that are part of a present-day critical reader's repertoire--ones that are not necessarily the same as those of Augustine's originally intended audience.

First, there is the awareness that today we are daughters and sons of Freud. We can employ such terms as addiction, compulsion, compensation, and sublimation. These refer to drives and instincts in ways that highlight unconscious elements behind an eminently rational facade (without being reductive). As a result, we can thus see beyond Augustine's extremely persuasive accounts (for he never lost his rhetorical skills) without totally discrediting them.

Also implicit in Margaret Miles' presentation is the contribution of hermeneutics--especially the realization, derived from Hans-Georg Gadamer, of the effective historical aspect of any text.[1] This term refers both to: (1) the historicity of any work, i.e., its embeddedness in a specific historical context, and (2) the history of the reception, i.e., the effects, that any work which has stood the test of time, brings with it.

Augustine's *Confessions*, as a classic of Western spiritual autobiography, comes replete with such an overweight baggage of effects that it may need many years of study, as Margaret Miles has undertaken, to reach the original (and I use that term advisedly) Augustine, undistorted by centuries of projections and idealizations. For this task, it is a "hermeneutics of suspicion" (adapted from Paul Ricoeur's initial usage of this term) that is required.[2] This suspicion also informs Margaret Miles' intelligent resistance, as a woman reader, to Augustine's beguiling self-disclosures.

Such interpretive aids to scholarship, plus a self-critical awareness of their appropriation, has led many contemporary women to startling discoveries. One of these discoveries is that of becoming cognizant (as Margaret Miles has) that many a text has been written by a man solely for other men without the slightest indication that women count as potential colleagues. This can have a devastating effect on a woman scholar. For there is a double awakening involved, both aspects of which Margaret Miles has alluded to:

1. The fact that women have in the past been denied the means to education that would have provided them with the motivation, opportunities, and drive either to write such a work as the *Confessions* or to be its intended audience, and

2. The fact that until very recently the women who have gained access to education were taught to read as men. Thus, the early questions that arose, with specific reference to the *Confessions*, never focused on the implicit masculinity of Augustine's language or his male point of view. His inclusiveness and relevance for all human beings, regardless of sex, race or class, were automatically assumed. Can we afford to maintain such a benign neutrality in our present comparatively privileged circumstances? This is where I believe that Margaret Miles makes some extremely pertinent observations concerning the role and place of women, sexuality, and the body.

I would like to remark on certain selected instances from Margaret Miles' presentation and then to raise some more general inquiries of importance for wider reflections on the notion of embodiment and its relation to philosophy/theology. To read the *Confessions* is to read a text regarding pleasure (or concupiscence) in a pleasurable way (i.e., to be enticed by what Roland Barthes calls the "pleasures of the text"). But if we are obedient readers, should we not also banish according to Augustine's admonitions, even this pleasure too? For, from Augustine's perspective, are there any pleasures that remain legitimate? Or, does concupiscence (identified as excessive passion) distort everything? Insofar as we are all innocent inheritors of original sin, this may initially seem to be the case. On the other hand, is it the body itself or just unbridled sensuality that is at fault?

Margaret Miles' appreciation of Augustine reflects a more complex approach to a classic male text. The early dismissive reading of Augustine as a simplistic dualist and misogynist by some feminists has given way to a more subtle interrogation. There is now acknowledgement that Augustine is not adamantly anti-body--it is only its wayward expressions that need to be brought (by grace) into perfect conformity with the will. Then sexuality, minus its ecstatic and non-rational expressions, can be performed in a tranquil and sober fashion without the trials and tribulations of the passions (and without the involuntary movements of what the Victorians euphemistically referred to as "the male member"). The intriguing questions that women now ask focus on just what it was that Augustine considered as legitimate pleasures, over and beyond his seeming preoccupation with sexuality. In Margaret Miles' assessment, the pleasures that remain acceptable promote the ideal of continence, exemplified as permanence and intensity. On this score, in responding to Augustine's recommendations, one could not only be a disobedient reader, as is Margaret Miles, who questions the viability of the coexistence of permanence and intensity. One (please note my rhetorical use of this term) could be an irreverent reader and ask (along with Julia Kristeva) if what Augustine was actually seeking was a symbiotic union with the eternal phallic (i.e., preoedipal) Mother in whose presence all frustrations and longings are eternally satiated.[3] This has implications for further discussions regarding the displacement of the "feminine" by celibate males from actual flesh and blood women to a remote and sinless Virgin Mother or to Mother Church.

Margaret Miles' nuanced reading also heeds the figurative language, preoccupied with images of male sexuality, that pervades the text. While Augustine's life of dissipation may have ceased with his conversion, its imagery continues to haunt him. Perhaps because his sexuality has not been integrated into his ultimate vision of the good life, Augustine cannot escape its subversions (conscious or otherwise). In saying this, I am not indicting Augustine on any charge of pretence or bad faith. His situation is quite consonant with that of any reformed compulsive character (if we accept Augustine's own self-descriptions of his obsessions.) But the intriguing question is, why did someone not remark on this obvious fact earlier? Again, one could be an irreverent reader and ask an impertinent question, as Elizabeth Clark has done. For, if in Augustine's portrayal of the human condition, it is the woman who remains the passive vessel that receives the male seed, and if it is this male seed that conveys the sin of Adam and Eve, is it not the male of the species (and not the female) who deserves to have borne the responsibility for our irrevocably flawed nature?[4] Why has woman been the scapegoat for so many centuries?

My final reflections have to do with the explorations women are undertaking today because of their new-found awareness that sex as well as gender are socially constructed. Initially, many feminists became aware that those qualities deemed "feminine" and indicative of gender were culturally relative. A more recent perception, however, is that the sexual body itself, as distinct from attributions of gender, is not simply a physiological entity, with predetermined natural or biological functions. It is a surface which is sculpted according to societal expectations regarding normality, sanity, health, etc. (In this connection, the legacy of Foucault on the insidious yet seductive operations of power need to be acknowledged.) The response of women to these insights is not unanimous, and I believe that there will be much continuing debate in the years to come concerning alternate models. However, I would like to suggest some of the issues that are crucial for these discussions.

For it is all too apparent that a social devaluation of the body has accompanied the exclusion or oppression of women. At the root of these discriminatory attitudes is a binary system, endemic to Western philosophy/theology that has associated men, and things qualified as male, with the superior state of spirituality or rationality. At the heart of this system is, what Elizabeth Grosz has termed "a profound somatophobia."[5] How is the body then to be rehabilitated and what forms of relation could be proposed for both men and women?

Three suggestions:

1. The view of the body as natural and of women as closer to its rhythms needs careful re-evaluation. Without implying that we are totally determined by cultural forces, we need to acknowledge that nature is constructed just as much as culture, and artificial associ-

ations of women with nature simply reinforce traditional misapprehensions and convenient justifications.

2. "Thought" needs to be given to a philosophical mode which does not glorify the mind to the detriment of a weak or erratic body. In so doing, the established mind/body dichotomy should give way to forms of "embodied subjectivity" or "psychical corporeality." (Here I am again indebted to E. Grosz). Care should be taken to not simply reverse the binary pairs. To aid this process, a judicious application of the work of the French thinker, Luce Irigaray, could prove helpful.[6]

3. Embodiment should not be considered the sole domain, or specific quality of one sex. In addition, consideration needs to be given to the way in which culture manipulates bodies to its own ends. Could not a plurality of images be entertained, so that no single image of the "body beautiful" (be it male or female) can impose its artificial standards? A further recommendation is that any ideal type (be it that of a sexual object, or of a disembodied intellect, or of youth's unwrinkled and flab-free proportions) needs to be replaced by a respect for the diversity of shapes, sizes and colors that characterize our all too mortal and aging frames.

Finally, a closing thought. I especially identified with Margaret Miles when she remarked on her sympathy with St. Augustine's "wanting to have it all." What a dynamic phrase, evocative of the human longing for infinity, which will ever elude its grasp. My own problem in this area, perhaps one which I share with many women today, is no longer one of disillusion before an impossible task, but one of settling too soon, because of perceived, or imposed, limitations. How ironic it is that it is not Augustine's call to continence that impresses Margaret Miles. Instead, what surfaces in her presentation, and what communicates itself to me, is an elemental energy that is infectious. It is something akin to Mary Daly's "pure lust," and to what Audrey Lorde named the "erotic." It is an affirmation of life that has nothing to do with indiscriminate sexuality, and nothing whatever to do with the deformations and defamations we have supposedly inherited because of original sin.

NOTES

1. Hans-Georg Gadamer, *Truth and Method* (New York: Crossroad, 1982), 267-274.

2. Paul Ricoeur, *Freud and Philosophy: An Essay on Interpretation*, trans. D. Savage (New Haven: Yale University Press, 1970), 32-36.

3. Julia Kristeva, "Stabat Mater," *The Kristeva Reader*, ed. T. Moi, (New York: Columbia University Press, 1986), 161-163.

4. Elizabeth Clark, "Vitiated Seeds and Holy Vessels: Augustine's Manichean Past," *Ascetic Piety and Women's Faith* (Lewiston, N.Y.: E. Mellen Press, 1986), 291-297.

5. Elizabeth Grosz, *Volatile Bodies* (Bloomington: Indiana University Press, forthcoming), chapter one.

6. Luce Irigaray, "This Sex which is not One," *This Sex which is not One*, trans. C. Porter with C. Burke (Ithaca: Cornell University Press, 1985, 23-33); *je, tu, nous: Toward a Culture of Difference*, trans. A. Martin (New York: Routledge, 1993).

The Antiochene Tradition

Regarding the Role of the Body

within the "Image of God"

Frederick G. McLeod, S.J.

The early Fathers regarded the scriptural phrase "created in the image and likeness of God" as a deep mine from which they could unearth rich nuggets of theological and anthropological truth. They looked upon it as providing a divinely revealed source from which they could explore such questions as: what are the relationships between God and humans and between humans and the rest of creation and how creatures can come to know who God is and what is the way they can encounter Him in life. Yet while all agree in general that human beings enjoy a uniquely privileged position within creation because they are God's image, the fathers offered widely divergent views as to how human beings actually image God and where exactly this gift of image can be said to reside within them.

The purpose of this paper is to sketch what the Antiochenes held to be the right way to interpret how humans image God. It is an outlook that differs notably, at least in emphasis, from what the Alexandrian School and Saint Augustine have espoused. It is also one very rarely mentioned in theological literature, past or present. We will begin our study first with a brief survey of what contemporary exegetes hold to be the meaning of the phrase to be created "in the image and likeness of God." Then so that we might have a backdrop against which we can contrast the Antiochene tradition on this question, we will offer several vignettes that highlight the Platonic, Alexandrian, and Augustinian viewpoints. Afterwards, we will present what the major Antiochenes, especially Theodore of Mopsuestia, affirm about the meaning of image. We will supplement this with what three East Syrian Christians, especially Narsai, have to say. We will conclude with some observations on how our present topic dovetails with this volume's theme on "Religion and the Body."

CONTEMPORARY SCRIPTURAL EXEGESIS

In their commentaries on Genesis 1:26-27, contemporary scriptural exegetes address, for the most part, three interrelated issues regarding these verses: 1) what do the terms "image" and "likeness" denote in Hebrew; 2) whence does the term "image" originate, and 3) what is its most likely meaning in the Genesis context. Because the main focus of this paper is not scriptural, we will merely mention here the opinions of scholars who can be regarded as spokespersons for the differing interpretations cited below.

First, Geoffrey Bromiley in *The International Standard Bible Encyclopedia* believes that the Hebrew words for image and likeness are an example of a synonymous parallelism, where the words do not differ in meaning from one another.[1] Reginald Fuller, however, sees different nuances in the two terms, with the Hebrew word for image ("selem") denoting an exact reproduction or duplicate of another, and the word for likeness ("demut") signifying a resemblance.[2] According to this interpretation, the author or redactor of Genesis is asserting that Adam is to be looked upon as a "copy" of God, but not exactly so. The term "likeness," therefore, is to be understood as both qualifying and restricting the meaning of "image."

In regard to the origin of the term "image," Edward Curtis in his article on the "Image of God" in *The Anchor Bible Dictionary* points out that in Egyptian and Mesopotamian literatures, the image of a god was to be looked upon not as the "picture" of a particular god but as a temple, where this god could be both encountered and truly worshipped.[3] If an image, however, was unavailable, no cult was possible. But on those occasions when the image was present, the worshipers would employ a morning ceremony, called the "Opening of the Mouth." By means of this rite, they believed that they could magically animate the image and thus be able to present their cult and petitions to their god. Curtis suggests that this practice may explain the background looming behind Genesis 2:7, in which God is said to have fashioned the figure of a man out of the clay of the ground and then animated it by breathing life into it.[4]

If the author of Genesis has been influenced by this Egyptian and Mesopotamian understanding of the function of a divine image, he would, of course, be adapting it to the Jewish view that looked upon Yahweh as a transcendent God. His intent would be to portray human beings, and not merely the king, as standing in a special, unique relationship to God because of their functional role within creation. They would be, as it were, the "place" where all other creatures can come in contact with God and offer their worship. If this is the author's purpose, then the meaning of the phrase to be "in the image of God" has less to do with what God looks like than with the position and role that human beings play in the created order of things.[5] In other words, the term "image" in Genesis 1:26-27 is to be understood not in a graphic but in a cultic, functional sense.[6]

While Curtis' interpretation offers an insightful view of what may be the literary background of the term "image" in the Genesis account, it is still not clear in what precise way the author of Genesis understands how human beings image God. In his article in *The Interpreter's Dictionary of the Bible*,[7] N. W. Porteous cautions that physical resemblance cannot be totally excluded. For Adam is said in Genesis 5:3 to have given birth to Seth, "in his likeness, after his image." Many other passages in the Jewish Scriptures also manifest a curious uncertainty over whether God can or cannot be seen. Yet as John McKenzie in his *Dictionary of the Bible* points out, the Jews of ancient times considered it be like an article of faith that any attempt to picture Yahweh by an image was rejected. For it was tantamount to reducing him to the level of nature and thus bringing him down to the level of the gods who were worshipped through empty images.[8]

As regards those who hold for a spiritual interpretation of how humans are made in the image and likeness of God, Geoffrey Bromiley in *The International Standard Bible Encyclopedia* lists a variety of possibilities. Humans can be said to image God by reason of their "personality," "self-consciousness," "self-determination," "reason," "an ability to pass judgment," "freedom of the will," "moral capacity" and "immortality,"[9] His own scholarly preference is for "personality," but with the proviso that "this must not be understood in the sense of the autonomous, self-legislating self of the philosophers."[10] A somewhat similar view is proposed by John McKenzie, who writes: "In the OT Yahweh is distinguished from the other gods by the designation 'living;' He is an extremely vigorous and sharply defined personality who plans, desires, achieves, and responds personally to the words and deeds of men. In this 'living' quality man resembles Him."[11] To state this another way, humans image God by the ways they act as spiritual beings who are rational and free. The emphasis is upon their spiritual activity.

Other scholars refuse to apply "the image of God" to human spiritual faculties. Fuller maintains that the author of Genesis would not possess our understanding of the human psyche and would therefore find it impossible to comprehend how image can be said to relate to the rational soul and its faculties. He insists that "it is man himself, not merely his nature, that is in the image and likeness of God; the author's conception is existential rather than essential."[12] In other words, it is the whole person who is in the image of God rather than some specific aspect to the exclusion of others. According to Curtis, such a holistic view of image is truly "consistent with the way humanity is viewed throughout the Hebrew Bible."[13]

A change of view towards the meaning of "image" occurs in the New Testament, particularly in the Pauline writings. Saint Paul employs the term in reference to Christ "who is the image of God" (2 Cor. 4:4). N. W. Porteous sums up the significance of this, when he notes:

> Nothing could make clearer the tremendous impact of the revelation of God in Christ than the fact it has almost completely obliterated the thought of humans as being in the image of God and replaced it with the thought of Christ as being the image of God, that being understood in the sense of perfect correspondence to the divine prototype.[14]

For Paul, therefore, Christ is the image par excellence.

Paul, however, also looks upon humans as images of God. When applied to humans, image seems to be understood as a some sort of a dynamic element within a person that grows towards fullness as one becomes, in the words of Saint Paul, more "conformed to the image of his Son" (Rom. 8:29) and "transformed into the same image from glory to glory" (2 Cor. 3:18). John McKenzie interprets these two passages as clearly affirming that the "image of glory" is "not to be found only in the attributes of grace and virtue, but ultimately in the resurrection which alters the physical form of man also into the glory of Christ."[15] On this point, N. W. Porteous points out that "Paul's identification of Christ with the man in the image of God of Gen. 1:26 springs, not from a cosmological, but from a soteriological, concern."[16] In other words, "image" for Paul refers not to Christ's pre-existence as "the image of the invisible God, the first-born of all creation" (Col. 1:15), but to the primary and central role that he plays in the economy of salvation.

This brief scriptural overview highlights the considerable amount of disagreement among contemporary exegetes as to the exact meaning of the phrase created "in the image and likeness of God." We will encounter the same wide divergence of opinions, as we now move to consider the patristic understanding of these terms. For the fathers have split into two camps regarding "image," with some maintaining that it is a spiritual reality residing in the soul and others insisting that it is a dignity and function belonging to the whole human composite, body as well as soul.

THE ALEXANDRIAN, CAPPADOCIAN AND AUGUSTINIAN TRADITIONS

In this section, we will touch very briefly upon the views of those who contend that the "image of God" is to be sought only in the highest "reaches" of the rational soul. We will present the thought of Philo, Origen, Cyril of Alexandria, Gregory of Nyssa, and Augustine regarding the image.[17] This treatment is meant solely to provide a backdrop against which the Antiochene position can be more sharply highlighted and contrasted.

Philo

Philo (ca. 20 B.C.- 41 A.D.) was an Alexandrian Jew, who employed Platonic thought as a means to grasp the meaning of the Hebrew scriptures.[18] He considered the Genesis chapters not as a series of myths, but as "modes of making ideas visible, bidding us to allegorical interpretation."[19] His view of image is expressed in the following quote:

> For just as God is the Pattern of the Image [the Logos] . . . so does the Image become the pattern of others, as Moses makes clear at the beginning of the Law Code by saying, 'And God made man after the Image of God' (Gen. 1:27); thus the Image has been modeled after God, but man after the Image.[20]

In other words, Philo regarded the Logos as God's primary image according to whose pattern all human beings have been created.

For Philo, the story of Adam's fall reveals how the human soul forgot its true nature as image of the Logos. To regain its true nature, the soul must follow the path of mystic contemplation.[21] For since the Logos is the personified divine Reason who binds creation to the divine, it follows then that humans made in the Logos' image are themselves persons by virtue of their reason. This outlook has exercised a profound impact upon the fathers that we will presently be treating. For when they applied Philo's thought to scriptural texts, especially from Paul, they "christologized" Philo's Logos. This also led them to appraise the Christian life as a dynamic but gradual process of restoration of the image lost or distorted at the original fall and to stress the importance of controlling one's passions, so that one may be able to contemplate God's Word.[22]

Origen

Origen (ca. 185-254) considered image as applicable only to Christ's divine nature, as seen in the following quotation: "He [Celsus] did not realize that the image of God is the firstborn of all creation, the very Logos and truth, and, further, the very Wisdom Himself . . . whereas man was made 'in the image of God'."[23] As to how humans image God, Origen sought to find the answer, as Philo did, by seeking an allegorical explanation of the Genesis account. He believes that this is referring to the first creation when human beings were spiritual intellects fashioned after the pattern of the Logos.[24] Then due to some fall (that also affected angels and demons), humans were placed in their present corporeal bodies. They are able, however, to regain their original state of likeness to God when they unite their efforts to those of the Logos and His Spirit. We see this in the following:

> The remaining possibility is that that which is made in the image of God is to be understood of the inward man, as we call it, which is renewed and has the power to be formed in the image of the Creator, when a man becomes perfect as his heavenly Father is perfect.[25]

For Origen, therefore, to be created "in the image" indicates that humans are imperfect images who image God through their souls--not their bodies. Though fallen, they are nevertheless capable of progressing and retrogressing, depending on how they respond to the activity of the Holy Spirit in their lives. For they possess within themselves a spiritual ability enabling them to come into contact with the Logos through contemplation and to grow thereby in their state of holiness. This is stated briefly but clearly in Origen's exhortation: "Let us always, therefore, contemplate the Image of God, so that we can be transformed to his likeness."[26]

Cyril of Alexandria

Cyril (376-444) rejects the opinion that humans can image God in any way that implies a similar bodily structure within God. He asserts: "He [Adam] has been honored by God, by having been made in His image and likeness--not in his bodily shape, that is, but rather because he is capable of being just and good, and fitted for all virtue."[27] Cyril elaborates upon what he means by this in his letter to Calosyrius:

> A human being's formation to God's image has other meanings --meanings on the surface and meanings deep within; for a person alone, of all the living creatures on earth, is rational, compassionate, with a capacity for all manner of virtue, and a divinely allotted dominion over all the creatures of the earth, after the image and likeness of God. Therefore, it is inasmuch as a person is a rational animal, a lover of virtue, and earth's sovereign that a human being is said to have been made in God's image.[28]

In other words, Cyril looks upon image as being rooted in the powers that the soul possesses to act in rational, volitional, virtuous, and authoritative ways that resemble the "ways" that God acts towards His creation.[29]

Gregory of Nyssa

The theme of the "image of God" holds an important place in the writings of one of the outstanding Cappadocians, Gregory of Nyssa (ca. 335-95).[30] He sees no difference in meaning between the terms "image" and "likeness." When he approaches the question of where the "image of God" resides in human beings, his interest is mainly practical and ascetical. He focuses at times upon the many divine gifts--freedom, "apatheia," "gnosis," mercy, immortality--with which God has endowed humans and tries to determine which should be spiritually cultivated as being the more godlike.[31]

But as the following quotations indicate, he seems to regard the image primarily as a spiritual character whose dynamic power a person can use to grow into a likeness with God, as seen in the following two quotations: "The aim of the life of virtue is to become like God,"[32] and "He who has truly come to be in the image of God and who has in no way turned aside from the divine character bears in himself its distinguishing marks and shows in all things his conformity to the archetype; he beautifies his own soul with what is incorruptible, unchangeable, and shares in no evil at all."[33] For Gregory, therefore, to act in a virtuous way, which presumes the balanced, rational use of one's freedom, is the way that human beings image God and grow in their likeness to Him, enabling one to not only resemble God's way of acting but to become in the process divinized.

Augustine

Augustine (354-430) clarifies his understanding of image in his great work, *De Trinitate*.[34] Though he uses the terms "image" and "likeness" interchangeably in his commentary on Genesis 1:26 as being a "certain intelligible form of an illuminated mind,"[35] there are a few places where he distinguishes between "imago" as a particular kind of likeness by which something relates to and is expressive of its source and "similitudo" as any form or likeness between two things. He writes:

> Certainly, not everything in creatures, which is in some way or other similar to God, is also to be called His image, but that alone to which He Himself alone is superior; for the image is only then an expression of God in the full sense, when no other nature lies between it and God.[36]

When Augustine makes his final distinction as regards the meaning of the phrase "image of God," he holds that only the Verbum is the true Image and that all other created spiritual beings are images in a secondary sense. These latter, however, are capable of becoming more completely an image of God through the transforming activity of the Verbum. We see this expressed in Book 7 of the *De Trinitate*:

> For we are, likewise, the image of God, not indeed an equal image, since [ours] was made by the Father through the Son, not born of the Father as His is. And we are so, because we are enlightened by the light, but He is the light that enlightens.[37]

In his *De Trinitate*, Augustine explores in what specific ways human beings can image the Trinity. He holds that the image of God resides only in the higher dimensions of the soul, as seen in the following passage: "man was made to the image of God in that part of his nature wherein he surpasses the brute beasts; this is, of course, his reason or mind or intelligence or whatever we wish to call it."[38] Augustine then proposes an experience of love as best providing an insight into how the human mind reflects the Trinity and how the human image can be refashioned.[39] But when this failed to explain how love partakes of the Trinity, he then later developed an analogy rooted in the three immanent operations of the soul. He compares, first, the Father to the mind itself, secondly, the Son to both the intellect's knowledge which is its offspring and the word which comes from it, and, thirdly, the Holy Spirit to love.[40]

After establishing this latter analogy as the basis on which humans can image God, Augustine then treated what were the purpose and function of the human image. We find this affirmed in Book XIV, Ch. 16, of the De Trinitate:

> Hence, what is read in that other place: 'Put on the new man that has been created according to God,' means the same as that which is said in this place: 'put on the new man, that is being renewed according to the image of him who created him.' There he says 'according to God,' but here 'according to the image of him who created him.' Instead of the expression that he employed there 'in justice and holiness of truth,' he says here 'in the knowledge of God.' Consequently, this renewal and reformation of the mind is made according to God or according to the image of God. He says 'according to God,' therefore, that we might understand this renewal to be wrought in that thing where there is the image of God, namely in the mind.[41]

Bernard McGinn interprets the meaning of this well, when he writes:

> This is why Augustine insists that the introspective activity involved in our personal recognition of the trinity within our own consciousness is not meant to be a pure mental exercise in and of itself--it is intended to lead the soul to that participation in Divine Wisdom which is not just the recognition that the "mens" does indeed bear the image of the Trinity, but also the conviction that the whole purpose for which this image was created was to attune itself more consciously and more directly to its heavenly source.[42]

In other words, humans, because they possess the image of God in their minds, are able to attain to a vision of God through God's primary image, the Verbum. When attained, this vision restores the human image to its most fundamental purpose: to be--through grace --in union with the triune God and thus able to experience to some degree the state that originally existed before Adam fell.[43]

Summary of the Alexandrian, Cappadocian, and Augustinian Positions

Clearly the theologians just treated reflect Philo's views on image. They hold that the "image of God" applies primarily to the Word and in an applied sense also to humans. They also look upon the human image as residing in the highest part of the soul.[44] For they insist that only a spiritual image can reflect and share in God's transcendent nature. This leads them to look upon image as an agent of divinization, whereby a person can become through contemplation of the Logos or Verbum more like unto God. While this kind of outlook has helped to develop an understanding of grace, it also has had an unintended downside: it effectively minimizes the role that the human body plays in the economy of salvation.[45] It is against this kind of view that the Antiochenes have written.

THE ANTIOCHENE TRADITION

While those belonging to the Alexandrian school were heavily influenced by Philo's Platonic views regarding the human being as a soul existing in a body and his distinction between the "first" and "second" creations (supposedly described in Genesis 1:27 and 2:7),[46] the Antiochene tradition,[47] which was eclectic in outlook,[48] offered a far different theological view. It held that humans were a unified whole of body and soul and identified the image of God, not as Philo did with the "first" creation, but with the person of clay fashioned at the "second" creation.[49] It is this latter view that we now wish to attend to. As we proceed, we will treat of those fathers who are traditionally regarded to be the exponents of Antiochene thought[50] and follow this up with the teaching of those East Syrian fathers who have promoted it.[51]

Diodorus of Tarsus

Diodorus of Tarsus, who became a bishop in 378 and died before 394, is regarded as one of the founders of the so-called

Antiochene School. If we can accept as authentic a passage attributed to him in Migne,[52] he rejects the arguments of those maintaining that the image of God resides in the invisible power of the soul. He points out that, if this position be true, then both angels and demons who are invisible ought also be called images. Yet in the same passage he interprets Saint Paul's statement about men being the image of God and women the glory of man as indicating that men are God's image in that they possess mastery and power. He sums up his comments by asking rhetorically: "How, then, is man God's image?" He responds: "By way of dominion, in virtue of authority." While the right to exercise this power of domination is spiritual, it is an extrinsic power given to men as such, enabling them to act in an authoritative way as God's steward or representative.

Because only fragments of Diodorus' numerous writings have survived, it is difficult to draw conclusions as to his view on whether the phrase, "image of God," refers to the whole person and, if so, in what sense this is so, particularly as he believes that only men have been created in God's image. Since John Chrysostom repeats Diodorus' statements on image as signifying dominion and not applicable to women, Chrysostom's elaborations can most likely be taken as indicative of Diodorus' position. But as we will see below, Theodore of Mopsuestia maintains a different view or emphasis in his extant writings. While Diodorus stresses man's authoritative role, Theodore emphasizes more its symbolic, cultic, and unifying roles.

John Chrysostom

John Chrysostom (ca. 347-407), who seems to have been a fellow pupil of Diodorus along with Theodore of Mopsuestia, espouses the same view as Diodorus' noted above. John excludes the possibility of the image residing in the soul. For otherwise the angels who are invisible would also have to be called images.[53] For him, man has been fashioned in the image of God "according to his preeminence and dominion, not according to anything else: for God made man to be the leader of everything on the earth and nothing is greater than man, but everything is under his power."[54] And like Diodorus, he too strictly interprets Paul's assertion in 1 Cor. 11:7 that: "man ought not to cover his head. For he is the existing image and glory of God; the woman however is the glory of man." We see this in his response to a question as to whether women possess the "image of God":

Our answer is that men and women have one form, one distinctive character, one likeness. Then why are men said to be in the
"image of God" and women not? This is because what Paul says
about the "image" does not pertain to form. The "image" has
rather to do with authority, and this is what the man has. The
woman has it no longer. For he is subjected to no one, while she
is subjected to him. For as God has said: "Your desire shall be
for your husband, and he shall be your master" (Gen. 3:16).
Therefore men are in the "image of God" since they have no
one above them, just as God has no superior, but rules over
everything. Women, however, are "the glory of man," since she
is subjected to him.[55]

Though Chrysostom speaks here of men alone as being the
image of God, he qualifies this in other places, not as regards to
women but in its relationship to Christ. He holds, as do all the
fathers we have considered, the view that "image of God" strictly
speaking pertains only to Christ. For only he can fully image God.[56]

Theodore of Mopsuestia

The great luminary in the Antiochene School was Theodore of
Mopsuestia (350-428). Although many of Theodore's writings have
been lost, yet various fragments have survived that reveal his thought
concerning the meaning of image. These are found in J.-P. Migne's
Patrologia Graeca, in Edward Sachau's translation of a Syriac text
containing Theodore's *Introduction to and Commentary on Genesis
1 and 2*,[57] and in Françoise Petit's translation of unedited Greek
fragments of Theodore's writings on image recently discovered in a
ninth-century florilegium.[58] Since the thought contained in these
fragments corresponds to what we will see present in the writings of
those who have acknowledged their dependence upon Theodore,
they can be accepted, I believe, as being truly authentic, despite the
fact that all these manuscripts are relatively late and that Petit
considers the redactor of the florilegium to be "more careful in his
calligraphy than in his orthography or grammar"--a failure that
entails the need at times to conjecture as to what is the meaning of
a particular text.[59]

In his *Commentary on Genesis*, Theodore asserts that at creation
God fashioned humans last of all, in order to indicate not only their
preeminence over all other creatures but their role as the fundamental bond uniting the spiritual and material beings within the

universe.[60] Theodore explains this latter role thus:

> For He [God] fashioned Adam with an immortal, invisible, ra-
> tional soul and a mortal, visible body. By the former, he is like
> unto invisible natures, and the latter is akin to visible beings. For
> when God willed to gather all of creation into one, so that, al-
> though made up of diverse natures, it might be held together
> by one bond, He [then] created and animated this [bond] which
> is related by its nature to the whole of creation, that is, He
> created man.[61]

Theodore elaborates upon how humans function both as the
bond of the universe and God's image, in the following quotation:
He [Moses] wrote: "He created him [Adam] in the image of God,"
to indicate that he excels in his fashioning, because all beings are
bonded in him so that by the means of his image they might draw
near to God. When they [the rest of creation] fulfill the laws imposed upon them by God to minister unto him, they are pleasing to
the Legislator by [their] diligence to him. Since God needs nothing
and is invisible, they offer the glory due to Him by serving the one
who is needy and visible.[62]

Theodore offers a comparison to illuminate the role that Adam
plays within creation. He likens God to a king who has constructed
a magnificent city and set his image in its center to prove that he
is its founder. By so doing, the king expects that his image will be
venerated by all the inhabitants. In a similar way, God has placed
Adam within the city of the universe, intending thereby that the
veneration that all creatures owe Him as their transcendent God be
expressed through His chosen image.[63] This analogy mirrors what we
have seen in the scriptural interpretation above.[64]

Though the fragments we possess only hint at it, Theodore
appears to regard Christ as the true and primary image of God. We
see this in the following quotation that has apparently survived from
his *De Incarnatione*. It spells out in detail how Christ functions as
God's true image and foreshadows God's eternal plan to renew and
restore all of creation in and through Christ.

> And he [Christ] holds the place of image on two accounts. For
> those who love certain [people] very often set up images of them
> after [their] death [and] consider they have sufficient solace for
> [their] death; and by looking, as it were, upon an image, they
> think that they see the [loved] one who is not seen, nor present,

thus appeasing the flame and force of [their] desire. Also, those who have images of emperors within cities seem to honor by cult and adoration those who are not present, as though they were present and to be seen. Both of these [cult and adoration], however, are fulfilled through him [Christ]. For all those who are with him and pursue virtue and are prompt returners of debts to God love him and greatly honor [him]. The invisible divine nature receives love through him who is seen by all. They believe that they are seeing God through him and that by being always present to him, they are bestowing the entire honor [on God]. He is viewed as being [God's] imperial image, since the divine nature is, as it were, in him.[65]

One other fragment in which Theodore distinguishes between "image" and "likeness" deserves attention. Because of what he has affirmed about the role of image, it is evident that, like both Diodorus and John Chrysostom, he rejects the opinion of those who hold that image resides in the higher reaches of the soul. Yet he does believe that the faculties of the soul can provide a person with some knowledge of God and of His triune nature. He maintains that human faculties imitate those, as it were, present in the Divinity--though, of course, in an inferior analogous way.[66] We find this expressed in a text that is partially defective but still understandable:

And from the designation of 'image' [lacuna], he affirmed that the divine nature is to be understood as one. Then as regards the statement [that Adam was created] 'according to our likeness,' we take it to be a sign of the number of persons within the divine nature.[67]

It seems, therefore, that Theodore understands the term "image" as referring to Adam/Christ as the bond of the universe who reveals the existence of God and as the medium through whom worship is to be extended to God. "Resemblance" looks, rather, to ways that humans can be said to be analogously like unto God or that can be imagined as imitating God's actions. In other words, "image" should be taken more as a symbol; and "resemblance" as an analogy.

Theodoretus of Cyrensis

The last major theologian of the School of Antioch was the renowned Theodoretus of Cyrensis (ca. 393-466). His view on image is found in a fragment published in Migne.[68] He insists against those holding that the human body images God that they fail to take into account how Scripture is employing accommodated language when speaking of God's visible appearances.[69] He then rejects the view of those holding that the "image of God" resides in the invisible soul, arguing that otherwise angels ought also be called God's images.[70] After this, he proceeds to discuss what certain doctors have asserted about image. He presents their positions favorably, without saying in the fragment whether he has made these his own.

Theodoretus first mentions how certain doctors have understood that:

> the God of all, when He created a sensing and intellectual creature, finally formed man, as a certain image of Himself, by placing him as a medium between animate and inanimate, sensing and intellectual beings, in order that both the animate as well as the inanimate beings might serve him as a form of the tribute [that they owe to God], while the intellectual natures might demonstrate their benevolence for [their] Creator by exercising care for man.[71]

As we have just seen, this is Theodore of Mopsuestia's position on how human beings image God by being the bond of the universe. They are the mediators who enable all the rest of creation to serve God.

When Theodoretus addresses the issue whether humans have been created in the image of God according to their power to dominate over the irrational world, he simply observes that there are other kinds of ways that humans can be said to imitate God, such as in fabricating things, making judgments, and thinking discursively of all sorts of possibilities.[72] Since the fragment ends here, we can offer only a conjecture as to how Theodoretus relates this to what he previously asserted about image. Perhaps, his choice of the word "imitation" to describe how human actions can be regarded as being analogous to God's way of acting is indicative of the distinction Theodore of Mopsuestia has earlier made between image and likeness. The examples just cited would be instances of how humans are like unto God. They would be referring to the ways that humans have been created in God's likeness, rather than in His image.

If we can judge from the limited sources presently available to us, Theodoretus' passing remarks on image as it pertains to humans as the bond of the universe may be manifesting a shift in Antiochene thought away from both Diodorus' and John Chrysostom's emphases upon image as being first and foremost a reflection of God's creative and dominative power. As we will see repeated below in our treatment of the Syriac understanding of image, Theodore of Mopsuestia seems to have introduced a new and more coherent way for looking upon how humans actually image God. "Image" now signifies not only the pre-eminence and dominion that human beings possess within the universe but also the way that the rest of creation can know, love, and serve their God.

THE EDESSENE TEACHING ON THE IMAGE OF GOD

In the fifth century, Edessa (now the Turkish city of Urfa) began to supplant Antioch as the center of theological thought for the Antiochene tradition.[73] Its school, then known as the Persian school, dates back at least until the time of Ephrem (ca. 306-384).[74] When Narsai, a Syriac Christian from the Persian lands, was elected as the head of the school around the middle of the fifth century, it became a strong bastion in defense of Diodorus, Theodore, and Nestorius.[75] After Narsai was forced to flee for his life, he then established a school at Nisibis which was at that time under Persian control. The school quickly became the intellectual center for East Syrian (or as it is often popularly referred to, Nestorian) Christianity. It was responsible for maintaining and promoting the theological thought of Theodore.

In this section, we will discuss the views of three writers from the fifth, sixth, and ninth centuries who reflect the East Syrian ideas on image. The first is Narsai whom we have just mentioned;[76] the second is Cosmas Indicopleutes, a sixth-century Egyptian merchant, who travelled to the Black Sea and reports about the conversations he held with the East Syrian Catholikos Mar Abba I (540-552) concerning the teaching of Diodorus and Theodore;[77] and the third is the East Syrian scripture exegete, Išo'dad of Merv, who lived and wrote in the mid-ninth century.[78]

Narsai

Narsai's teaching on image is explicit and richly detailed.[79] He affirms in Homily 66: "The Creator willed to call it [the human soul] and body His image."[80] But he is also careful to point out in Homily 4: "He [the Creator] called him [Adam] an image of His majesty in a metaphorical sense. For everything created is vastly inferior to the divine essence. [God's] nature is so immeasurably exalted over that of creatures that it does not possess, as corporeal beings do, a visible image."[81] In other words, "image of God" is a dignity bestowed on the whole human being. It does not denote a photographic kind of image, but is understood more in the contemporary sense of a symbol. It points to and says more about the reality of God than any abstract explanation. Not only does this human image reveal something about God but it shares in His power. We see this expressed in Homily 49 in language clearly dependent upon Theodore: "The Creator set His image in the world, the city of the kingdom, and by a visible image He makes known the power of His transcendent divinity."[82] Narsai elaborates upon this in Homily 1: "With the name of a nature not constituted by a maker, I have called the image of man, when I fashioned him. For his sake I have created everything that is invisible and visible, and I have set him as a steward over my fashioning."[83] For Narsai, therefore, image bestows upon Adam a dignity and an authority that enables him to function as God's viceroy before all other creatures.

Like Theodore, Narsai envisages a close connection between human beings as the images of God and the bond uniting the material and spiritual dimensions of the universe. We see these two outlooks telescoped in Homily 66 when Narsai declares: "He [the Creator] fashioned and skillfully made a double vessel, a visible body and a hidden soul--one man. He depicted the power of His creatorship in him as an image: mute beings in his body and rational beings in the structure of his soul."[84] In other words, for Narsai, the universe is an organic whole whose rational and irrational worlds are bonded together and summed up in Adam.

Narsai specifies more clearly how human beings function as both image and bond of the universe in the following citations; first, in Homily 4: "He [the Creator] has exalted his image with the name of image, in order to bind all [creatures] in him, so that they might [thus] acquire love by knowing Him through knowledge of His image."[85] We see this same idea expressed also in Homily 62: "I [the Creator] set him like an image for creatures, so that they might consider him, in order that by love to him everyone might know me."[86] Human beings, therefore, are the divinely appointed ways for other creatures to know, love, and serve God. They bind the spiritual and corporeal worlds on a horizontal plane and unite them vertically to God by enabling them to know and love God.

Narsai refines this twofold understanding of the meaning of image even more. Doubtless reflecting the teaching of Colossians

1:15, he carefully points out that Jesus, not Adam, is in point of fact God's image. Homily 62 expresses this well:

> He [the Creator] called the first Adam by the name of image in a secondary sense. The image in reality is the Messiah, the Second Adam. Thus 'Come, let us make man in our image' was fulfilled when the Creator took His image and made it a dwelling place for His honor. The promises to Adam came to be in reality in the Messiah.[87]

For Narsai, therefore, the bestowal of the name of image upon Adam is a foreshadowing of that time when God will dwell within His primary image, Jesus Christ.

Narsai describes how Jesus will function as the image of God in the following two extended quotes that speak of his role in heaven before the angels and the elect:

> By the yoke of his love will be united together angels and men, and they will celebrate him as the image of the hidden king.... They continually worship in the temple of his body that One who is hidden in him and offer therein the pure sacrifices of their minds. In the haven of his body come to rest the impulses of their thoughts, as they become worn out in search for the incomprehensible hidden One. For this reason, the Fashioner of the universe chose him from the universe, that by his visible body he might satisfy the need of the universe. A creature needs to seek out what is hidden and to discover the meaning and intent of what is secret. Because it is impossible that the nature of the hidden One appear openly, He limited their inquiries to his visible image.[88]

> He [the Word] assumed him [Christ] for the peace of rational beings as the first fruits for us all, in order that He might bind in him the love which Adam loosened by [his] transgression of the divine command. He honored the whole nature of rational beings by assuming him, because He made those akin to him by nature share in his honor.[89]

In other words, by assuming our human nature and enabling it to attain immortality in heaven, the Word has affected the nature of all humans and, because human nature bonds together the rest of the universe, all created natures. The risen Christ, therefore, is the central link uniting other human beings and all other created beings, both spiritual and corporeal, to God. The soteriological role that Jesus plays at the end times as the true image of God helps us to understand what happened to the image when Adam fell in Paradise. Though Adam cannot destroy his double role as both image of God and bond of the universe, he can nevertheless distort and corrupt it. When he sinned, he turned his image into a sign of contradiction by means of his disobedience and corrupted it by his introduction of actual death into the world. When death severed Adam's soul from his body, his image was split apart. He could no longer fulfill his function as the unifying bond between the spiritual and material worlds and as the true image who reveals God and the way He is to be worshipped. Narsai describes in Homily 4 how all the rest of creation reacted when death entered into the world: "rational and dumb beings became strangers to the race of men and, because of his fall, lost hope that he would ever rise again."[90] Jesus, however, radically alters this whole situation for himself and for those who share in his nature, when he gains immortality and entrance into heaven.

One final point needs to be made about Narsai's view on how humans have been created "in the image and likeness of God." While insisting that humans do not have a natural likeness to God, Narsai does see similiarities that can afford some insight into who God is. In a passage similar to the one by Theodore of Mopsuestia cited above, Narsai observes:

A figure, signifying the name of the Divine Essence, is found in the generation [of Adam's soul] . . . . Its likeness faintly resembles [and] signifies the Persons [of the Trinity]. Its nature resembles the Father; and its [mental] word, the Son; and [its] life, the Spirit. Its nature does not have a natural likeness to the Nature of the hidden One, but only a typical likeness.[91]

As with Theodore, the resemblance between human faculties and the Persons in the Trinity seems to be one way that humans possess a likeness of God. Whereas "image" is used to express the symbolic role that humans, especially Christ, plays within creation, "likeness" refers to the analogies and the typical/archetypal relationships existing between human nature with its faculties and, as it were, their counterparts within the Trinity.

Cosmas Indicopleustes

In his work on *Christian Topography*, Cosmas Indicopleustes claims to be reflecting the conversations he held with the East Syrian Catholicus, Mar Aba I, concerning the theological views of Diodorus and Theodore.[92] In Book III, when he discusses in passing the creation of human beings, he writes in terms similar to those that we have already encountered in Theodore and Narsai:

> After arranging the inside of his house [i.e. the created universe], so that it is complete and harmonious, this king founded and completed a city and then placed there his own proper image painted and embellished with diverse colors. Likewise God, who is sovereignly wise, reunited, one could say, his diverse and varied works, the rational and irrational, mortal and immortal, corruptible and incorrptible, those perceptible to the senses and to the intellect, and completed [these] by realizing a living being, namely man, who is composed of all these natures. And He placed him in the house so prepared as an image of Himself, revealing the existence of a unique creator of the universe. This is the reason why the angels, marvelling at the image and being well disposed towards God, treat man with care and serve him openly. And the same holds true for all creation.[93]

We see the same idea expressed in the following, where God is said to have fashioned Adam as "having all things in himself--things visible and invisible, things that are perceived by the intellect and by the senses, things that are corruptible and incorruptible. [This] indicates that there is one Creator of all that is."[94] In other words, human beings insofar as they are the bond unifying the diverse elements within the universe image to themselves and to others that there is only one Creator.

Išo'dad of Merv

The final Syriac source that I wish to mention is Išo'dad of Merv, a dedicated exponent of Theodore's historical-grammatical exegesis. In his treatment of Genesis 1: 26, he lists various interpretations offered for the meaning of the phrase, "image of God."[95] He first likens God to a king who has placed his image in the middle of a city that he has built and adorned. Then after a series of general meanings, he notes how God has made man like to visible and invisible beings, so that these may not only honor him as God's image but love him because of their affinity with them.

Išo'dad then proceeds to reject the position of those who held that "image" and "likeness" are applied to human beings by reason of their rational natures and domination. For angels are recognized as reasonable and intelligent and inanimate natures as dominating, but neither of these are ever called images of God. He then offers a number of ways that humans can be considered to be images of God. First, they alone symbolize both the unity and persons within the Trinity. For example, he compares the soul to God the Father, the mental word engendered by the soul to the Son, and its spirituality to the Holy Spirit. Secondly, humans are called image because they are the synthesis of the world. For they enclose and unite in themselves the entire creation of spiritual and corporeal beings.

Thirdly, human beings are like unto God by their operational power, though they differ in the ways they fashion things, humans out of matter and God out of nothing. Fourthly, they are like unto God by reason of their intelligence. They can grasp the whole span of creation in heaven and earth in an instant, whereas the divine nature exists everywhere already. Fifthly, they are like unto God by the royal and judiciary power they exercise. Sixthly, they are called image because from their race will later come the man Jesus Christ, who will be the image of the invisible God.

While Išo'dad does not identify from whence he has drawn these different explanations, he is evidently indebted to Theodore and/or those Syriac fathers who acknowledge him as their mentor, at least as regards the six views that we have just treated above. He seems to have compiled these from writings that he had at hand and would be expressing--out of context--different usages of "image."

CONCLUSION

As our brief survey has exposed, there exists a wide disparity of understanding among the scripture exegetes and fathers of the church regarding the meaning of the phrase "to be created in God's image." While all agree that it indicates that Adam and Eve enjoy not only a special but even a unique relationship with God, they disagree, however, over whether the body is to be understood as a constitutive element within the image of God and, if so, how does it function as such.[96] The Alexandrians, Cappadocians, and Augustine readily maintain that the body is good, serving as the temple in which the image resides. But they restrict image to the highest reaches of the mind, arguing strongly that only a spiritual reality can image the transcendent nature of a spiritual God.[97] As regards the Antiochenes, the extant writings, particularly that of Diodorus and Theodore, are relatively sparse. Yet they do provide us, when taken together with that of the East Syrian theologians, a logically consistent understanding of image that is pregnant with theological meaning regarding the role that the body plays in the drama of salvation. Their view is unmistakably Pauline in that it emphasizes how Christ is the mediator, savior, and recapitulator of the universe.

For Theodore and those who follow him, the body not only is an essential part of what constitutes the human person as God's image but actually plays a necessary and central role within God's plan for salvation. For its essential union with the soul makes it the bond uniting both the material and spiritual worlds. Its union reveals who the God is who created the world. The body is also like a statue placed in the center of a city whose founding ruler wants to be reverenced as though he himself were present. By manifesting care for the corporeal image that God has set up within the world, other creatures can fulfill their dutiful love for their Maker. In other words, image has a cultic, as well as a revelatory, function to play within the created world. This purpose becomes clearer when the primary image, Jesus Christ in whom the Word dwells, overcomes death and attains a glorious union with God in heaven. The risen Christ stands in the midst of heaven as the primary image enabling all created beings to enter into heaven and to know, love, and worship their transcendent God.

Christ's role as the primary image of God explains too why dominion is associated with image. The dominion bestowed upon Adam at creation looks to the universal and total authority that belongs to Christ, as the one in whom the Word resides and as the Conqueror of death. As such, Adam's dominion both foreshadows and images the total power that will be given to Christ. Or to put this in another way, universal dominative power resides internally within Christ, because of his union with the Word. Other humans share in this by extrinsic denomination in that they possess the same human nature composed of body and soul that prepares the rest of creation for the coming of Christ. While Christ is the primary image, Adam and his offspring can also be called images in a secondary, received sense.

The view of Theodore on the meaning, place, and role of image differs at least in emphasis from the Alexandrian outlook on image. Yet these two outlooks ought to be regarded as complementary rather than as solidly opposed to each other. The Theodorean understanding stresses the totally personal, communal, and functional aspects of the special, unique relationship that humans enjoy with God. That of the Alexandrians, on the other hand, is focussed mainly on the essentially spiritual nature of an individual's union with God and of its dynamic possibilities for growth. But if both positions are taken together, they can be seen as filling out the major elements that constitute the personal and communal dimensions of an act of religious faith in God. They raise questions for each other and for all seeking to understand the nature, role, and dignity of human beings within the divine economy of salvation.

THE SIGNIFICANCE OF THE ANTIOCHENE VIEW FOR THIS VOLUME

The Antiochene outlook on image, as expressed by Theodore of Mopsuestia, offers, I believe, a number of important points that are relevant to our present volume's general theme on "Religion and the Body." Three stand out. First, the Antiochenes make us aware of and much more sensitive to the deeper implications for the role that the body is meant to play in the mysteries of both Christ's incarnation and resurrection. They point to how the human body is not merely an adjunct or appendage to the soul but an essential constitutive element within God's salvific plan for the universe. The body is necessary insofar as it provides a concrete way for a transcendent God to reveal Himself and to manifest His love for all that He has created. Also the visible body that Adam and other human beings possess offers a medium whereby other creatures may know where and how to extend their love to God. This highlights a twofold truth fundamental for our Christian life: that love for one's neighbor is in fact love for God and that love, at least in its spiritual dimensions, needs the body and its activity to be able to express itself in a symbolic way to others.

Secondly, the Antiochene fusion of humans as image of God and the bond of the universe accents the basic, radical relationship of kinship that exists between the human body and the rest of the material universe. As the root meaning of our word "atonement" so clearly signifies, we are called to be "at-one-with" not merely God, ourself, and other human beings, but also all the rest of creation. This bond we possess with the physical world is hard to grasp, let alone to experience, especially for those conditioned by the western, technological attitude that regards the corporeal world as something simply to be used as an object and even abused.

The Antiochene view brings home to us in a striking way at least the realization that God has created humans in a symbiotic relationship with the entire organic and inorganic world. It can make us sensitive to the fact that our human body is truly the medium par excellence of relationship and of dialogue--not merely with other human beings but with nature itself. It gives added meaning to what Saint Paul asserts so movingly in Romans 8:18-23 about creation's eager awaiting to share in the redemption of our bodies. Its outlook provides us with a Christian, theological basis that both explains and justifies the Native American and Oriental religions' insistence upon the need for humans to exist in harmony with nature.

Finally, the Antiochene outlook on the role Christ's body plays in reconciling all to God can afford us some insight into the meaning of the Pauline and Irenaean statements on how all creation, spiritual and material, will be recapitulated in the man-God, Jesus Christ. It is a topic that we rarely find treated today, other than in an occasional reference to Teilhard de Chardin, even though we live in an age that has become strongly sympathetic to ecological issues and to the evolutionary outlook on life so prevalent in our society. The value, therefore, in reflecting upon the Antiochene synthesis is that it instills within us a critical awareness of a cosmic dimension to life. At creation, all beings were bonded in Adam; and at the consummation of the ages, the corporeal as well as the spiritual worlds will be brought together into a unified whole. Since no one has expressed this more eloquently than Saint Paul, I can think of no better and more fitting way to conclude our paper on the Antiochene outlook on how humans have been created "in the image and likeness of God" than to repeat his stirring and thrilling words in Colossians (1:15-18, 19-20) about who Christ is and what he has accomplished:

> He [the Christ] is the image of the invisible God, the firstborn of all creation. For in him were created all things in heaven and earth, the visible and the invisible . . . . He is before all things, and in him all things hold together . . . . For in him all the fullness was pleased to dwell, and through him to reconcile all things for him, making peace by the blood of the cross, whether those on earth and those in heaven.

NOTES

1. Geoffrey W. Bromiley, gen. ed., *The International Standard Bible Encyclopedia* II (Grand Rapids: William B. Eerdmans, 1979), 803. A similar conclusion is found in N. W. Porteous' article on "image" in *The Interpreter's Dictionary of the Bible* II (New York: Abingdon Press, 1962), 683. He writes: "The linguistic evidence which has been thus summarily reviewed would suggest that that there is not much difference in meaning between the two nouns." From this, he concludes: "This disposes of the dogmatic interpretation which goes back to Justin and Irenaeus that the 'image' is reason, which man retained after the Fall, whereas 'likeness' is 'justitia originalis,' which he lost."

2. Reginald C. Fuller, gen. ed., *A New Catholic Commentary on Holy Scripture* (New York: Thomas Nelson, 1969), 175. The same view is expressed in the exegesis of Gen. 1:26-27 in *New Jerome Biblical Commentary* (Englewood Cliffs: Prentice Hall, 1990), 11. Cf. also Edward Curtis' article on the "Image of God" in *The Anchor Bible Dictionary* 3, ed. by D. N. Freedman (New York: Doubleday, 1992), 389-91.

3. See Curtis, 389-91. Another question Curtis enters into is what effect ought the Hebrew preposition have upon the present translation: should it be understood as meaning that Adam and Eve were created not "according to" but "as" the image of God. He maintains that it is not clear that the preposition has ever had this latter meaning, though he allows that this may be what the biblical author of Genesis wants to convey. Cf. also John L. McKenzie's article on "image" in his *Dictionary of the Bible* (New York: Collier Book, 1965), 384.

4. Curtis believes that it was fear of idolatry that prevented the use of the term "image" in the period before the Exile. But afterwards, when idolatry was no longer a problem, Jewish writers were free to employ the imagery. He writes: "In the new religious context created by the Exile and return, the 'image of God' motif was again taken up and developed both in the intertestamental period and in the NT." See 391.

5. Curtis, 391.

6. Richard Clifford and Roland Murphy express this view in their commentary on Genesis in the *New Jerome Biblical Commentary*, 11, when they write that: "the human is a statue of the deity, not by static being but by action, who will rule over all things previously created. In the ancient Near East, the king was often called the image of the deity and was vested with God's authority; royal language is here used for the humans."

7. Porteous, 683.

8. McKenzie, 384.

9. Bromiley, 683.

10. Bromiley, 684.

11. McKenzie, 385.

12. Fuller, 175. E. F. Sutcliffe reminds us too that "in the Old Testament categories soul and body are so intimately one that the body is the soul in its outward form, its external expression." See his article in *A Catholic Commentary on Holy Scripture*, ed. B. Orchard, et al. (New York: Thomas Nelson, 1953), 183.

13. Curtis, 350.

14. Porteous, 684.

15. McKenzie, 385.

16. Porteous, 684.

17. For a summary treatment of some of these writers as well as others from the early church, cf. Lars Thunberg, "The Human Person as Image of God" in *Christian Spirituality: Origins to the Twelfth Century*" I, ed. by B. McGinn and J. Meyendorff (New York: Crossroad, 1985), 291-312; and especially A.-G. Hamman, *L'homme, image de Dieu* (Paris: Desclée, 1987).

18. The patristic views on the meaning of the phrase the "image of God" are rooted not only in the Jewish and Christian Scriptures but in the Greek philosophical speculations of their day. For two survey studies on Philo's influence, see A. Solignac's "Philon d'Alexandrie II. Influences sur les pères de l'église," *Dictionnaire de spiritualité ascétique et mystique, doctrine et histoire*, 12a (Paris: Beauchesne, 1983); and the articles on "Philo" and "Platonism" in the *Encyclopedia of the Early Church*, ed. by Angelo Di Berardino (New York: Oxford Press, 1992).

19. Philo, *Works. Philo Supplement* I, trans. by Ralph Marcus (Cambridge: Harvard University Press, 1953), 125.

20. David Winston, tr., *Philo of Alexandria: The Contemplative Life, the Giants and Selections* (New York: Paulist Press, 1981), 101.

21. For a fuller treatment of this, see Bernard McGinn, *The Foundations of Mysticism* I (New York: Crossroad, 1992), 38-39.

22. Cf. McGinn, 71-2.

23. Henry Chadwick, tr., *Origen: Contra Celsum* (Cambridge: Cambridge University Press, 1953), 378. For a list of citations from Origen's remarks on image, see the thematic anthology that Hans Urs von Balthasar has compiled, *Origen: Spirit and Fire*, trans. Robert J. Daly, (Washington: The Catholic University of America Press, 1984), 51-59. For a thorough study of how Origen understands image, see Henri Crouzel, *Théologie de l'image de Dieu chez Origène* (Paris: Aubier, 1957); and for a study on the role that the "image of God" played in the Origenist controversy, see Elizabeth A. Clark, *The Origenist Controversy: The Cultural Construction of an Early Christian Debate* (Princeton: Princeton University Press, 1992), 43-84.

24. Origen, *Homélies sur la Genèse*," tr. Louis Doutreleau, "Sources Chrétiennes" (Paris: Cerf, 1976), 56-57.

25. Daly, 378-79.

26. Origen, "ibid." Cf. also McGinn, 114.

27. Cyril of Alexandria, *In Mattheum, Patrologia Graeca* 72, ed. J.P. Migne (Paris: D'Ambroisi, 1859), 384. For the definitive work on Cyril's understanding of image, see Walter J. Burghardt, S.J., *The Image of God in Man According to Cyril of Alexandria* (Washington: The Catholic University of America Press, 1957).

28. Cyril of Alexandria, "Epistola ad Calosyrium" in Philip E. Pusey's *Sancti Patris Nostri Cyrilli Archiepiscopi Alexandrini in d. Joannia Evangelium* III (Oxford: Clarendon Press, 1872), 605.

29. See especially Chapters Two and Seven in Burghardt. In the latter, Burghardt points out a major inconsistancy in Cyril's position. Since Cyril affirms that our divine resemblance will be perfected only at the end of the time when we shall be like to Christ in his incorruptibility and superiority over death, it then ought to follow that the human body is here and now somehow imaging its future incorruptibility.

30. See R. Leys, *L'image de Dieu chez Grégorie de Nysse: Esquisse d'une doctrine* (Paris: Desclée de Brouwer, 1951); and H. Merki, *Von der platonischen Angleichung an Gott zur Gottähnlichkeit bei Gregor von Nyssa*, Paradosis VII (Freiburg: Paulusverlag, 1952).

31. Leys, 59-63 and 72-78.

32. Gregory of Nyssa, *In Cantica, P.G.* 44, 960-961.

33. Gregory of Nyssa, *The Life of Moses*, tr. A. J. Malherbe and E. Ferguson, (New York: Paulist Press, 1978), 136.

34. For an extended treatment of Augustine's view of image, see John E. Sullivan, O.P., *The Image of God: The Doctrine of St. Augustine and its Influence* (Dubuque: Priory Press, 1963).

35. Migne, *Patrologia Latina* 34, 292-93. Later in 749, he writes: "the only relation that I can see [between image and likeness] is that he [Moses] wished to signify the very same reality by these two words."

36. Saint Augustine, *De Trinitate*, tr. Stephen McKenna, "The Fathers of the Church" (Washington: Catholic University of America Press, 1963), 327-28. For a fuller treatment of this, see McGinn, 243-62 and Hamman, 256-58.

37. Saint Augustine, *De Trinitate*, 227.

38. Augustine, *Commentarium in Genesim, P.L.* 34, 292.

39. For a treatment of the role love plays in Augustine's understanding of image, see McGinn, 246-7.

40. Augustine, *De Trinitate, P.L.* 42, 972.

41. McKenna, tr., *De Trinitate*, 443.

42. McGinn, 247.

43. McGinn, 255-56.

44. Cf. Crouzel, 71 ff.

45. Bernard McGinn, "The Human Person as Image of God: Western Christianity," in *Christian Spirituality: Origins to the Twelfth Century*, ed. Bernard McGinn and John Meyendorff, (New York: Crossroad, 1985), sums up well the weakness of this approach: "The concentration on the soul, or inner person, as the true image and the difficulties that thinkers in this tradition had in expressing the substantial union of body and soul led to systematic ambiguities that encouraged depreciation of the body and sometimes skewed the sanity of ascetical observances" (328).

46. Procopius of Gaza (465-530) was an adherent of the Alexandrian position, especially that of Origen, and an opponent of Theodoretus of Cyrenis. He holds, however, an outlook similar to that of the Antiochenes regarding human beings as the bond of the universe and the symbolic representative of God to whom all the rest of creation must show reverence and service. See Procopius in *P.G.* 87, 123.

47. The School of Antioch is an umbrella designation for a group of exegetes and theologians who lived and wrote in the fourth and fifth centuries. Unlike the School of Alexandria that functioned as a unified, scholastic institution with a rather clearly defined program of study, the School of Antioch was a much more loosely organized grouping of scholars teaching in a personal capacity and sharing with others in their circle a basic commitment to the same literal and historical approach to exegesis and theology. They were especially opposed to what they deemed to be an excessive emphasis on the part of the Alexandrians to an allegorical interpretation of Scripture. They were also adament in their defense of the full integrity of Christ's human nature which they believed was being compromised by the Alexandrian stress upon Christ's divinity. The School's outstanding members were Diodore of Tarsus, Theodore of Mopsuestia, St. John Chrysostom, and Theodoret of Cyrrhus. Cf. the article on "Antioch: V. School" in the *Encyclopedia of the Early Church* I, 50.

48. For an understanding of the philosophical influences affecting the Antiochene fathers, see R. A. Norris, Jr., *Manhood and Christ* (Oxford: Clarendon, 1963), 3-20.

49. This may also explain why in their exegetical interpretation that the Antiochenes are suspicious of what they believe to be an overemphasis upon the spiritual or allegorical meaning of a text to the detriment of its 'bodily' meaning.

50. For a fine summary of the Antiochene position, see Jules Gross, *La divinisation de chrétien d'après les pères grecs* (Paris: J. Gabalda, 1938), esp. 253-276.

51. While the ante-Nicene fathers strongly maintained that humans were created in the image of God in a non-anthropomorphic way, they reveal very little elaboration on this subject, at least in those works presently available to us. A few, (e.g. the author of *De resurrectione*, a work attributed to the second century Justin Martyr in *P.G.* 6, 1585; Cyprian's *De Bono Patientiae* in *P.L.* 4, 634; and Lactantius in his *Divinae Institutiones* in the "Corpus Scriptorum Ecclesiasticorum Latinorum" 19, 147) refer to the whole person as being made in the image of God, but without explaining what they mean by this. Irenaeus is the one exception. He distinguishes between image and likeness, understanding image as referring to the whole human composite of body and soul and likeness as indicating the presence of the Spirit's activity in completing human nature and making it stable. For a further study of Irenaeus' understanding of "image" and "likeness," see Jacques Fantino, *L'homme image de Dieu*

chez saint Irénée de Lyon (Paris: Cerf, 1986). He also provides a summary of excerpts on how "image" was understood in the ancient world up to the second century.

52. This citation of Diodorus is found in *P.G.* 80, 107-10.

53. John Chrysostom, *Epistola ad Colossianos: Homilia III, P.G."* 62, 317-18.

54. John Chrysostom, *Commentarium in Genesim: Homilia VIII, P.G.* 53, 72. The same idea is expressed also in *Homilia IX*, 78: "It [image] refers not to the dignity of one's substance, but to a kind of dominion."

55. Migne, *P.G.* 54, 589. Cf. also 53, 74.

56. See John Chrysostom, *Epistola Secunda ad Corinthious: Homilia VIII, P.G.* 61, 456.

57. Edward Sachau, ed., *Theodori Mopsuesteni Fragmenta Syriaca* (Leipzig: G. Engelmann, 1869). William Wright has authenticated the Genesis text as being truly from Theodore. For additional passages of Theodore's "Commentary on Genesis," see R.-M. Tonneau, "Théodore de Mopsueste, Interprétation (du Livre) de la Genèse (Vat. Syr. 120, ff. I-V)," in *Le Muséon* 66 (1953), 45-64; as well as the fragments contained in *P.G.* 66, 109-13.

58. Françoise Petit, 'L'homme créé "à l'image" de Dieu quelques fragments grecs inèdits de Théodore de Mopsueste,' in *Le Muséon* 100 (1987), 269-81.

59. Petit, 269.

60. Sachau, 15 and 18.

61. Sachau, 5.

62. Sachau, 15.

63. Petit, 275-77.

64. See pp. 24-25 above.

65. Theodore of Mopsuestia, *De Incarnatione*, XIV, *P.G.* 66, 991.

66. Petit, 277-81.

67. Sachau, 14. Cf. also Petit, 272-73.

68. Theodoretus, *Quaestiones in Genesim*, *P.G.* 80, 103-07.

69. Theodoretus, *P.G.* 80, 103.

70. Idem.

71. Theodoretus, *P.G.* 80, 103-05.

72. Theodoretus, *P.G.* 80, 106-07. For a different conclusion, see E. Montmasson's "L'Homme créé à l'image de Dieu d'après Théodoret de Cyr et Procope de Gaza," *Échos D'Orient* XV (1912), esp. 158-60. I believe that Montmasson has missed the significance of how image relates to humans as the bonds of the universe and how Theodoret's remarks on image as dominion need to be interpreted in light of the distinction that Theodore of Mopsuestia makes between "image" and "likeness."

73. Cf. R. Lavenant's article "Edessa" in *Encyclopedia of the Early Church*, 263.

74. Barhadbshabba Arbaya, "Cause de la Fondation des Écoles", trans. A. Scher, *Patrologia Orientalis* 4, (Turnhout: Brepols, 1907), 377, asserts that Ephrem founded this school in 363 A.D. E.R. Hayes, *L'École d'Édessa* (Paris, 1930), 39-40, believes that a school already existed before Ephrem arrived at Edessa. Arthur Vööbus, *History of the School of Nisibis*, Corpus Scriptorum Christianorum Orientalium 266, Subs. 26, (Louvain: CSCO, 1965), 8, questions the reliability of the sources. But he believes that "there is no cogent reason for us to reject the tradition altogether. It may contain a historical kernel." In regard to Ephrem's view on image, we see this expressed in his *Commentarium in Genesim*, I, 29, Corpus Scriptorum Christianorum Orientalium, 153, 17, where he maintains that image pertains to Adam because of his freedom and his dominion over creatures. He understands that this is exemplified in three ways. First, just as the power of God is present in all things, so has Adam's dominion been placed over all. Secondly, Adam possesses a pure soul that can receive into itself all kinds of virtues and divine charisms. Thirdly, it can direct the rational part of the soul to any point and arouse images of anything that it wants. In other words, image for Ephrem is a spiritual power that is like unto God's in its ability to exercise dominion within the universe as well as to acquire all virtues and at least be able to conceive of all created things. This view of image commands interest because it comes out of a Syriac tradition that at least initially shows little or no influence from Greek philosophical thought. Beginning in the fifth century, Theodore of Mopsuestia's understanding of image will start to supplant that of Ephrem among the East Syrians.

75. Narsai's homily in defense of the three doctors attests to this. See F. Martin's "Homélie de Narses sur les trois Docteurs nestoriens," *Journal Asiatique* 14 (1899), 446-92; and 15 (1900), 469-525. Edessa was also noted as a center where Greek and Syriac texts were quickly translated into each other languages.

76. For a biography of Narsai, see Philippe Gignoux's *Homélies de Narsai sur la Création*, Patrologia Orientalis XXXIV/3-4, (Paris: Brepols, 1968), 419-23.

77. See Wanda Wolska-Conus, *Cosmas Indicopleustès Topographie chrétienne*, Sources Chrétiennes 141, 159, 197 (Paris: Cerf, 1968-1973).

78. See Ceslas van den Eynde ed., *Commentaire d'Išo'dad de Merv sur l'Ancien Testament, I. Genèse*, Corpus Scriptorum Christianorum Orientalium 156 (Louvain: L. Durbecq, 1955).

79. It is not clear whether Narsai holds, as Diodorus and John Chrysostom did, that Adam is the image of God and Eve the glory of man. But he frequently speaks of image in such general terms that he seems to embrace all of humanity without intending to make any distinction between male and female. For both possess a rational soul and a human body that join them to both the spiritual and material worlds. Yet Narsai, because he holds that Christ is the primary image and Adam is an image of this image, may simply not see any difficulty here. He may presume that it is evident that image applies only to Adam and to men in general. Whatever the reason, Narsai has seen no need to clarify what are his views on this matter.

80. See A. Mingana, ed., *Narsai doctoris syri homiliae et carmina* II (Mosul, 1905), 251.

81. Frederick McLeod, S.J., ed., *Narsai's Metrical Homilies on the Nativity, Epiphany, Passion, Resurrection and Ascension,* Patrologia Orientalis 40/1 (Turnhout: Brepols, 1979), 39.

82. Mingana II, 100.

83. Mingana I, 17.

84. Mingana II, 239.

85. McLeod, 39.

86. Gignoux, 599.

87. Gignoux, 603.

88. McLeod, 177. For a very similar passage, cf. Thomas of Edessa, *Tractatus De Nativitate Domini Nostri Christi*, ed. Simon Joseph Carr, (Rome, 1898), 39.

89. McLeod, 131.

90. McLeod, 39.

91. Mingana II, 239.

92. Mar Aba I is considered to be one of the principal promoters in recasting the doctrine of Theodore of Mopsuestia in the sixth century. See Wolska-Conus, 85.

93. Wolska-Conus, 470. We see a similar passage in Iso'dad of Merv, 49.

94. Wolska-Conus, 34.

95. Ceslas van den Eynde, 49-53.

96. For a detailed study of the attitudes of early Christians towards the body, see Peter Brown, *The Body and Society: Men, Women, and Sexual Renunciation in Early Christianity* (New York: Columbia University Press, 1988).

97. Those insisting that the image of God was to be sought in the highest reaches of the soul readily admit that the Incarnation and Jesus' bodily resurrection involve the body as an essential element that must be attended to within salvation. But they apparently did not see any need to reconcile their outlook on this point with what they held regarding image. They seem satisfied simply to state that the image of God resides in the body. Cf. Burghardt, 102-03.

BODY AS MORAL METAPHOR

IN DANTE'S *COMMEDIA*

James Gaffney

In his letter introducing the *Paradiso* to his friend and patron, Can Grande della Scala, Dante prefaces an observation about the entire *Commedia*: "To clarify what has to be said, it is essential to be aware that the meaning of this work is not single but that it is a work having multiple senses, a number of meanings."[1] He goes on to distinguish between a first sense, called "literal," and a second which he calls "allegorical, moral, or anagogic."[2] These three terms, which Dante does not distinguish from one another, were in common use among medieval interpreters of the Bible. Taken collectively, they represent the capacity of the text to signify not simply "things," but things that have themselves some further significance.[3]

Since Dante, in the same letter, identifies the "philosophical genre" of his poem as "ethics," his second meanings tend to be of a moral or moralizing nature. It is in this sense that I propose to review some of the more interesting ways in which bodies, and conditions and circumstances of bodies, serve the *Commedia* as moral metaphors. But since non-literal senses have their basis in a literal sense, it is well to recall what Dante, and his educated contemporaries, thought a body, i.e. a human body, was.

Dante's philosophical assumptions about bodiliness derive from the Aristotelian doctrine of matter as co-principle with form in constituting mutable substances. A human body is accordingly the material component of a human substance, or person, whose form, however, is a distinctively spiritual soul.[4] Indeed, the word in Dante's Italian properly translated as "body" is more often *persona* than *corpo,* the latter term tending to have more sheerly physical, and at times cadaverous connotations. To these philosophical data must be added, on theological grounds, the soul's capacity to exist separately from the body after death, and the body's destiny to be reunited with that soul in an eschatological "resurrection."[5]

There is a popular, practical implication of the soul's being the form of the human body, namely that the imperceptible condition of a person's soul is exhibited, to some degree, in the perceptible condition of that person's body. Most obviously, that is what makes possible the physical communication of thought and feeling. It also constitutes the psychosomatic basis of common-sense beliefs that bodies can reveal, even unintentionally, mental and moral characteristics as well as passing moods. In that sense, the understanding--and sometimes misunderstanding--of body language occurs frequently throughout the *Commedia* in Dante's more intimate social encounters. There is also a reciprocal implication, that bodily deportment can be morally formative. Hence the importance attached in the Middle Ages, as in the Classical period, to norms of modesty or bodily decorum. In codified form, many of these norms, actually pre-Christian in origin, found their way into modern Catholicism in the rule books of religious communities.[6] Dante's own rather austere taste in male dress, and his scorn for female cosmetics and plunging necklines, were not untypical of contemporary educated Florentines.

A theological perspective having special importance for Dante's poetical moralizing is the idea that bodily reality, being created and redeemed by God, reveals something of God and transmits something of divine influence. This notion is fundamental to Christian sacramentalism, according to which bodily things and their actions become signs and instruments of divine grace.[7] It is likewise implicit in Dante's understanding of his own use of allegory.[8] And it is inseparable from Dante's Aristotelian psychology, according to which all intellectual knowledge must originate in sense perception. Beatrice lectures him on this subject in Paradise, observing that "it is for this reason that Scripture accommodates itself to your faculty, even attributing a hand and feet to God, while signifying something quite different."[9]

One can only guess what ideas about the body Dante may have drawn from popular culture, but he is unlikely to have escaped altogether the influence of what seems to have been the most popular medieval metaphor for the body. That is the likening of the body to a house, a house that provides its occupants' most intimate and essential environment and establishes a domain of ultimate privacy.[10] Like a proper house, its outside should be fenced or hedged, and its doors and windows should be controlled by the resident. It has its properly adorned space for leisure and hospitality, and also nether regions, quite indispensable, but scarcely suitable for public viewing. Just as stability, decorum, and discretionary access were the chief attributes of a respectable house, so were they of a body. The popularity of this metaphor, which is exploited even by medical text-books, reminds us that among ordinary medieval citizens the body was not an object of shame or detestation, but rather of privacy and discreet management. This seems very much the attitude of Dante, who was not, after all, a medieval monk, much less a medieval Manichee. By the same token, I do not think the fact that nudity is so prevalent in the *Inferno* is meant to suggest its inhabitants' prurience or obscenity, but rather their ravaged interiority. Theirs is not the vigorous nudity of the gymnasium, nor even the salacious nudity of the bordello. More nearly, it is the nudity of the morgue, the sad transparency of houses in a devastated city. In the same way, Dante's infernal scatology, represented by rivers of excrement and demons who signal with trumpet-bursts of flatulence, suggests a kind of parody of neglectful sanitary indecency. Dante, unlike Milton, finds no place in Hell for grandeur; a realm forsaken by goodness and truth must, in his philosophy, be forsaken also by beauty.

To speak of human bodies at all in Dante's *Commedia*, some preliminary distinctions have to be made. In the strictest sense, only one human body participates in the action of the poem. That is the poet's own body, whose earthly, temporal conditions are repeatedly contrasted with its eschatological milieu. In the course of the poem it exhibits many of the frailties that flesh is heir to, but also many of its strengths. It faints, falls, hurts, reels, wearies, and recoils from sensory shock. But again and again, with encouragement and help, it recovers itself and goes on. All the other human beings in the poem are not, in the strict sense, embodied. In *Inferno* and *Purgatorio* they appear embodied, and experience the sensations and emotions normally mediated by bodily organs and tissues. A mythico-scientific explanation of this arrangement is supplied by the poet Statius, comprising a kind of medieval synopsis of biological development from gamete to ghost.[11] In view of current concerns over when, according to Christian teaching, a fetus acquires full humanity, it is interesting to note that, in the strictly embryological portion of this account, it is taken for granted that a human soul does not become the body's form until the embryonic brain is fully developed.[12] In any case, according to Statius's "metabiology," after death the body's form replicates the shape of the body by a kind of projection onto the circumambient atmosphere. The resulting likeness, appropriately called a "shade," or shadow (*ombra*), is endowed with sensory and motor powers, and is not, therefore, simply an illusion, even though its appearing to be a normal body is illusory. This curious blend of embodiment and disembodiment makes possible not only the punitive and penitential experiences of *Inferno* and *Purgatorio*, but also a great many symbolically ingenious "special effects." Dante's original conception of the shades undoubtedly came from Vergil's account of Aeneas's journey to the underworld, but he has modified it to accommodate the more complex circumstances of Christian eschatology.[13] By the same token, in *Paradiso* human individuals are encountered not as body-like shades, but as configurations of brilliant light, varying in shape and intensity. This device of Dante's serves the poem well, but has always posed a problem to graphic illustrators, who often seem stimulated by the first two cantiche and then daunted by all but the most pyrotechnical scenes of the third.

The attribute of Dante's bodiliness that is most often contrasted with the condition of the shades is his weight, or gravitational mass.[14] He has also a kind of opacity that casts a shadow, whereas the shades do not.[15] These qualities identify the poet as belonging to another world, and destined to return there, as we are several times reminded by astonished reactions among the spirits he visits. Indeed, Dante's weight, as an aspect and symbol of his mortal, embodied humanity, constitutes a metaphor of fundamental importance which permeates the entire poem. It is not an original metaphor, having been introduced into Christian tradition by the theological imagination of St. Augustine, who summarized it in the famous epigram, *amor meus pondus meum*, which unfortunately sounds silly when rendered into English as "my love is my weight."[16] To dispel the silliness and appreciate the point, one must recognize that Augustine is thinking in scientific, albeit pre-Newtonian terms of gravitational attraction. To have weight is, therefore, to be subject to attraction, and what is experienced as weight is pressure in the direction of what preponderantly attracts. "My weight" represents my experience of being drawn or pulled in a definite direction by an attracting force. And that is, in one sense of the word, what Augustine means by "love." Thus, "my love is my weight" means that I perceive my love as an experience of being drawn, with the implication that the direction in which I am drawn indicates the effective object of my love. For Augustine, of course, disordered love, which prevails over our fallen nature, draws us ever downward. The opposing upward pull of the love of God remains futile unless we are assisted and elevated by divine grace. (We may be reminded of the persistence and scope of this metaphor by Simone Weil's entitling her study of Christianity *Le pesanteur et la grace* which has been rendered into English as "Gravity and Grace"--not at all a bad alternative title for the *Commedia*.[17]

The first of Dante's three great journeys, the *Inferno*, is relentlessly downward. Interrupted and deflected only by the contours of the vast conical underworld, he tends where his own weight draws him, and encounters those who have been drawn by similar weight beyond all hope of returning. The levels of evil, although all damnable, grow increasingly detestable as the descent continues, corresponding to the ever greater weight of ever more disordered love. The lowest point where Satan himself is lodged, is at the very center of the planet, the center, that is, of gravity, the ultimate point to which bodies on earth can fall by their own weight. Dante experiences this physically when, after climbing down the giant inverted body of Satan, and continuing into the passage that leads to the opposite side of the world, he suddenly feels in his own body that he is no longer letting himself down, but, without any change of direction, is now hauling himself up.[18] Enjoyable in itself as a contrivance of medieval science fiction, the episode is a rich spiritual metaphor that recalls the reader to the very beginning of the poem where Dante, unable to ascend the "delightful mountain," learns from Vergil that, for such as he, it is only the downward path that can lead upward.

As *Inferno* was an abyss, so *Purgatorio* is a mountain, to the very summit of which Dante must now carry his own weight, exerting his natural strength against the downward tug of gravity, in resolute pursuit of his goal--the natural goal of human nature. And as he strives upward he finds, even though the way does not grow less steep, that his strength grows with the exertion, so that he carries his weight more and more easily.[19] Everyone he meets along the way, despite barriers, burdens, and delays, is filled with a sense of tranquility and assured progress. Already in Purgatory one experiences the positive force of that principle which is famously enunciated in Paradise, *E'n la sua volontade e nostra pace*--in his will is our peace.[20] Dante the climber is not, of course, wholly self-sufficient; he needs help from time to time, and when he needs it he gets it. Sometimes the help far exceeds the need, in a kind of largesse of grace, as when, during sleep, a saint carries him in her arms to the next level of his ascent.[21] It is natural goodness, assisted by grace, maturing in virtue. The long climb ends at last on level ground, in a setting of natural perfection, a beautiful, tranquil, outdoor world, full of vitality--and yet, devoid of human life. For this is the natural habitat of a natural goodness that perished with the corruption of human nature. The only way to get here now is by a journey that, like Dante's, travels beyond the realm of nature into the realm of grace.

For that final journey he cannot carry his weight, much less be carried by his weight. The motor power of his love is no longer efficacious. And so, in Paradise, Dante becomes in effect weightless. His passage from heavenly sphere to heavenly sphere is effortless and instantaneous. To the reader of *Paradiso* Dante still seems to be embodied, and yet freed from all restraints of bodily inertia. But Dante himself is not sure, and he deliberately renders the reader unsure when he says to God, "Whether I only was the part of me that you created last, you, governing the heavens, know."[22] There can be little doubt that Dante is here appropriating the reflection of his illustrious predecessor, St. Paul, who was also carried into the heavens during his mortal life, but, as he observes, "Whether in the body or out of the body I do not know, God knows."[23] In any case, the heavens themselves are corporeal, all the way through the Primum Mobile. Beyond that lies the Empyrean, where the poem and the journey end. The Empyrean is not corporeal, being "the heaven of pure light, intellectual light full of love, love of the true good, full of joy."[24] It is that love, which moves all things, that carries the poet through his final journey.

To turn from the pervasive metaphor of Dante's own body, and more precisely of his bodily weight, to more particular instances of body as moral metaphor raises problems of selection from an abundance of relevant material. The first bodies we meet in *Inferno* are dense mobs of those who, as the poet puts it, "never really lived," that is, never undertook any commitments, enlisted in any cause, embarked on any real course.[25] They are a herd of naked, sweaty, insect-stung bodies, following in crazy motion a meaningless banner in an endless procession that gets nowhere. Equally repulsive and absurd, they are bodies whose souls were, so to speak, superfluous, giving no direction, good or bad, to life. Here, if anywhere in the poem, we see Dante's contempt for what is sometimes meant by "the masses," stumbling along whatever path appears to be that of least resistance. The question spontaneously suggests itself, What are they for?, and the poet answers, "for themselves alone."[26] That is why, on the periphery even of Hell, their alienation is so total. They do not matter; not to God, not even to Satan. *Guarda e passa*, says Vergil to his companion: "Just take a look and move along."[27]

In Limbo, the classical heroes and sages are characterized by magnitude and solemnity.[28] They are strolling or seated, their voices modulated, their attitudes courteous and serious. Their facial expressions have no trace of sadness, but neither are they joyous. Their place of residence, full of light and natural beauty, affords our last sight of green and flowery brightness until the slopes of Purgatory.

Just below that classical serenity, darkness closes in, where a chaotic windstorm tosses the bodies of adulterers. The imagery expresses the classical judgment of lust as a surrendering of bodily life to forces of unpredictable and uncoordinated turbulence.[29] In this scene of randomly buffeted individual human bodies there is only one peculiar vestige of stability--Dante's one compromise between classical and romantic perceptions of sexual infidelity. The adulterers Paolo and Francesca, although at the mercy of the wind like all the others, remain, nevertheless, together. Dante weeps at the sight of this couple, and his sympathy is not reproved by Vergil. Eternally storm-tossed and yet eternally inseparable, the bodies of these famous lovers suggest the two powerful counter-currents of classical morality and courtly love present in the poet and his world.

The bodies of gluttons suffer a different kind of storm, a steady, dirty, winter downpour.[30] They are not flung about but stretched prone in the slush and mud, immobilized and barely distinct from the filth they lie in. This kind of intemperance, unlike that of sex, elicits no romantic mitigations.

With the greedy and the wasteful we meet for the first time purposefully striving bodies.[31] But their very strenuousness only emphasizes their futility, because their constantly clashing efforts only cancel one another out. Both groups move heavy weights, but always in opposite directions, constantly colliding and reversing themselves only to collide again. The economic irony of a society in which both enormous avarice and enormous waste combine to frustrate human aspirations was not less present to medieval Florentines than it is to modern Americans.

The plight of the wrathful and the sullen, their senses clogged and their limbs impeded by the Stygian mud, has a symbolism to which the sullen themselves give rueful expression.[32] Having shut out of their lives all the fresh air and sunshine of normal amiability, they are now swallowed up in the kind of atmosphere with which they polluted the communities that had to endure their presence.

Bodies of arch-heretics are actually entombed, in burning sepulchers, and it is only their eerie necropolis that meets Dante's eyes when he finally makes his way through the gates of the City of Dis.[33] Why this strange combination of entombment and cremation? Perhaps the fire recalls the familiar way of executing heretics. Perhaps the graves signify the spiritual lethalness attributed to heresy.

That the violent against their neighbors should be plunged in rivers of blood requires no subtle explanation.[34] The condition of the suicides, however, makes an important symbolic statement. In the form of blackened, burnt out trees and briars, they are more unlike human bodies than any other sinners.[35] And they tell us that when real bodies rise again on the last day, theirs are destined only to hang like tattered rags from their brittle twigs and thorns. For Dante, then, the malice of suicide is found less in the fact of killing than in the contemptuous implication of discarding God's great gift of the body. Accordingly, their bodies are to remain forever what they have made of them, a kind of trash.

The bodies of those whose violence is directed to God, such as blasphemers, crouch, lie, or crawl upon an arid wasteland under a slow shower of flames.[36] Perhaps we are invited to see here the ghastly parody which results from despising those gifts from above that saturate the world with fertile vitality. Curiously it is here, among the violent against God, rather than among the lustful, that Dante at first places the sodomites, though in *Purgatorio* he seems to revise this moral taxonomy. Nonetheless, it is noteworthy that here, as with Paolo and Francesca, we have one of the rare occasions of tender sympathy between the poet and one of the damned, in this case his old beloved teacher, Brunetto Latini. Their tender meeting ends with Brunetto forced to run in pain across the fiery desert. And yet he looks to Dante like one of the athletes who race across the meadows at Verona and, as his old pupil touchingly adds, not like a loser of the race, but like a winner![37]

A new kind of body symbolism is introduced by Vergil's recalling that in the mountains of Crete there stands a towering, ancient figure of a man, with golden head, silver shoulders, a brazen torso, and legs all of iron, except for the right foot, made of clay, on which he rests most heavily. Perpetual tears running down his immense body into the earth form the sources of the terrible rivers of Hell. Borrowed partly from the Bible and partly from Ovid, this body represents a human history in long, continual decline, that irrigates Hell and rests now on the two supports of Empire and Church.[38] The whole drift of Dante's social and political criticism leaves no doubt that it is the Church which is the foot of clay.

In the circle of fraud, the upside-down burial of the simoniac clergy proclaims their inversion of fundamental priorities, the twisted necks of the astrologers mock their pretended knowledge of the future, and there is an unmistakable appropriateness in the immersion in human excrement of those who corrupt by flattery.[39] Here too are the hypocrites, outwardly shining but weighted down by interior leadenness.[40] The thieves, who appropriate what is not their own, are here repeatedly despoiled of their very bodily identities in an endless cycle of metamorphoses into serpents.[41]

In the lowest depths of Hell, beyond the crucified Caiaphas, the bodies of great betrayers are variously lacerated in ways that recall the bloody consequences of their treacheries.[42] At the very bottom is the body of Lucifer, prodigious in size, but with nothing of Miltonic grandeur, shoved head downward into the funnel neck of Hell. For Hell's abyss was created by an outraged God's hurling that enormous body through the crust of the earth. But by a grotesque providence, symbolic of the Christian paradox of good arising out of evil, that same act had a constructive consequence. For it was the earth displaced by Lucifer's gigantic body that erupted on the opposite side of the globe to produce the "delightful mountain" of Purgatory.[43]

In Purgatory all the bodies are either in motion or eagerly ready to move. And there is no chaotic motion. It is progressive and ascending. Dante and those he meets are headed in the same direction now. They are fellow-pilgrims. This is a clean and, as its name declares, a cleansing place. Vergil must wash Dante's face clean of its hell-stains before they can proceed.[44] The air is bright and full of music. Biblical and liturgical themes abound in word and picture. There is no lack of arduousness, but the contrast is profound between the rigors endured here and those of the underworld. Basically, it is the contrast between harsh vengeance and vigorous discipline, between torture and training. And the contrast is reflected in a wholly different mood: confidence replaces hopelessness, and there is joy instead of bitterness. The proud labor under heavy weights, but only to learn not to be unbending.[45] The eyes of the envious are sealed, but only to teach kinder ways of looking.[46] The wrathful must move in a smoky darkness, until their inner smolderings cease to blight their society.[47] Here the slothful take lessons in running.[48] The greedy, fastened to the ground, consider how one is weighted down by excessive property.[49] The gluttonous mend their ways by fasting, until the contours of their thinned faces remind them what they are by outlining the name *omo*--man.[50] In interesting contrast to the

arrangement of *Inferno*, here the lustful penitents comprise hetero-
sexuals and homosexuals alike, and once cleansed by a purifying fire,
they innocently exchange kisses.[51]

Beyond all these is the earthly paradise, where the long penitential ascent, grown easier at each successive level by a gradual lighten-
ing and livening, finally ends. It is the idyllic habitat of humanity's
bodily life. The air, the water, the living things are all an environ-
mentalist's best dream, equally beautiful and wholesome. But the
spirits who ascend the mountain cannot remain or even linger here,
and Dante's solitary sojourn is for his unique education. For the
earthly paradise is humanity's paradise lost, that peaceable kingdom
from which the unruly ways of human beings required their expul-
sion.[52]

This place will be Dante's last earthly sojourn, and the occasion
of his last experiences of unequivocal bodiliness. He is welcomed by
a beautiful woman, reminiscent of Persephone as she gathers flowers
by the river side, with a singer's voice and a dancer's gait, known to
us only as Matilda.[53] It is she who escorts him to his long-awaited
rendez-vous with Beatrice--who is at first stern and veiled. Despite
the shock of this cold encounter, Dante recalls the turmoil of feelings this woman had so long ago stirred in his youthful body, and
"felt the great power of an ancient love."[54] Turning to share this
moment with his dearest friend and surest guide, he finds that Vergil
has silently vanished, and the face he had just washed is stained
again with tears.[55]

Beatrice has hard words for her errant lover, but at last she
removes her veil, resumes her gentleness, and exhibits a beauty that
from this moment on grows more dazzling with every stage of their
upward journey. Her sacramental role is delicately expressed as, each
time Dante gazes lovingly into her eyes, her own eyes turn from his
upward, inviting his to share her own climactic vision as, at the
poem's end, they do.

Much of Dante's sojourn in the earthly paradise is occupied at
a kind of theater-in-the-park, as spectator of an allegorical pageant
that summarizes, partly with bitter satire, the course of Christian
history. Dante's political and ecclesiastical views are plain in the final
scene of lascivious embraces between a jealous giant and a fickle
whore, parodying the political flirtations of Philip the Fair and
Boniface VIII.[56] We are reminded that identifying the bishop of
Rome with the whore of Babylon was not, as is often supposed, a
Protestant satirical invention, but a Catholic one.

The metaphor of the body does not find a great deal of nourishment in Paradise, where even Dante's own bodiliness is ambiguous, and where conversation of a decidedly abstract and metaphysical sort tends to predominate. Nevertheless, *Paradiso* does make some important contributions to this theme.

Given the strange, strong currents of dualism, especially of a Manichean kind, that had widespread influence during the high Middle Ages, it is worth emphasizing that Dante's own habitual attitude towards materiality in general, and human bodiliness in particular, is matter-of-factly positive. Although he has strong views about indecency and conventional assumptions about modesty, he is no more embarrassed by the sheer fleshliness of the human condition than would be Boccaccio or Chaucer. And to exclude any misunderstanding on this score, Beatrice delivers in Paradise a theological lecture on creation in which the divine origin and original goodness of matter are explicitly affirmed.[57] In all of this, Dante's views are simply and comfortably orthodox, very much in harmony with the Aristotelianism of Thomas Aquinas.

Even admirers of the general reasonableness of Thomas Aquinas, however, are likely to concede that there was something in the medieval air that often led even him into nonsense on one aspect of human bodiliness, that of sexuality. It is pleasant to observe that his admirer Dante seems to have kept well clear of the more grotesque features of the "sexology of the medieval church."[58] There is no suggestion in the *Commedia* that sex is supremely hazardous to Christian or natural morality, or that sexual immorality, when it does occur, is supremely heinous. It cannot be accidental that the lustful are situated farthest from the depths in Hell, and nearest to the summit in Purgatory. What is perhaps more significant, though less often remarked, is that active sexuality defines a location in Paradise.

That the third heaven should be Venus was dictated by the sky maps of medieval astronomy, a science in which Dante was uncommonly learned. But just how venereal Venus was to be in the scheme of the *Commedia* was left to the poet's discretion, and it is hard to doubt that, although the third heaven's representatives could not, of course, be lustful, Dante did want them to be unmistakably lusty. How otherwise could he have selected as his sole delegate from the pages of the Bible Rahab, the harlot, and even insisted that she was the very first one Christ admitted to this heaven after he liberated the Old Testament saints.[59] The love poet, Folco of Marseilles, minces no words about the erotic fervor which led to difficulties in his youth; but about such things, he delightfully comments, in heaven there can be no more remorse, but only laughter![60]

Perhaps most eloquent of the mood in Venus is Cunizza da Romano, who proudly declares that "I shine here because this planet's radiance conquered me," and complacently acknowledges that this may not be pleasing to the "vulgar-minded."[61] This oft-wed and sometimes not quite wed lady was a well-known elder contemporary of Dante's, whose reputation is summarized as follows by a younger contemporary: "She was, in all her ages, a woman in love, and so generous in her love that she would have counted it as great villainy to refuse it to any man who sought it courteously."[62]

This third heaven, perhaps because its theme is associated with reproduction, is also the setting of a lecture on genetics delivered by Charles Martel, occasioned by the observation that great men not infrequently beget disappointing children. This reflection prompts a discussion of the seeming randomness with which hereditary traits and combinations of them are distributed between one generation and the next. The discussion has a moral lesson as well as scientific interest. For this randomness is said to be providential, inasmuch as it engenders great individual variation within the species, and thereby makes possible the intricate complementarity of abilities and needs out of which civil society is constructed. Nevertheless, Martel observes, we continually spoil this process by deciding *a priori* what our offspring should be and do. As a result, our society overflows with misfits who, for that very reason, do immeasurable harm. That is why we have as rulers people who would have done better as preachers, and monks who would be fitter for soldiering. We ought to see what our children really are like, and then seek appropriate opportunities for them, instead of decreeing what they must be like and proceeding to make their lives ruinous for themselves and for others.[63]

The high value Dante sets upon the body is brought out in Paradise, when he inquires among the brilliantly luminous and joyous spirits there what significant effect they could anticipate from the resurrection of the body. There seems to be a suggestion that, for beings such as they, being reclothed in a mere body seems anticlimactic, and dulling rather than enhancing. On the contrary, he is assured, they are actually defective without their bodies, and once they are restored their brilliance will be intensified and every kind of experience mediated by the senses will be immeasurably heightened.[64] In Paradise that means, of course, greater joy, but in Hell the pains of the damned will likewise be intensified. In any case, Dante clearly does not regard the body and its senses as in any way obstacles to the richest kinds of experience.

In the eighth heaven, something happens to Dante the meaning of which has always perplexed commentators. Numerous inconclusive interpretations have been published over the centuries, including one of my own.[65] The context is a series of examinations on faith, hope, and love, administered to Dante by Saints Peter, James, and John.[66] Just before the last examination begins, Dante peers curiously, trying to discern if the legend were true according to which John the Evangelist, like the Blessed Virgin, was assumed bodily into heaven. The saint denies the legend and then, suddenly, Dante is struck totally blind. Deprived of the support of Beatrice's gaze, he marvels that such a thing could befall him there, in "the world of gladness." Out of this bewildering darkness he must discourse in response to the saint's questions about love. His answers are exemplary, and at the end he feels his eyes reopened by the probing gaze of Beatrice, with keener vision than ever before. Without belaboring the exegetical questions, I would suggest that the commonest explanation, that Dante's blindness is a punishment inflicted for his impudent curiosity about the body of St. John, is totally incongruous with the whole meaning of *Paradiso*, and that a more plausible symbolism is to be sought in the mystical tradition of an interior darkness that tests love in preparation for the highest reaches of contemplation.

At all events, it is the very pinnacle of contemplative ascent for which Dante is destined when, in the final canto, drawn beyond all heavens into the Empyrean, he is shown by the light of glory a vision of God. And our theme retains its relevance even to that supremely spiritual climax. For in the ecstasy of the divine vision itself the poet sees what is, unmistakably, "our image," the form, that is, of our bodily humanity. For inseparable from the vision of the triune God is the vision of the Word made flesh. Dante's Christology is visually confirmed. God, too, has a body. How such a thing can be surpasses his power of intellect. "But then my mind was struck by light that flashed and, with this light, received what it had asked."[67] And with that the poetry ends. For the poet's imagination is now superfluous, because "already desire and will were moved, like an evenly turning wheel . . . " and the motion of the poet's inner being becomes united with the motion of all the heavens he has traversed, driven now as they are driven, wholly by Love.

NOTES

1. Dante Alighieri, *Opere Latine* (Milan: Rizzoli, 1965), p. 205. [In this and all subsequent instances (unless otherwise indicated), the English renderings of Latin and Italian texts are my own.]

2. *Ibid.*

3. Thomas Aquinas, *Summa Theologiae* (Turin: Marietti, 1952), 1a.1.10. "That sense in which things, signified by words, themselves signify yet other things, is called a spiritual sense." Aquinas does distinguish the three non-literal senses, in a way that was sufficiently conventional to be summarized in a medieval mnemonic rhyme: *Litera gesta docet/quid credos allegoria/moralis quid agas/quid speres anagogia* (The literal sense teaches what has been accomplished; the allegorical, what you are to believe; the moral, how you are to behave; the anagogic, what you are to hope for.) *ibid.*, p. 561. For Dante's elaboration of this doctrine, see Dante Alighieri, *Convivio* (Milan: Rizzoli, 1952), pp. 70- 72.

4. *Purgatorio* XXV, 72.

5. *Ibid.*, 79.

6. One widely imitated by modern religious communities is the Jesuit *Regulae Modestiae*. The Christianization of these classical manners was mainly accomplished by St. Ambrose, whose *De officiis ministrorum* adapted them from Cicero's *De officiis*.

7. The orthodox understanding of sacraments is epitomized in Thomas Aquinas, *Summa Theologiae*, IIIa, qq. 50- 52.

8. Dante, *Convivio*, pp. 70-74.

9. *Paradiso* IV, 43-45.

10. Georges Duby, editor, *A History of Private Life*, Volume II: *Revelations of the Medieval World* (Cambridge: Harvard University Press, 1988), pp. 522-524.

11. *Purgatorio* XXV, 34-108.

12. *Ibid.* 68-72.

13. Vergil, *Aeneid* VI, 260ff.

14. Dante's "weightiness" in embarking on the rivers of the underworld, e.g. *Inferno* VIII, 27, was evidently inspired by Vergil's *Aeneid* VI, 413, but the "tightening" that ensues progressively in the ascent of Purgatory, e.g. *Purgatorio* IV, 92, represents Dante's theological elaboration.

15. *Purgatorio*, III, 16-30.

16. Augustine, *Confessions* XIII, 9.

17. Simone Weil, *Gravity and Grace* (NY: Octagon, 1979).

18. *Inferno* XXXIV, 109-111.

19. *Purgatorio* XXII, 8-9.

20. *Paradiso* III, 85.

21. *Purgatorio* IX, 55-57.

22. *Paradiso* I, 73-75.

23. 2 Corinthians 12.2.

24. *Paradiso* XXX, 40-41.

25. *Inferno* III, 64.

26. *Inferno* III, 39.

27. *Inferno* III, 51.

28. *Inferno* IV, 83-84.

29. *Inferno* V, 28-33.

30. *Inferno* VI, 7-9.

31. *Inferno* VII, 25-30.

32. *Inferno* VII, 121-122.

33. *Inferno* IX, 110-120.

34. *Inferno* XII, 47-48.

35. *Inferno* XIII, 4-6.

36. *Inferno* XIV, 13-39.

37. *Inferno* XV, 121-124.

38. *Inferno* XIV, 103-111. See Ovid, *Metamorphoses* I, 89ff. and Daniel 2.31ff.

39. *Inferno* XVIII, 112-114.

40. *Inferno* XXIII, 64-66.

41. *Inferno* XXIV, 94-105.

42. *Inferno* XXXII, XXXIII.

43. *Inferno* XXXIV, 121-126.

44. *Purgatorio* I, 127-129.

45. *Purgatorio* X, 115-121.

46. *Purgatorio* XIII, 667- 72.

47. *Purgatorio* XVI, 1-6.

48. *Purgatorio* XVIII, 97-98.

49. *Purgatorio* XIX, 121-124.

50. *Purgatorio* XXIII, 30-33. The cheek bones, brows, and the ridge of the nose form the M; the eye-socket on each side an O.

51. *Purgatorio* XXVI, 31-33.

52. *Purgatorio* XXVIII, 91-96.

53. *Purgatorio* XXXIII, 119. No historical counterpart of the character bearing this name has been plausibly identified.

54. *Purgatorio* XXX, 39.

55. *Purgatorio* XXX, 49-54.

56. *Purgatorio* XXXII, 148-153. See Revelation 17.1-3.

57. *Paradiso* VII, 13-138.

58. The phrase is that of C.S. Lewis, who summarizes this aspect of medieval thought in *The Allegory of Love* (NY: Oxford University Press, 1958), pp. 13-18.

59. *Paradiso* IX, 118-120.

60. *Paradiso* IX, 103.

61. *Paradiso* IX, 36.

62. Jacopo della Lana, cited in *The Divine Comedy of Dante Alighieri, Paradiso*, translated by Alien Mandelbaum (NY: Bantam Books, 1984), p. 341.

63. *Paradiso* VIII, 115-148.

64. *Paradiso* XIV, 43-60.

65. James Gaffney, "Dante's Blindness in *Paradiso* XXV- XXVI: An Allegorical Interpretation," *Dante Studies* 91 (1972) 101-113.

66. *Paradiso* XXIV-XXVI.

67. *Paradiso* XXX, 140-141.

Sex, Celibacy, and the Modern Self

in Nineteenth-Century Germany[1]

William Madges

Introduction

This essay intends to describe some of the changes in sexual practice that occurred in nineteenth-century Germany and to describe some aspects of the theological discussion of obligatory clerical celibacy that occurred during the same period. My thesis is that both the dramatic increase in illegitimacy and the campaign against obligatory clerical celibacy in the early nineteenth century were the result of the dispersion of a modern mentality that emphasized personal autonomy and individual development. This modern mentality had begun to penetrate European society in the eighteenth century. It came to significantly affect diverse segments of the German population in the early nineteenth century. To identify with some degree of certainty all the causes of the emergence of this modern sense of self is a difficult, if not impossible task. Convinced materialists or convinced idealists, however, might not feel daunted. Marxist materialists might attempt to explain the emergence of the modern self exclusively in terms of the demise of the previous mode of production and the rise of the new capitalist mode of production. Hegelian idealists, by contrast, might attempt to explain it exclusively in terms of the emergence of Englightenment ideas about authentic personhood. Both interpretative schemes, because they are reductionistic, are in my judgment untenable. This essay adopts a line of interpretation that seems to be more reasonable. It begins with the assumption that socio-economic factors, cultural practices, and intellectual ideas all played a role in the development of modernity. It then takes a look at the phenomena of changing sexual practices and public critiques of mandatory clerical celibacy and asks whether we can perhaps discern behind or under these phenomena socio-economic factors, cultural practices, or intellectual ideas that might explain their emergence.

A second assumption influences the interpretation of nineteenth-century Germany that this essay offers. I assume that socioeconomic factors and intellectual currents will impinge upon the lives of members of different social classes differently. Insofar as the economic situation and educational opportunities of the middle and upper classes in the nineteenth century provided them readier access to intellectual currents, it seems reasonable to expect that intellectual movements, rather than changes in the mode of production, had greater influence in changing their ideas about sexuality and personhood. Conversely it seems reasonable to expect that economic and social factors, rather than intellectual movements, had greater influence in changing the ideas and practices of the lower classes with regard to sexuality and personhood.

I do not wish to suggest, however, that only one set of factors influenced each of the different social classes. Ideas and practices seem to condition each other mutually. Therefore, instead of saying that practices generate certain ideas or conversely that ideas generate certain kinds of practices, it is better to say, as Charles Taylor reminds us, that with regard to any concrete development in history, change is occurring both ways. With reference to the period under consideration here, Taylor notes that an important relation links the notion of possessive individualism with the economic practices of capitalist, market society, and that this relation is not a unidirectional causal one.[2]

Before turning to the phenomena I wish to describe in this essay, perhaps a few words are in order about why these two quite different phenomena have been chosen. First, I am interested in describing some of the changes in sexual behavior and in ideas about sexuality and marriage that emerge among church members in nineteenth-century Germany. Although the specific issues of sexual morality and obligatory celibacy affect the laity and the clergy in the church in different ways, it seems fruitful to include consideration of both groups in an essay that wants to get a fuller, rather than narrower, picture of the attitudes and behavior of church members with regard to sexuality and marriage. Second, I find the two phenomena --changes in sexual practice among the laity and public criticism of obligatory celibacy among the clergy--not to be unrelated. I wish to suggest that both phenomena reflect the interiorization of a modern sense of self, in which concern for one's autonomy, one's rights, and one's personal fulfillment comes to have an urgency it did not previously have. Whether caused primarily by economic and social factors or by political and intellectual ideas, the effect nonetheless seems the same: people of different social classes and from different states in the church began to assert their autonomy and their desire for personal development free from the constraints of traditional, external authorities. This heightened sense of autonomy and heightened concern for personal development came to expression in a freer sexual practice and in vocal, public criticism of obligatory clerical celibacy.

The official response of the Roman Church to these phenomena, and the motivation underlying them, was negative. Throughout the nineteenth century, both popes and Catholic apologists attributed the evils of liberalism, socialism, indifferentism, pantheism, atheism, and the radical use of historical criticism of the Bible to the Protestant apotheosis of private judgment. What began with Luther's challenge to ecclesiastical tradition and institutional authority in the sixteenth century was believed to have culminated in the late eighteenth century with Kant's exaltation of the Enlightenment virtue of thinking for oneself. The campaign against obligatory celibacy, as well as the other political, social, and religious upheavals of the late eighteenth and the nineteenth century, were all considered to be the fruit of this elevation of personal autonomy and freedom.[3] Consequently, from the time of the French Revolution to the Second Vatican Council, the Roman Church's leadership engaged in a battle against the social and political manifestations of the modern sense of autonomy and freedom.[4]

Although Vatican II opened the door to a positive appreciation of modernity, the Roman Church continues to wrestle with modernity's vexatious aspects, including the demands for self-fulfillment in sexual matters. At the very least it is interesting to note that more than 150 years ago church and society began to deal consciously with these demands. Perhaps a study of these phenomena in the nineteenth century will also help us to understand better some of the forces that have shaped our own modern self-understanding.

Changes in Sexual Behavior

It is a fact that both legitimate and illegitimate fertility of young European women rose late in the eighteenth century and that both legitimate and illegitimate fertility declined late in the nineteenth century.[5] Scholars, however, are not in agreement about the reasons for these movements. There is little unanimity particularly with regard to the causes of increased illegitimacy. Some have attributed the increase in illegitimate fertility to the spread of urbanization and industrialization. Others have attributed it to processes of secularization and modernization that affected both rural and urban life.[6] In the following paragraphs I will sketch some of the factual data, particularly as they refer to the situation in Germany, and then suggest some promising explanatory theories.

Increase in Marital Fertility

During the eighteenth century, and in some parts of Europe during the first half of the nineteenth century, a substantial increase occurred in the number of children that a married European woman would be likely to have had in her twenties. Studies of five villages in different parts of Germany, for example, indicate that the greatest increase in fertility occurred during the early part of the nineteenth century among women in their early twenties.[7] This increase in fertility meant that women who married in their early twenties usually had at least two children more than women who had married at the same age in the eighteenth century.

How are we to account for this increase in fecundity? A plausible response might be more frequent intercourse. But why was intercourse more frequent? Edward Shorter offers a plausible theory, which can be stated succinctly: Women who began to acquire a new sense of personal autonomy sought companionate marriages much more often than did women with traditional mentalities. The frequency of intercourse was higher in such marriages than in traditional marriages because women in them experienced sex as a pleasurable act. In the absence of birth control, more intercourse led to more pregnancies and therewith to increased marital fertility.[8]

What evidence is there to support this theory? Some specialized studies of family life indicate that there was a gradual shift in the understanding of marriage in Europe during the seventeenth to the nineteenth centuries.[9] The shift began to occur first in Anglo-Saxon countries and France, and it appeared in other countries later. Already in the seventeenth century, marriage came to be seen among the upper social classes to be a consequence and continuation of romantic love. These romantic sentiments gradually trickled down to the working classes, many of whom began to see marriage as a means to individual fulfillment and happiness. The limited evidence available suggests that the initial appearance of the companionate marriage among the middle and lower classes probably occurred in the eighteenth century. What is clear is that beginning at that time (i.e., the end of the eighteenth and the beginning of the nineteenth century), there was a steady decline in the power wielded by parents and by wider kinship groups in the choice of marriage partner, and more and more the choice was seen as the couple's.[10] Whether or not the emergence of companionate marriages was its primary cause, marital fertility did increase among young married women in Europe during the early part of the nineteenth century.

The decline in fertility during the last few decades of the nineteenth century, moreover, does not necessarily indicate a lower rate of intercourse among married couples later in the century, because by that time effective contraceptive techniques were more widely used. The increased use of contraception indicates that more people were thinking of sex as an expression of love and means of pleasure, and not just as the vehicle of procreation, and it suggests that people were thinking of family size in a different economic and moral light.[11]

THE INCREASE IN ILLEGITIMACY

At approximately the same time as the increase in marital fertility, there was also an increase in extramarital fertility. A sharp increase in illegitimate fertility occurred in many parts of Europe in the second half of the eighteenth century. Illegitimacy further accelerated around the time of the French Revolution, and continued to increase in many parts of Europe until the middle of the nineteenth century.[12] Between 1750 and 1850 the magnitude of the increase in illegitimate fertility for much of Europe was four or fivefold.

> In all but a handful of villages and cities for which data are available, illegitimacy rose, departing from modest plateaus of one to three per cent of all baptisms, to often ten or fifteen per cent. Also prebridal pregnancy--that is, women who are already pregnant when they marry--climbed dramatically. . . . Thus not only were couples who did not marry having premarital intercourse more often than before, couples who did marry were doing so as well.[13]

Although increased fecundity or fewer abortions might account for the increase in illegitimate births, heightened sexual activity among young adults seems to be a more plausible explanation. The fact that prenuptial conceptions rose simultaneously with illegitimate births suggests that the total volume of premarital intercourse was rising.[14]

Why was there an increase in sexual activity among young adults in the late eighteenth or early nineteenth century? Did young adults come to a new appreciation of their bodies and of sexual intercourse? If, as seems tenable, people came increasingly to see sexual expression as an integral factor in personal human development or to appreciate sexual intercourse as an expression of love, we still need to ask about the factors that contributed to this new understanding of sexuality. Three sets of factors seem to have had the biggest impact on facilitating this new understanding: economic, social-political, and intellectual. A few words about each.

Economic modernization was one cause of changes in sexual attitudes and behavior, especially among young women of the lower classes. According to Misner, the rise of the "putting-out" system, according to which contractors (the so-called putters-out) organized cottage industries (such as weaving) for greater productivity and for more distant markets, contributed to a breakdown in the limitations on marriage and to a rise in the number of illegitimate children.

> By a process easy to imagine, the young couple starting to earn money from weaving or making clocks would feel that they had the wherewithal . . . to support themselves and a child or two. Instead of just being a seasonably employed farmhand and milkmaid, they would actually earn money during the winter. With or without the sanction of authority, they could have their baby and go on living.[15]

In the nineteenth century, where agriculture was modernized, where the putting out of textiles thrived, where factories were established, a new working-class subculture emerged. This new subculture weakened traditional moral taboos; it legitimated sexual behavior differently from the traditional European culture prior to 1750.[16]

One way to interpret this working-class subculture is to regard it as having been permeated by an emerging marketplace mentality; another way to interpret it is to regard it as having been permeated by an increasing sense of individual dignity and autonomy, to which the ability to provide economically for one's dependents and/or the freedom to make some choices about one's kind of work contributed. Whereas the former interpretation emphasizes the working class's commitment to the maximization of individual profit, the latter interpretation emphasizes its growing concern for personal development. In either event, concern for self, one's rights and automony takes on new importance. This development was particularly significant for women. As women learned autonomy or maximization of self-interest in the economy, they began to transfer these concepts to their personal lives.[17] The emergence and spread of wage labor facilitated this transfer. Because paid employment meant that women brought a distinct, quantifiable contribution to the family's resources, women came to feel entitled to a greater voice in the disposal of these resources. The balance of power in the family began to shift.

Politically and socially the late eighteenth century was an age of revolution. The French Revolution and the subsequent secularization of large parts of Europe unleashed social forces that had effects on sexual attitudes and behavior. Prior to the Revolution, a variety of forces worked to limit the illegitimacy ratio. Social, legal and psychological factors, such as partial community control over the assignment of non-inherited properties, the politics involved in obtaining a marriage license, and the threatening exhortations of preachers to observe sexual chastity, made sexual abstinence or restraint "not so much a matter of personal choice as a simple fact of life."[18] S. Ryan Johansson writes:

> Low rates of illegitimacy were related to the fact that the sexual lives of both ordinary single women and men (who lived for the most part in small villages) were closely monitored by the local representatives of state and church, as well as by their own neighbors. The unmarried had no general right to privacy or any form of sexual expression with another person. When moral deviance was detected by the authorities, it was swiftly and harshly punished.[19]

Many of these restrictions on marriage were relaxed or repealed in most German states at the very beginning of the nineteenth century in response to a more liberal spirit emanating from the Revolution.

The liberal reforms of the Napoleonic era gave more freedom to the individual, and thus also made possible a freer sexual practice. As serfdom was suppressed, ordinary people were able to come and go as they pleased, without fear of legal reprisal. As a greater degree of personal freedom was guaranteed by law, parents could no longer dictate the religious choices of their children or impose marriage partners on them. The auctioning of church property made necessary by secularization allowed thousands of Germans to purchase small plots of land and to become more autonomous. When the legal system in many cases no longer punished fornication publicly and corporally and when foundling homes were built where unwed mothers could place their babies while preserving anonymity, many people concluded that "sexual indulgence had become legal, and they equated civil with moral legality."[20]

The relative freedom, however, did not last long. The number of impoverished persons, and the concomitant demand on public relief, eventually increased due to problems in agricultural economy. The increasing numbers of poor were not only a financial drain, but also a source of social unrest. Consequently, during the third decade of the nineteenth century restrictive legislation began to be reinstated in southern and middle German states, sometimes stipulating even stricter requirements for marriage than had existed before.[21] Although marriage restrictions were not uniform among the different German states in the first half of the nineteenth century, they were similar in spirit: that is, they were usually directed against people who were considered to be in an unfavorable economic situation or otherwise socially undesirable, e.g., those who had recently received public financial support, those without stable employment and a secure income, those who had been convicted of theft or had reputations as drunkards or loafers.[22] These marriage restriction laws may have contributed to an increase in illegitimacy.[23]

Intellectually the late eighteenth century was the age of Enlightenment; the age of seeking, in Kant's famous words, release from one's self-incurred tutelage. Some who followed Kant's advice to dare to think for themselves apparently concluded that the traditional prohibitions against premarital intercourse, by both church and state, no longer applied to them. Of course, only the educated elite were conversant with the literature of the *philosophes*, and consequently only this small segment of the population had its sexual attitudes and behavior directly influenced by this intellectual current. Still, other intellectual or educational forces may have played a role in shaping the sexual attitudes and behavior of the lower classes. W. G. Lumley, writing in the second half of the nineteenth century, believed that there was a positive correlation between bastardy and the level of education one received. Whether or not there is a causal connection between illegitimacy and education, it is nevertheless significant that the illegitimacy explosion "coincided closely in time with the spread of primary education, and in space with the diffusion of literacy among the population."[24]

It would be unwise to suggest that any one factor--economic, political, legal, or intellectual--determined the change in sexual behavior and the increase in illegitimacy. As in other aspects of life, so too in the matter of sexual activity a number of factors work together in shaping human behavior. For our purposes, it is important to highlight the point that changes in economy, law, and society enabled individuals in the nineteenth century to further develop their sense of autonomy and to come to see sexual fulfillment as an integral part of their humanity. From this perspective, the increased frequency of sexual intercourse among married couples as well as the increase in illegitimacy can be regarded as expressions of a more holistic self-understanding, rather than the mere unleashing of wild carnality.

CLERICAL CELIBACY AND THE ENLIGHTENMENT CRITIQUE

The Enlightenment encouraged people to think critically about many church practices, including priestly celibacy. Diderot argued that sexual abstinence violated human nature; Rousseau claimed that the obligation of celibacy in the Latin tradition of the Roman Church violated a fundamental human right.[25] In response to the Enlightenment's call for greater personal autonomy and the obligation to think for oneself, many individuals began to debate the issues of clerical celibacy and priestly marriage. In the eighteenth century, hundreds of treatises challenging or defending ecclesiastical celibacy were published.[26]

Whereas many could discount the critique of celibacy by the French philosophers as deriving from allegedly anti-Christian men, it was a different matter when Catholic Abbé Pierre Desforges advanced theological arguments against priestly celibacy in his 1758 book, *Avantages du mariage, et combien il est nécessaire et salutaire aux pretres et aux éveques de ce tems-ci, d'épouser une fille chrétienne.* Desforges, about whose life little is known, pointed out that priestly marriage occurred in Christian antiquity, and he claimed that the Hebrew Bible gave support to his claim that marriage and priesthood were compatible according to divine will. From the fact that the high priests of the Old Testament were married, Desforges derived the conclusion that Christian bishops should follow their example.[27] The French Parliament had the book burned and the author confined in the Bastille. Desforges' two-volume work had little effect in France.

The French Revolution thirty years later, however, raised the question again. The Constitution of 1791 provided that no profession could prohibit a person from marriage and that no public official could refuse to ratify a marriage on such grounds. Moreover, the recognition of marriage as a civil, not a religious contract, meant for sympathetic revolutionaries--in France and elsewhere--that priests could be "laicized" without requiring the consent of church authorities. After the Concordat of 1801 well over 2,000 of the more than 3,000 priests and religious who had married during the Revolution chose marriage rather than ecclesiastical reinstatement to active priestly duties.[28]

Between 1790 and 1810, the German discussion of the issue was largely dependent upon political events in France. German, Enlightened clerics hailed the French recognition of marriage as a civil contract, and they hoped to follow the example of French married priests. Even after Napoleon's 1801 concordat with the pope, German opponents of clerical celibacy continued to expect to win from the state, if not from the pope, the right of laicization. Although there were renewed attempts after the Congress of Vienna to win legal recognition of this right, they were unsuccessful, as the Bavarian Concordat of 1817 demonstrates.

Throughout the first half of the nineteenth century, the debate in Germany concerning the necessity of priestly celibacy continued with some vigor. The thesis of Desforges's book, which had little initial effect in France, was made known to Germany through a lengthy review of the book by Protestant C. W. F. Walch (1726-1784), who observed with surprise that there was some lively support for priestly marriage within the Roman Church.[29] In 1802 Heinrich Ignaz von Wessenberg, the vicar general of Constance, began to mold his diocese in accord with the Enlightenment spirit. In addition to a reform of the missal and the use of the vernacular in the liturgy, he criticized the principle of celibacy.[30] The following year (1803), Benedict Maria Werkmeister (1745-1823), novice master in the Benedictine monastery in Neresheim, published anonymously his *Proposal for the Gradual Introduction of Priestly Marriage in the German Church*. Werkmeister, one of the most indefatigable opponents of priestly celibacy in Germany, asserted that celibacy was contrary to nature. Moreover, he criticized the usual education of priests, which encouraged the seminarians to despise, even hate, women. Like other Enlightenment critics of contemporary church practice, Werkmeister advocated the reformation of the entire church along Enlightened guidelines and the abolition of priestly celibacy.[31]

In the second and third decades of the nineteenth century, the debate between the supporters and the opponents of clerical celibacy became increasingly polarized. On the one side were those "genuine" Catholics, whose authentic catholicity was proved by their unconditional acceptance of priestly celibacy and their unswerving loyalty to Rome. On the other side were those Enlightened or "liberal" Catholics, who valued the autonomy of the local church and from which they expected to win a change in the regulations concerning priesthood and marriage. The arguments made by those who were against mandatory celibacy were sometimes so vehement that they left little room for the possibility of *voluntary* celibacy.[32] It is interesting to note that most of the early nineteenth-century clerics who opposed mandatory celibacy argued against it primarily because it violated "nature" or the natural "rights" of the individual. The use of "natural rights" or "rights of the individual" language demonstrates that a new, modern sense of self suffused the perspective of public critics of celibacy in early nineteenth-century Germany.[33]

The Proposals of J. B. Hirscher

Johann Baptist Hirscher (1788-1865), sometimes associated with the Catholic Tübingen School, joined the debate in 1820 with a lengthy review of two recently written works on celibacy by J. A. Sulzer and F. G. Weinmann.[34] Hirscher used the occasion of writing this review to express his dissatisfaction with the current practices for preparing seminarians for the priesthood. He observed that few candidates for the priesthood in his day seemed to have sufficient authentic zeal for their future spiritual office and sufficiently developed moral sensibilities to be good priests. Hirscher believed this to be the case because few candidates for the priesthood had received the appropriate upbringing and education.[35] From Hirscher's perspective, the first question that had to be addressed was: what promotes the best possible spiritual and moral development of individuals so that they can become good priests? Celibacy or priestly marriage has significant value only insofar as it promotes the moral and religious development of the priest. Having stated this conviction, Hirscher then turned to criticize some traditional assumptions in the Roman tradition about the value of virginity and celibacy.
        First, Hirscher challenged the assumption that virginity and celibacy, in and of themselves, promote spiritual perfection. He claimed that, on the contrary, experience demonstrated that celibacy

had not advanced the morality of the clergy. Without citing numerous examples of moral turpitude, Hirscher did suggest that "not a small number of the clergy had fallen into a state of serious sinfulness on account of the celibacy requirement."[36]

Second, Hirscher rejected the assumption, defended by one of the authors (J. A. Sulzer) under review, that a celibate lifestyle automatically placed an individual on a higher spiritual plain than a married lifestyle. Without denying the spiritual value of virginity, Hirscher stated that his own observations had led him to conclude that the celibate state was spiritually salutary for only a small number of people. In Hirscher's opinion, only a few people are truly called to a life of virginity. The majority of the clergy, however, "is not called to viriginity; and they lug the yoke of celibacy without any moral blessings."[37]

Hirscher believed, on the other hand, that at least at the present time in Germany, marriage had to be regarded as "morally advantageous" for the majority of the clergy. As warrant for this belief, Hirscher offered the assertion that marriage and the sexual impulse were divinely intended for more than the propagation of the species.

> Certainly the sexual impulse, which extends to the entire human race, compels us in light of all our experience--if we otherwise believe in divine wisdom--to conceive the thought that it cannot be designed merely for human reproduction, but rather that it will intervene in human upbringing in diverse and salutary ways . . .[38]

Some of the salutary effects of sexual attraction and marriage, according to Hirscher, are a peaceable disposition, kind-heartedness, a more focused life-plan.

Hirscher was also convinced that the intimacy required in marriage would develop the individual's concern for the well-being of others--beginning, of course, with the well-being of one's spouse and children, but then broadening out to include a concern for the well-being of one's neighbors, one's town, and one's country. Rather than thinking that concerns about the economic welfare and physical health of one's family would hinder a relationship with God and with others outside one's immediate family, Hirscher argued that such concerns promoted and enriched these relationships by heightening one's sense of need for God and by deepening one's empathy with the plight of others.[39] Hirscher's assessment of married life is so positive one might suspect that he has created a romanticized ideal that has little basis in reality.[40] Yet Hirscher does admit that marriage does not always live up to its full potential. Even then, however, it has a deeper and more positive influence upon the religiosity and morality of individuals than does bachelorhood.[41]

Hirscher knew that not all clerics agreed with his point of view, but he hoped that all would agree that the spirit of the gospel required the church not to force its members to remain in a lifestyle that was not life-giving for them. Appealing to this gospel spirit, Hirscher thus supported the right of laicization for priests who had come to realize that they had not been authentically called to a life of celibacy.[42]

Although he did not support a law of permanent and obligatory celibacy for priests, Hirscher also did not fully agree with F. G. Weinmann, who advocated the immediate and universal repeal of the celibacy law. Hirscher believed that there were good pastoral reasons for moving toward repeal gradually and with respect for diverse circumstances in different countries. Hirscher thought that, prior to the abolition of mandatory celibacy, it would be necessary to prepare members of the church for this change by providing comprehensive education programs. Hirscher observed that many people would be opposed to the idea of a married clergy "as long as one did not impart to them correct ideas about the connection of marriage and celibacy with human religiosity and morality, and as long as one did not enlighten them about the history of the law of celibacy--at least to the point of seeing it as not a divine law."[43] Another obstacle to gaining popular support for the abolition of mandatory celibacy, according to Hirscher, was the popular understanding of married life. As Hirscher saw the situation, many people had neither an appropriately Christian understanding of the way spouses should relate to each other nor an appropriately positive and full appreciation of sexual intimacy. Consequently, many spouses harbored a feeling that there was something base or unworthy in their relations with each other, and they thereby concluded that married relations were incompatible with the ordained state. Hirscher responded:

> If, as Christianity desires, the sensual drive of the married couple were guided in a manner appropriate to Christian dignity; if sensual pleasure were elevated and humanized through the *mutual* love and modesty of the spouses; then one could find nothing in married relations that one had to consider beneath

the dignity of the clergyman.[44]

Many people were willing to continue to believe that the celibate life is a spiritually higher way of life because they wrongly believed that there is something dirty about sexual relations and because they failed to see that marriage could be an enriching experience for both spouses.[45] Hirscher's reference to the idea of mutuality in marriage and his suggestion that marriage could be an enriching experience for both spouses seem to confirm the fact, alluded to earlier in the essay, that the value of companionate marriages was perceived by educated Germans already in the first quarter of the nineteenth century.

As he drew to the conclusion of his review, Hirscher appealed to the church hierarchy to examine seriously the issue of celibacy and to consult widely on the issue. He observed that despite the fact that so many scholarly and popular opinions about the issue had been published and despite the fundamental importance of the issue for the well-being of the church, the leaders of the church had not engaged in an intensive consultation on the issue. But to engage in such consultation and deliberation was their obligation.[46]

Hirscher concluded his review with the proposal of a flexible and gradual approach to the abolition of mandatory celibacy. He made three final points. First, mandatory celibacy is not an eternal, divine law, but a disciplinary law; and disciplinary laws are subject to change. Second, each country has different needs and perhaps a different attitude toward priestly marriage; consequently, the decision about the obligatory nature of priestly celibacy should be made by the church in each individual country. Third, those countries that abolish mandatory celibacy should introduce the change gradually; in this way, the possibility of widespread confusion or scandal among the people is reduced.[47]

Other Voices in the Discussion of Celibacy

In the first half of the nineteenth century, other voices in Germany were heard in the celibacy debate. Professors Zell and Amann, professors of philology and canon law respectively at the University of Freiburg, published anonymously in 1828 their *Reflections in Favor of the Abolition of Mandatory Celibacy for the Catholic Clergy.* This publication summarized many of the standard arguments against celibacy. Moreover, it intended to inform the public on the issue and to give support to the petitions that had been forwarded to the state authorities in Baden asking for the abolition of mandatory celibacy. Although the work advanced historical, practical, and legal arguments against celibacy, the authors emphasized that their critique was primarily directed against the mandatory character of the present discipline.[48] Johann Adam Möhler (1796-1838), one of the most famous members of the Catholic Tübingen School, responded with a defense of celibacy.[49] Möhler declared that those who petitioned the government for the abolition of mandatory celibacy should be more concerned with those things that could actually improve the spiritual, theological, and pastoral qualities of the Baden clergy. He denied that priestly marriage would necessarily lead to such improvement. Although he did not believe that every individual who opposed celibacy was also an opponent of fundamental Christian doctrines, Möhler was convinced that the manner of thinking of such an individual was closely related to the un-ecclesial or anti-ecclesial attitudes becoming popular in some educated circles in Germany. Möhler regarded it as irresponsible for Catholic professors to advance arguments against celibacy in the public press.[50] With these preliminary comments out of the way, Möhler then responded to the historical and theological arguments that the Freiburg book had advanced. In addition to controverting its interpretation of the historical record, Möhler argued that allowing priestly marriage would have a negative effect upon the life of the church because it would open the door to greater state interference in the church's life. For Möhler celibacy constituted "unmistakeable evidence of the non-identity of church and state"; and for this reason, he did not welcome the abolition of "perhaps the only means of permitting free-thinking candor to germinate in our clergy."[51]

Agitation about celibacy reached such a level that Pope Gregory XVI was compelled to comment on it. In his encyclical *Mirari vos* (1832), the pope admonished bishops to defend the law of celibacy with all the power at their disposal:

> Now, however, We want you to rally to combat the abominable conspiracy against clerical celibacy. This conspiracy spreads daily and is promoted by profligate philosophers, some even from the clerical order. They have forgotten their person and office, and have been carried away by the enticements of pleasure. They have even dared to make repeated public demands to the princes for the abolition of that most holy discipline. But it is disgusting to dwell on these evil attempts at length.[52]

Pope Pius IX followed his predecessor's lead. In his first encyclical, *Qui pluribus* (1846), Pius condemned the conspiracy against clerical celibacy that was being promoted by churchmen who "have wretchedly forgotten their own rank and let themselves be converted by the charms and snares of pleasure." And proposition 74 of the *Syllabus of Errors* (1864) repeated his earlier condemnations.[53]

From 1832 on anyone who publicly spoke against mandatory celibacy was to be regarded as no longer authentically "Catholic." Thus when the German Catholic movement, begun by Johannes Ronge (1813-1887) and Johann Czerski (1813-1893) in the 1840s, raised its voice against celibacy it did not receive recognition as a genuinely *Catholic* phenomenon. And when Hirscher touched upon the celibacy issue again in 1849, in his book *The Present State of the Church*, he was accused of separating himself from the Roman Catholic Church.[54] In this book, Hirscher again recommended that mandatory celibacy be abolished and that laicization be permitted. He further proposed that those priests who felt compelled to laicize themselves not be automatically excommunicated, but rather "be allowed to continue in full communion with the Catholic Church."[55] His book was promptly put on the Index of Forbidden Books.[56] As a result, further public discussion of abolishing mandatory celibacy was effectively stifled in Germany.

CONCLUDING REMARKS

In this essay I have described attitudinal changes toward marriage and sexuality and changes in sexual behavior in Germany during the late eighteenth century and the nineteenth century. These changes consisted in an increase in marital fertility, a sharp rise in illegitimacy, and some significant vocal criticism of mandatory clerical celibacy, particularly in the first half of the century. In addition to describing these changes, I have attempted to identify socio-economic factors, cultural practices, and philosophical ideas that might explain their emergence.

The identification of the causes of these phenomena is an interpretative act and, like all acts of interpretations, is open to challenge. Although the interpretation offered in this essay may be imaginative, I submit that the evidence adduced in its support is not imaginary. The increase in marital fertility began to occur at a time when the notion of companionate marriage was filtering down from the upper to the lower social classes. The increase in illegitimacy occurred at a time when the spread of wage labor and changes in the mode of production were causing changes in traditional family structure and town life. The public critique of celibacy by clerics in Germany emerged in the wake of the French Revolution, as the ideas of inalienable rights, governmental representation of the people, and democracy were spreading throughout Europe. I have suggested that, whether occasioned primarily by socio-economic factors or by political and philosophical ideas, an emergent modern sense of self underlies these changes in sexual behavior and the public critique of celibacy.

This modern sense of self insisted upon greater autonomy in decisions about individual development. Insofar as questions about whether to marry or not, with whom to be sexually intimate, and how to relate to one's spouse are questions at once deeply personal and extremely significant for one's human development, it is no surprise that as the sense of self changed, so too did attitude and behavior with regard to these important personal issues. Although the population studies of nineteenth-century Germany did not give us direct proof of changes in self-consciousness, the different public criticisms of celibacy reviewed in this essay did provide us with some evidence of changes in self-consciousness. For example, in Hirscher's arguments in support of the moral and religious benefits of clerical marriage, we can see the expression of an appreciation of the place of sexual and marital intimacy in the development of the human person. In his critique of the church's refusal to allow a change in its discipline of celibacy we can see an expression of the demand for greater personal autonomy and freedom. When these two aspects of Hirscher's thought are put together, we can see that Hirscher criticized the church because its refusal to modify its celibate discipline was a refusal to allow individuals to develop more fully as human beings.

Whether or not significant numbers of the German people in the nineteenth century *consciously* developed a new understanding of the connection between sexuality and human development, they did develop a heightened sense of personal freedom and autonomy. The evidence for this heightened sense of autonomy is to be found in the changes in sexual behavior.[57] People wanted to have a voice in matters that were important to them, and sex and marriage mattered to many of them. Hirscher testified to the importance of having a voice in matters of importance when he wrote:

> The same spirit which manifests itself in political matters, works also in the Church. In the one case, as in the other, men will

88   BROKEN AND WHOLE

have their parts in public interests of grave importance to themselves. The constitutional and democratic principle has penetrated the nations, and every where, if the Republic does not already exist, the Monarchy at least takes the constitutional form. Pure Monarchy has become an impossibility. It is equally true in the Church. The purely monarchical direction of a diocese, for example, runs in a direction so opposite to all the characteristics of the age, that such a thing, or at least its perpetuation, side by side with the constitutional and popular vitality of the State, appears possible in no other way, than by the apostasy of the entire intelligence of the community, or by the prevalence of a religious indifference the most complete.[58]

In both phenomena described in this essay--changes in sexual attitudes and behavior and public critique of mandatory clerical celibacy--we can discern the voice of the emergent modern self, a self which increasingly came to insist upon its autonomy, its rights, and its personal fulfillment. This self sought to be heard in the nineteenth century. And both society and church today continue to wrestle with its demands.

Notes

1. Research for the section of this paper dealing with arguments against clerical celibacy was made possible in part by a 1992 summer stipend from the National Endowment for the Humanities.

2. Taylor writes: "What is more, the balance between the two directions may change with time. In the case of some of the crucial idées-forces discussed here, the facilitation may be mainly from idea to economic practice in the early period, where the ideas found their original source in religious and moral life. This seems to be the case with possessive individualism, which emerges before the explosive development of market relations in the industrial revolution. But in the later phase, when some of the new ideas originating among the social elite became the common property of the whole society, the preponderant direction was often reversed. It is clear for instance that the forceful imposition of proletarian status on masses of ex-peasants who were chased off the land into the new centres of industrialization preceded and caused the acceptance of atomistic self-consciousness (frequently combated by new formulations of working-class solidarity) by so many of their descendents today." Charles Taylor, *Sources of the Self: The Making of the Modern Identity* (Cambridge: Harvard University Press, 1989), 206-7.

3. We do not have record of significant statements from the hierarchy in the nineteenth century concerning the rise of illegitimacy, but we do have record of local pastors and bishops complaining about the sexual immorality of some church members in their area. Presumably, the hierarchy was unaware of the extent of illegitimacy across national borders and therefore did not respond to the phenomenon as a serious problem affecting the universal church. By contrast, the critique of obligatory celibacy was public and not confined to one country. Consequently, the nineteenth-century hierarchy did respond officially to this phenomenon.

4. Joseph Komonchak has argued that it was the social and political consequences of the Enlightenment that principally engaged the Roman Church's attention during this period and that it was to combat these that the Church chose to deal with intellectual issues as it did. See his "The Enlightenment and the Construction of Roman Catholicism," in the *Catholic Commission on Intellectual and Cultural Affairs 1982 Annual* (Notre Dame, 1984), 31-59, especially 34. Georg Schwaiger comments: "One of the tragedies of Church history is that the promises embodied in that Catholic Enlightenment were prevented from coming to fruition. The 19th century saw the rise of a Church policy which damned any criticism of the restored Church, any suggestion of reforms adapted to the age, as pernicious 'Enlightenment,' as tending toward a 'Febronian nationalistic church' and therefore as unorthodox and 'liberal' and a betrayal of the papacy." Schwaiger, "Catholicism and the Enlightenment," in *Progress and Decline in the History of Church Renewal*, ed. by Rogert Aubert (New York: Paulist Press, 1967), 91-107; here 106-07.

5. John Knodel and Steven Hochstadt, "Urban and Rural Illegitimacy in Imperial Germany," in *Bastardy and its Comparative History*, ed. by Peter Laslett, Karla Oosterveen and Richard M. Smith (Cambridge, Mass.: Harvard University Press, 1980), 284. For the specific information about the situation in Germany see the studies cited by Edward Shorter, "Female Emancipation, Birth Control, and Fertility in European History," *The American Historical Review* 78 (1973):605-40; here, 634. John Knodel points out that married women in the nineteenth century have at all age levels beneath age 39 higher fertility than those who married in 1692-1799. See his "Two and a Half Centuries of Demographic History in a Bavarian Village," *Population Studies* 24 (1970):353-76, especially 369. Ilse Müller's study shows that the average number of children in three villages of Württemberg who were born to women married between the ages of 20 and 24 increased substantially from the 1750-1799 period to the 1800-1849 period, whereas the average number of children born to women married at age 25-30 increased in the last half of the eighteenth century, but thereafter declined. See her "Bevölkerungsgeschichtliche Untersuchungen in drei Gemeinden des württembergischen Schwarzwaldes," *Archiv für Bevölkerungswissenschaft und Bevölkerungspolitik* 9 (1939):185-206, 247-64.

6. For a discussion of this issue and some of the literature on both sides, see Robert Neuman, "Industrialization and Sexual Behavior: Some Aspects of Working-Class Life in Imperial Germany," in *Modern European Social History*, ed. by Robert J. Bezucha (Lexington, Mass.: D.C. Heath and Co., 1972), 270-98, particularly 270-71, 281-2. See also Edward Shorter, "Illegitimacy, Sexual Revolution, and Social

Change in Modern Europe," *The Journal of Interdisciplinary History* 2 (1971):250-51; Knodel and Hochstadt, 287 and 292.

7. Shorter, "Female Emancipation," 607.

8. Shorter, "Female Emancipation," 626.

9. See Philippe Ariès, *L'Enfant et la vie familiale sous l'ancien régime* (Paris: Seuil, 1973). Helmut Möller, *Die kleinbürgerliche Familie im 18. Jahrhundert: Verhalten und Gruppenkultur* (Berlin: de Gruyter, 1969).

10. "In this revolution in family life, the two facets of the growing moral consciousness are interwoven. The rebellion against the patriarchal family involves an assertion of personal autonomy, and voluntarily formed ties, against the demands of ascriptive authority. But the rebellion is fired by the sense that what is at stake is a fulfilment that nature has made centrally significant." Taylor, *Sources of the Self*, 290.

11. See John E. Knodel, *The Decline of Fertility in Germany: 1871-1939* (Princeton: Princeton University Press, 1974), 75; S. Ryan Johansson, "The Moral Imperatives of Christian Marriage: Their Biological, Economic, and Demographic Implications in Changing Historical Contexts" in *One Hundred Years of Catholic Social Thought: Celebration and Challenge*, ed. by John A. Coleman (Maryknoll: Orbis Books, 1991), 135-154, here 145-146.

12. Shorter asserts that the years 1790-1860 were, "in virtually every society or community we know about, the peak period of illegitimacy." "Sexual Revolution," 246. See 265-272 for graphs charting the rise in illegitimacy in specific European locations.

13. Shorter, "Female Emancipation," 607-08. On average, the rate of prebridal pregnancy rose by 12% between 1810 and 1840 in those parts of Germany for which data are available. In one German town the increase was as much as 26%, while in another it was only 3%. See the table in Shorter, 637.

14. See Shorter, "Sexual Revolution," 239-40.

15. Paul Misner, *Social Catholicism in Europe: From the Onset of Industrialization to the First World War* (New York: Crossroad, 1991), 14.

16. For evidence of a kind of demystification of sex among the working class, based upon working-class autobiographies, see Neuman, 270-98. For a broader discussion of some of these issues, see Lee Rainwater, "Some Aspects of Lower Class Sexual Behavior," *The Journal of Social Issues* 22 (1966):96-108, and Rainwater's "Sex in the Culture of Poverty," in *The Individual, Sex, and Society*, ed. by C. B. Broderick and J. Bernards (Baltimore: Johns Hopkins Press, 1969), 129-40. Also see Shorter's "'La Vie Intime' Beiträge zu seiner Geschichte am Beispiel des kulturellen Wandels in den bayerischen Unterschichten im 19. Jahrhundert," *Kölner Zeitschrift für Soziologie* 16 (1973):530-49.

17. There is some question whether the shift in family relations was more pronounced at the beginning or end of the nineteenth century. Whereas Shorter's work underlines the early part of the century, Peter Stearns's review of pertinent German literature finds a significant shift in family patterns and a recognition of

greater female independence toward the *end* of the nineteenth century. See Stearns's "Adaptation to Industrialization: German Workers as a Test Case," *Central European History* 3 (1970):303-31. Cf. Shorter "Female Emancipation," 622.

18. Michael Phayer, *Sexual Liberation and Religion in Nineteenth Century Europe* (London: Croom Helm, 1977), 23; see 15-22 for a discussion of the factors contributing to sexual restraint in pre-modern Europe.

19. Johansson adds that "punishment for breaking the rules came more often and more swiftly for deviant women." "The Moral Imperatives of Christian Marriage," 136. For a description of the traditional, often violent, response to sexually libertine behavior, see Oscar Helmuth Werner, *The Unmarried Mother in German Literature with Special Reference to the Period 1770-1800* (New York: Columbia University Press, 1917). The fact that illegitimacy did remain low before 1750 is remarkable in light of the fact that marriage took place at a relatively late age, that is, between 24-27 years old rather than 12-16 years old. During the period 1500-1750, moreover, approximately 10-15% of all men and women remained single throughout their adult lives. The fact that so many adults remained unmarried could have led to high illegitimacy rates, but did not. Until the eighteenth century the illegitimacy rates remained between 2-7% of all recorded births.

20. Phayer, 25. Another way to look at this development is to say that perhaps attitudes toward personal autonomy, rather than towards sexuality, began to change with the dawn of modernity. Charles Taylor, for example, suggests that in the modern period respect for human life became connected to the notion of autonomy. Respect for individual autonomy, as the corollary of respect for the human person, came, under the influence of the Romantic appreciation of individual difference, to entail acceptance of the idea that people ought to be free to develop their personality in their own way, even if it is repugnant to the moral sense of others. See Taylor, *Sources of the Self,* 11-14.

21. John Knodel, "Law, Marriage and Illegitimacy in Nineteenth-Century Germany," *Population Studies* 20 (1967):280.

22. See Knodel, "Law," 280-81. For a detailed description of some of the laws and the states in which they existed, see Friedrich Thudichum, *Über unzuverlässige Beschränkungen des Rechts der Verehelichung* (Tübingen: Laupp and Siebeck, 1866). See also Karl Braun, "Das Zwangs-Zölibat für Mittellose in Deutschland," *Vierteljahrschrift für Volkswirtschaft und Kulturgeschichte* 20 (1867):1-80; Eduard Schübler, *Die Gesetze über Niederlassung und Verehelichung in den verschiedenen deutschen Staaten* (Stuttgart, 1855); Mack Walker, "Home Towns and State Administrators: South German Politics, 1815-30," *Political Science Quarterly* 82 (1967):35-60.

23. One indication of this contribution is that when restrictive marriage laws were repealed in the final third of the nineteenth century, those states that previously had the most comprehensive and restrictive legislation--such as Württemberg, Baden, and Bavaria--experienced sharp declines in illegitimate fertility. Knodel, "Law," 289-91. He estimates that there were 53% more illegitimate births in Württemberg and 55% more in Baden as a result of the marriage restrictions in force between the 1830s and the 1860s. Shorter adds a caveat: "It must be borne in mind that these laws were not responsible for the initial take off of illegitimacy, postdating that explosion

by several decades. Other factors were behind central European illegitimacy as well, for even in the absence of such legislation several German states experienced the highest incidence of bastardy on the continent." "Sexual Revolution," 254-55.

24. Shorter, "Sexual Revolution," 252. See W. G. Lumley, "Observations upon the Statistics of Illegitimacy," *Journal of the Statistical Society of London* 25 (1862):219-74. Cf. Johansson, 145.

25. In his encyclical *Rerum Novarum*, Pope Leo XIII asserted something quite similar. And Pope Pius XII quoted Leo in his own encyclical *Casti Connubii*: "No human law can take away from man the original human right to marry." *Acta Apostolicae Sedis* 22 (1930), 542. Cited by Heinz-Jürgen Vogels, *Celibacy--Gift or Law? A Critical Investigation* (Kent: Burns & Oates, 1992), 98.

26. See Augustine de Roskovany, *Coelibatus et breviarium: duo gravissima clericorum officia, e monumentis omnium seculorum demonstrata. Accessit completa literatura,* 11 vols. (Pest-Neutra, 1861-1881), vol. 7, no. 5023b-5312 and *Supplementa ad collectiones monumentorum et literaturae. De coelibatu et breviario* (Neutra, 1888), 4, no. 1135-1164, 1706-1780.

27. See Roskovany, 4, no. 1201. See also Paul Picard, *Zölibatsdiskussion im katholischen Deutschland der Aufklärungszeit: Auseinandersetzung mit der kanonischen Vorschrift im Namen der Vernunft und der Menschenrechte* (Düsseldorf: Patmos Verlag, 1975), especially 57-64. For a good sketch of the motives offered in support of celibacy during the first four centuries of the church, see Gerard Sloyan, "Biblical and Patristic Motives for Celibacy of Church Ministers," in *Celibacy in the Church,* ed. by William Bassett and Peter Huizing (New York: Herder and Herder, 1972), 13-29. Sloyan's conclusion, 29, that celibacy was promoted by church officials because it regarded the marriage act as defiling is developed and confirmed by Heinz-Jürgen Vogels in his book, *Celibacy--Gift or Law?* (Burnes & Oates, 1992). For documentation about the genesis of a negative view of marriage, also see Bernard Lohkamp, "Cultic Purity and the Law of Celibacy," *Review for Religious* 30 (1971):199-217.

28. See John Lynch, "Critique of the Law of Celibacy in the Catholic Church from the Period of the Reform Councils," in *Celibacy in the Church,* 65-66. For more detailed information about the status of married priests in France after the Revolution, see Simon Delacroix, *La réorganisation de l'Eglise de France après la Révolution 1801-1809* (Paris; Éditions du Vitrail, 1962), 443-56.

29. Christian Wilhelm Franz Walch, *Neueste Religionsgeschichte,* 9 vols. (Lemgo: Meyer, 1771-1783), 2:429-448.

30. Lynch, 67. For a brief exposition of the impact of the Enlightenment upon Catholic Germany, see Schwaiger, 99-107.

31. Werkmeister's *Unmaßgeblicher Vorschlag zur Reformation des niedrigen katholischen Klerus* (1782) and his *Vorschlag, wie in der deutschen Kirche die Priesterehe allmählich eingeführt werden könnte* (1803) were both published anonymously. In the former work, which was his first publication, he expressed only in footnotes his hope that priests would soon be allowed to marry and his belief that a natural or biological father would make a better spiritual "father." His *Beiträge zur Verbes-*

serung der katholischen Liturgie in Deutschland, which contained an expanded version of his 1782 *Unmaßgeblicher Vorschlag,* was initially published under his own name, but its further publication was prohibited by Duke Carl Eugene of Württemberg. See August Hagen, *Die kirchliche Aufklärung in der Diözese Rottenburg:Bildnisse aus einem Zeitalter des Übergangs* (Stuttgart: Schwabenverlag 1953), 9-21.

32. For a summary, see Picard, 217-223.

33. Concerning the modern, Western notion of rights and its connection with the modern sense of self, see Taylor, *Sources of the Self,* 11-14.

34. *Theologische Quartalschrift* 2 (1820):637-70. According to the prevailing custom, Hirscher's review or "Recension" of J. A. Sulzers, *Die erheblichsten Gründe für und gegen das katholisch-kirchliche Cölibatsgesetz zu nochmaliger Prüfung dargelegt* and J. G. Weinmanns *Soll der Cölibat der katholischen Geistlichkeit ferner fortbestehen; oder soll er aufgehoben werden?* appeared unsigned. Concerning the appropriateness of the term "Catholic Tübingen School," see Rudolf Reinhardt, *Tübingen Theologen und ihre Theologie* (Tübingen: J.C.B. Mohr, 1977).

35. [Hirscher], "Recension," 649. Hirscher distinguished between instructional plans and lessons, on the one hand, and comprehensive education and formation, on the other. In this regard, Hirscher praised the Jesuit model of education for addressing the whole person. Hirscher believed that neither priestly marriage nor celibacy would improve the spiritual and moral quality of priests unless candidates for the priesthood first were selected much more carefully and second were given an education more appropriately and intelligently directed to their future ministry.

36. [Hirscher], "Recension," 662. Concerning other deleterious effects of enforced celibacy, see 652-53.

37. [Hirscher], "Recension," 652. See also Franzen, "Die Zölibatsfrage im 19. Jahrhundert," 351-354. H. J. Vogels makes this point the centerpiece of his contemporary critique of celibacy in *Celibacy--Gift or Law?* He argues that the ability to lead a celibate life is the result of receiving such a charism from God. Without the charism, celibacy is a legal imposition under which many priests suffer. Vogels writes: "This book's argument can be summarized in two sentences: 1. A gift is necessary for celibacy; this is not given to all priests and without it celibacy leads to illness; 2. The law on celibacy, on the other hand, has taken its origin from the interest in the cultic purity of Old Testament priests, which nowadays is no longer recognized as a sound reason." 22.

38. [Hirscher], "Recension," 654.

39. "Recension," 655, 656.

40. For example: "Die Ehe hat überhaupt einen so wohlthätigen Einfluß auf die Erziehung der Menschen zur Religiosität und Moralität, daß keine andere Welteinrichtung in dieser Beziehung neben sie gestellt werden kann." "Recension," 654.

41. [Hirscher], "Recension," 656.

42. [Hirscher], "Recension," 660-661. Although he moderated his criticism of mandatory celibacy in later years, Hirscher differentiated himself from other members

of the Catholic Tübingen School by publicly articulating arguments against the practice.

43. [Hirscher], "Recension," 664-665.

44. [Hirscher], "Recension," 665, emphasis added.

45. "Will man also das Volk mit der Priesterehe versöhnen, so muß man aus allen Kräften dahin arbeiten, daß der eheliche Umgang der Christenwürde entspreche, und einmal der Wahn verschwinde, als könne durch die eheliche Einsegnung das aufhören thierisch und Sünde zu seyn, was man thierisch treibt, und sündlich. Man muß wenigst dahin wirken, daß die Christen die christliche Weise, im Ehestande zu leben, erkennen; und einsehen, daß das Gefühl einer gewissen Unwürdigkeit, das man oft heimlich mit dem Geschlechtsgebrauch auch in der Ehe verbindet, der unchristlichen Weise dieses Gebrauches zuzuschreiben sey; und daß dagegen in der christlichen Ehe durchaus nichts liege, was der Menschenwürde überhaupt, und der Würde der Geistlichen insbesondere widerstehe." [Hirscher], "Recension," 665-666.

46. [Hirscher], "Recension," 662-63.

47. [Hirscher], "Recension," 668-69.

48. [Amann and Zell], *Denkschrift für die Aufhebung des den katholischen Geistlichen vorgeschriebenen Cölibates. Mit drei Actenstücken* (Freiburg: 1828), 65. For a contemporary, multi-paged critique of celibacy, see Vogels, *Celibacy*, 70-88, 98. Vogels makes *historical* evidence of the right of apostles to take a wife as a companion his strongest argument against the prohibition of clerical marriage. He interprets the historical evidence as suggesting that clerical marriage does not violate divine law. Arguments deduced from the universal human right to marry are secondary in Vogels' critique. Vogels ultimately claims that there are five grounds on which compulsory celibacy is invalidated. He sums them up (p. 105): "The law of compulsory celibacy is against human rights, against apostolic rights in scripture, against the inamenability of charisms, against the holiness of marriage (in its original motivation), against the requirements of equality in the rules of admission to priesthood."

49. [Möhler], "Beleuchtung der Denkschrift für die Aufhebung des den katholischen Geistlichen vorgeschriebenen Cölibates," *Der Katholik* 30 (1828):1-32, 257-297. In the same year it was also published as a self-standing pamphlet. Both publications were issued anonymously. See Möhler's *Gesammelte Schriften und Aufsätze*, ed. by J. J. I. Döllinger, 2 vols. (Regensburg: 1839), 1:177-267. In order to understand Möhler's critique of the Freiburger *Denkschrift*, it is important to keep in mind that the book asserted the right of the laity to have a voice in the determination of church practices and politicies. Amann and Zell proposed the abolition of celibacy as the first application of the principle of legitimate lay authority in the church. To Amann and Zell's opponents, this proposal appeared to be an expression of an Enlightened, anti-ecclesial mentality. See Picard, 331. Stephan Lösch claims that prior to 1826 Möhler had already proposed the idea of forming an anti-celibacy association, but that Möhler quickly came to regret this idea. See Lösch's *Prof. Dr. Adam Gengler, 1799-1866. Die Beziehungen des Bamberger Theologen zu J. J. I. Döllinger und J. A. Möhler* (Würzburg: 1963), 245-251.

50. Here he may have had Hirscher in mind as well as the Freiburg authors of the *Denkschrift*. Concerning Möhler's quarrel with Hirscher over his public statements on celibacy, see Stephan Lösch, "Die Diözese Rottenburg im Bilde der öffentlichen Meinung (1828-1840)" *Rottenburger Monatschrift* 11 (1927-28): 66.

51. [Möhler], "Beleuchtung der Denkschrift," 100, 112.

52. Pope Gregory XVI, "Mirari vos," para. 11, in *The Papal Encyclicals, 1740-1878*, ed. by Claudia Carlen (McGrath Publishing: A Consortium Book, 1981), 237.

53. Pope Pius IX, "Qui Pluribus," para. 16 in *The Papal Encyclicals*, 280. "Syllabus of Errors," reprinted in *Readings in Church History*, ed. by Colman J. Barry (Westminster: Christian Classics, 1985), 992-96; here 996.

54. F. X. Dieringer, *Offenes Sendschreiben "über die kirchlichen Zustände der Gegenwart" an Dr. J. B. von Hirscher* (Mainz: Kirchheim & Schott, 1849), 26-28. Fr. Teipel, *Offenes Sendschreiben an den Herrn Professor von Hirscher in Freiburg. Eine Stimme aus Westphalen* (Paderborn: 1849), 5-7. *Hirscher und die katholische Kirche. Eine Beleuchtung der Hirscher'schen Reformpläne vom kirchlichen Standpunkte. Von einem Priester der Diözese Limburg* (Regensburg: 1850), 11-15. Johann Baptist Heinrich, *Die kirchliche Reform. Eine Beleuchtung der Hirscherschen Schrift: "die kirchlichen Zustände der Gegenwart,"* 2 vols. (Mainz: 1850), 2:92-126. For Hirscher's response to his critics, see Hirscher, *Antwort an die Gegner meiner Schrift: 'Die kirchlichen Zustände der Gegenwart'* (Tübingen: Laupp & Siebeck, 1850).

55. Hirscher, *Die kirchlichen Zustände der Gegenwart* (Tübingen: Laupp & Siebeck, 1849), 64. For an English translation, see *Sympathies of the Continent or Proposals for a New Reformation by John Baptist von Hirscher*, trans. and ed. by Arthur Cleveland Coxe (Oxford: John Henry Parker, 1852), 191.

56. His statements concerning celibacy were not exactly the only reasons for the book's condemnation. In this book, Hirscher argued for a decentralization of power or a democratization of church structure. Appealing to the testimony of the New Testament, he pointed out that the ruling principle in the early church was neither Peter nor the apostles, but rather the entire community of Jesus' disciples. See Hirscher's *Die kirchlichen Zustände*, 16-20; 106-11. See Hubert Schiel, *Johann Baptist von Hirscher. Eine Lichtgestalt aus dem deutschen Katholizismus des XIX. Jahrhunderts* (Freiburg: 1926), 1:138.

57. Evidence is also to be found in new demands for privacy and in the explicit articulation of a greater appreciation for the sentiments of love and affection in the family. See Taylor, *Sources of the Self*, 290-96.

58. Coxe, 125-26; Hirscher, *Die kirchlichen Zustände*, 26-27.

Contemporary Perspectives

on

Christianity and the Body

CHRISTIANITY, INC.

Jill Raitt

Our concern with the body is a way of asking, with a different emphasis, the question: "What is it to be human?" I think that for those of us who study and teach religious studies, that is the fundamental question with which we deal. When we study the religions of the world, among which we must include indigenous religions, we see that it is religious initiation that, for the most part, makes a newborn a member of the people, a human being, a person, capable of human and divine relations. In the patriarchal Rome of the Caesars, a new-born remained a fetus until its father picked it up and owned it as his child. If the father failed to own the child, it was abandoned on the doorstep for someone else to pick up or let die unrecognized as a human being.[1] In other words, the very notion "human being" is a social, and in many cases a religious, category as well as a biological one. In fact, the ways of making human or recognizing one's humanity are fundamental to religions world-wide.

In this address which opens our conference, I would like to share with you ideas about Christianity as a body that are both political and mystical. I do not claim originality, but rather a review, in the context of indigenous religions, of the pros and cons of corporate Christianity. In doing so, I will touch upon many of the topics listed in the program for this conference and which will be expanded upon in greater depth and, I hope originality, in particular sessions.

During the last three years, I have been privileged to participate in a series of conferences at the East-West Center in Honolulu. The conferences drew together scholars from around the world to discuss spirituality. It was in Honolulu that I began to be interested in the spirituality of the Polynesian people. The study has proved to be fascinating and I look forward to learning more. An advantage to learning more about the religions of other peoples is the increased understanding I gain concerning my own religion. Studying Protestantism taught me more about Catholicism; studying indigenous religions has taught me more about Christianity.

Through my contacts with Polynesians, I have gained insight into the interaction of majorities and minorities. The most searing and salutary, the most painful and instructive experience I have had in this regard occurred during the conference held last January at the East-West Center which focussed on indigenous religions in contact with Christianity. I was the only one there speaking from the Christian tradition. Most of the rest of the participants were Polynesian or spoke from the point of view of Polynesian religions. The burden of many of their papers was the trauma that Christian missionaries brought to their cultures and the ways they had accommodated that imposition. My own paper also mourned the liaison, frankly stated by a missionary to Hawaii in the early nineteenth century, that Christianity, commerce and culture were inseparable. Even though I was apologetic, my culture, my point of view, made me an "outsider," the representative of the oppressor. I was marginalized and at last rendered speechless, a *ha'ole* or "one without breath" as the Hawaiian scholar John Lake explained the Hawaiian word for white people. I experienced what marginalized people experience: lack of confidence that one will be understood, that one can say anything that will contribute to the conversation, and on top of all that, guilt for what my people had done and become. It was painful and valuable. Rarely, I think, has a member of the culture that now dominates the world the opportunity to learn what it feels like to be side-lined.

These conferences led directly to my four-week trip to Samoa, New Zealand and Rarotonga (one of the Cook Islands) that ended only two months ago. My hosts were, for the most part, the very people who had made me feel so insecure. They welcomed me with the hospitality and generosity for which the Polynesians are rightly known. And they appreciated the fact that I came with a mind prepared to listen and to learn. That much said by way of prologue, I turn now to my paper, "Christianity Inc." I shall begin with the negative implications of my title.

No single comment on the missionaries sent to Hawaii impressed me more deeply and made me more sad and ashamed than that of Edward Joesting:

> The great damage the missionaries did was an unintentional
> one, a harm they would have been hard pressed to understand.
> Christianity was a Western religion, and to be a Christian one

had to have the conscience of a Western man. The Hawaiians were Polynesians, and the concept of Christian sin missed the Polynesian mind. So missionaries attempted to destroy the old Hawaiian standards and substitute Western ideals of right and wrong. Only when this had been done would the concept of sin be realized and the need for a Christ be apparent. The missionaries preached endlessly about how depraved and stupid the Hawaiians had been. The Islanders were told they must feel great shame for what they had been, for their unenlightened parents and hero ancestors. It was a long, humiliating experience, . . .[2]

The preparation of the Congregationalist missionaries sent from New England, often via Yale College or Amherst College, to the shores of Hawaii was the least fitted to understand the values of the Polynesian peoples. These serge-clad, top-hatted missionaries could not so much as conceive the possibility that indigenous peoples had anything to offer Christians. The Congregationalist missionary, Hiram Bingham, gathering his journals after twenty one years in Hawaii, summed up traditional Hawaiian culture bluntly: "The whole policy of Satan here, seemed to be, *to make that to be sin which is no sin, and that to be no sin which is sin.*"[3] The Reverend A. W. Murray[4] of the London Missionary Society wrote that in 1835 Christianity was already "triumphant" in Polynesia. The Reverend Murray wrote in his journal, "Never have I enjoyed a season of deeper, purer interest than in meeting these tamed savages, these happy Christian converts from amid darkness the most deep, depravity the most profound, and pollutions the most loathsome."[5] He rejoiced that in Rarotonga there were no idols at all; all were Christians![6] While in Samoa there were "savages of the best type." They were not cannibals, nor were they blood-thirsty like Fijians or revengeful like New Zealanders, nor contaminated by the "deep moral pollution of the Tahitian and Hervey Islanders and the Hawaiian." But Samoans were still not innocent. They were "deeply polluted" as one could tell by the noise and debauchery of their all-night dances and occasional polygamy.[7] The Reverend Murray rejoiced that by 1857, an Hawaiian missionary society had been established and was sending out Hawaiian missionaries. These "Hawaiian" missionaries, however, had been made thoroughly Christian, we may be sure, and appeared dressed in dark suits, white shirts and black ties!

But before the missionaries, before the whalers, the Pacific Islands were already the objects of European bargaining. As soon as the Philippine Islands were observed and placed on a sixteenth-century map, Charles V, Holy Roman Emperor from 1519-1556, sold them to Portugal for 350,000 ducats.[8] Of this sale of their land, the Philippine people knew nothing. I was also bemused by Hiram Bingham's constant iteration of how salutary Christianity is for the character combined with his tales of the sinful misbehavior of the sailors, at least nominally Christians, from the whaling ships. Bingham's journals did not speculate upon the probability that the good and the bad exist among all peoples, regardless of their religion. Bingham, and the other missionaries, also spoke of the importance of "civilizing" the "savages." They must be taught to wear clothes and to speak and read English. The very commercialism of the Americans and Europeans is a means of bringing this "inferior" race to civilization and to Christianity.

> From what has been exhibited of native character previous to the commencement of intercourse with whites, it will readily be admitted that it was degraded in the extreme. Consequently the contact of a better race must necessarily cause some moral improvement . . . . The very fruits of civilization displayed to their covetous eyes in the superior knowledge, and above all in the property of the whites, begot in them a respect and desire for the faith which to their minds teemed so rich in temporal blessings.[9]

They must also build houses and churches after the manner of New England. The original instructions to the American missionaries in Hawaii stated in part: "Your views are not to be limited to a low or a narrow scale; but you are to open your hearts wide, and set your mark high. You are to aim at nothing short of covering those islands with fruitful fields and pleasant dwellings, and schools and churches." In sum, in the spirit of liberal Calvinism, the missionaries were not only to Christianize the Islands but also to transplant there the folkways of distant New England.[10]

For the "liberal Calvinists," opening their hearts wide did not pertain to learning the ways of the Hawaiians, although they had to learn their language. Rather it was to turn Hawaiians into candidates for Yale College and Hawaii into a little New England. They succeeded quite well by some measures, since Hawaiians did attend Yale College and even became Congregational ministers. Parts of the islands were organized into neat little squares with white-washed cottages built along their regular streets. Charles Nordhoff, writing about Honolulu in 1874, remarked:

... if you are an American, and familiar with New England, it will be revealed to you that the reason why all the country looks so familiar to you is that it is really a very accurate reproduction of New England country scenery. The white frame houses with green blinds, the picket-fences whitewashed until they shine, the stone walls, the small barns, the scanty pastures, the little white frame churches scattered about, the narrow 'front yards,' the frequent school-houses, usually with but little shade: all are New England, genuine and unadulterated; . . . The whole scene has no more breadth nor freedom about it than a petty New England village, but it is just as neat, trim orderly, and silent also.[11]

Judd, the anthologist, took this passage to be confirmation of the missionaries' success; it is evident to me that Nordhoff was not so pleased.

Nor are many of us "pleased." Christianity, Incorporated, has destroyed peoples' cultures, their dignity, their languages. It has carted off their religious works of art, their loved and beautiful gods and put them in museums. I was taken aback when the minister of education on the island of Rarotonga told me that not a single carving of the pre-contact Rarotongans remained. The islanders have never seen the work of their ancestors. All were either burned or shipped to the British Museum. Worse than that, the bones of indigenous peoples over the world have been taken for study or put in cases in museums for the irreverent to gaze upon. Only recently have some of them been returned to their people for ceremonial burial, among them the bones of Hawaiians.

These behaviors together with the commercialization of the cultures of indigenous peoples, a commercialization that went hand in hand with the building of churches and the gift of Bibles, are matter for a corporate *nostra culpa* from all Christians. The indictment is summed up by Ron Crocombe in a frequently reprinted book, *The South Pacific: An Introduction.*

The main commandments of the religion of commerce . . . are to value:
1. Yourself over others
2. Consumption over production
3. Waste over conservation
4. Immediate effects over long-term consequences.[12]

Although these commandments of the religion of commerce were not the intended effects of Christian missionaries, we recognize them as the offshoots of the marriage of Christianity, Culture and Commerce to the peoples of Polynesia, a marriage celebrated by the missionaries.

I would like to share here a bit more of my own spiritual history. When I understood how damaging Christianity has been to so many indigenous peoples in all parts of the world, I could no longer own my Christianity. Re-owning it has been a gradual process that has included the following elements, among others. I had to accept that Christianity is the religion of my tribe. I can no longer endorse the conversion of other tribes through the display of commercial goods and military arms which once accompanied eager missionaries bringing Bibles. Although many missionaries today no longer proceed in so crude a manner, the assumptions of missionizing are no longer plausible to me.

But the most important step for me was putting the corporate church, the body of Christ made up of you and me and folks like us, into the Easter liturgy to be forgiven and renewed. When we come before God we see ourselves whole, all at once, our lives taken up and our sins forgiven in the timeless moment of God's blessing. I hope it may be so also for the church so that its blunders and sins may be acknowledged and forgiven in the blessing God bestows on it as the body of Christ. The whole life of the church has brought it to this moment as our lives have brought us here. In any given moment, the turn to God can effect the gathering up of an entire life for its healing and restoration. It is on that reality that I count for myself and for the church for without it, I could neither be nor call myself a Christian.

It is to that side of Christianity incorporated that I now turn, to the side that stands graced and through those who pray and work, supports those who err unknowingly and even sin knowingly. Christians are incorporated, are in the body, are the body of Christ. The Christ who lives in the world today, the Christ into whose body we are baptized and by whose body we are fed is the Christ who is each of us. The Christ who lives in the world today is therefor male and female, and the names of Christ are the names of each of us who are willing to be called Christian. For even though Christianity has made powerful claims backed up by signs of aggressive power, military and commercial, it is also a religion that can be persuasively presented and gracefully, beautifully lived. In spite of its missionary impulsion and its theological sophistication represented by uncounted volumes of technical and scholastic development, the Christian story is an appealing one and its sacraments are powerful symbols. I would like to look again at some of those symbols while maintaining my conversation with indigenous religions.[13] Where else should I begin but with the focus of this conference, the body?

BODY

To consider the body requires that we reconsider our relations to the rest of material reality. Since the Reformation and the Enlightenment, the split between body and spirit, symbol and word has deepened and Christians have almost forgotten Christianity's early emphasis on bodiliness and its place in the Christian liturgy. I do not think that we need to return to the past to recover this emphasis. We can recover the body-centeredness of Christianity from scripture and the sacraments. And indeed we are doing so prompted by conversations with indigenous traditions who see themselves as whole as well as wholly related to the earth's body on which we all live and move and have our being.

The liturgical inheritance of Christendom is richly diverse, encompassing the Eastern Orthodox high mass and Quaker meditation. Central to all forms of Christianity, however, is the person of Jesus, called the Christ. In traditional Christian understanding,[14] God took a body, a real body. Jesus was God incarnate. God did not inhabit a body, did not pick up and put down a body; God was not only a spiritual being, but became a corporal being. Jesus rose bodily and appeared to his disciples and ate with them, even inviting Thomas to put his hand in the wound in Jesus's side.

Christians are recovering that appreciation of the body. Some Christians, including some of my students, are offended by the emphasis on body in early Christianity. But they and we must come to terms with the words of Paul, "If Christ is not risen, then vain is your faith." What does that mean? It means that the resurrection of Christ was not simply spiritual; the Greeks believed in a spiritual immortality. It means that the whole Christ, the man born-of-woman, rose bodily. Having risen, that body is now present as Eucharist and Church. But wait a moment. How easily the familiar concepts slide through the mind, the words come to the lips. How can it possibly be that the body born of Mary is both Eucharist and Church? How can it be that instead of the eaten becoming the eater, the eater becomes the eaten? In short, how do sacraments, and particularly the Eucharist, build the Church, the body of Christ? Are Christians unique in this complex religious perception?

SACRAMENTS

Eating together, eating the god or the powerful ancestor, or even the enemy as was once done among some Polynesian peoples, has only one object, to obtain life and the power of life which bodies manifest, while they live. It is through common actions made uncommon by ritual that religious peoples reach for the power and life of the gods. It is possible to conceive of such transference of life and power only when there is an analogous likeness between divine and earthly life and power. This concept is employed by some scholars[15] as the primary way of understanding the continuity among godly, heroic, political and cultural life among the Maori through a corrected interpretation of the concept of *tapu* (Maori) or *kapu* (Hawaiian) and called *taboo* by Captain Cook and the stream of anthropologists who, in his wake, invaded the South Pacific.

The principle meaning of *tapu* is life, powerful life. It is given by the gods and invested primarily in chiefs, but it can exist also in foods like the *kumara*, a yam-like plant that is ceremonially planted, harvested, prepared and eaten, and in war canoes, ceremonially built. Where there is no *tapu*, there is no life, hence the restrictions against its pollution or harm (those restrictions wrongly given the name of the power itself, hence our word, not theirs, of *taboo*).[16] From "indigenous" traditions like those of the Maori and many others, we learn a basic human relation to the earth and its products, to our processing of them and to their sanctified use in rituals.

In this context, let us return to our Christian understanding of sacraments and the language so familiar to us. From Christ's command, from his table-fellowship and post-resurrection sharing of himself as body and as bread comes Christian practice centered in sacrament. Sacraments are nothing other than the earth and its products becoming, analogously, vehicles of transcendent realities. The products of the earth pass through human hands, becoming bread, oil, wine, etc. These elements of our existence, these necessities of our lives, become the means of deep spiritual contact and growth. But let us be careful not to separate body and spirit. We can emphasize one or the other, but to split them apart is false to what it means to be a human being. Life is in the body; spiritual life is in the body, yours and mine and Christ's who with us is the church. We cannot separate body and spirit and live.

Material reality cooperates in a divine activity which incorporates people into God's body. Indeed, the body of God is not only our body but the earth which we speak of as created by God. However we speak of it, it manifests the power and life of God and the sacramental circle is completed. Although the goal of Christians is spoken about in terms of the life of resurrection, Christians need to remember that the life of the resurrection is lived *first* on earth through bodily birth and sacramental rebirth, bodily life and death blessed by the other sacraments, and lastly, bodily resurrection.

CHURCH

But this path is not a solitary one. Indigenous religions teach us also that however important the individual may be, no individual can survive physically or spiritually without a supporting community. In fact, no individual has any importance at all apart from the community, the group of people who bestow humanity on their newborns and through ritual, bring those new human beings into a dynamic relation with their ancestors and their gods.

St. Paul teaches the communal solidarity of Christians through an image made powerful by its appropriate relations to the body of Christ risen and eucharistically present: Christians are one body. That is basic. It is what the scriptures say; it is what the sacraments say. All who are baptized and participate in the Eucharist are one body: you are many grains ground into the one bread; you are many grapes crushed into the one wine; and all are Christ. Augustine's challenge to neophyte Christians is startling: "Know your dignity, O Christian; you are Christ." But to belong to, to become, to participate in one's deity are not new ideas. Neither rebirth nor incorporation are peculiar to Christianity. Christian initiation has continuities with all the religions who initiate, name, and call their "new-borns" to pass through death into new life.

BAPTISMAL INITIATION AND RENAMING

It is useless to be born if one is not reborn. Initiation rites of many religions say this explicitly or implicitly. Birthing rites and puberty initiations make the initiate a member of the religion of the people and provide the protection and knowledge one must have to deal safely with divine powers. Baptism is the Christian introduction to knowledge of the divinity and to the restorative sacrifice. Without such initiation, one is not allowed to participate in the Eucharist. Baptism is a new birth effected through the waters which signify death of the old and birth of the new. Water is life. Let me say again that life is here understood analogously for all life, divine and

earthly. The water of life is also a most appropriate metaphor and
aptly stands for the life poured out, the Spirit given by God at
Baptism. That life can be like the ocean, or a surging, rushing river,
or a quiet stream or a pool or lake. When those waters rise in a
surge of life, they may result in new humans; when they rise in
worshipers, they water the dry places of the soul and so, because the
waters circulate, they enliven the whole body of Christ. One is
immersed in the death of Christ and rises with the risen Christ to
participate in the Eucharist, to join that fellowship called the
Church, the corporation that is Christ.

EUCHARIST

After baptism, Christians are called to participate in the bread
which symbolizes, presents, and in some way, is the Body of Christ.
I know how theological battles over the Eucharist have torn Christianity apart. The "sacrament of unity" became the primary sacrament
of disunity, particularly between Catholics and Protestants, but also,
and not less fiercely, among Protestants as well. But fundamentally,
the Eucharist is the presentation of Christ to Christians for their
incorporation into the Christian body. The Church is an incorporation, an incarnation. The sacrament to which scripture calls Christians lifts them to heaven, and at the same time binds them to the
earth which Christians should revere as God's mirror and the earthly
source of the sacraments. This sacramental unity with each other
and with the earth gives Christians deep roots from which they can
draw strength to address the ecological and social problems of the
twenty-first Century.

SACRIFICE

A generic view of sacrifice is that it is intended to restore an
upset relationship between the deity and believers. While my Eliad-
ean notion of sacrifice is undergoing considerable change in dialogue
with Lawrence Sullivan's discussion of it in *Icanchu's Drum*,[17] the
basic sharing is not altered. That is, the sacrifice is a symbolic act by
which the power and life of the deity is made available to the community offering the sacrifice. The power may be invoked for many
reasons, but I think that those reasons may be summed up under the
broad notion of *power and life*. The community may be threatened
by physical or political dangers or it may seek to retain a life-giving
relation to divinity that has come under threat from the running

down of time, or the misbehavior of some member or members of the group.

For Christians the sacrifice of Christ on the cross has a deep history reaching through many peoples. It is specifically related to the Exodus of the Hebrews from Egypt and the sacrifice of the lamb whose blood protected the Hebrews from the destroyer. The families who sacrificed the lamb were directed not to break its bones, a condition dramatically recalled by the Gospel of John with regard to Jesus. Both Hebrews and Christians must look back even further to the sacrifices of nomadic herders who offered kids from their flocks to preserve animals and humans from the many threats of the desert. Whether one looks upon the sacrificial animal as a messenger that passes through death to plead before the divinity for those who sent it [Eliade] or as a means of dismissing primal beings to make possible the temporal and symbolic order [Sullivan], the basic likenesses obtain. The sacrifice is itself a bodied being. It is only through bodies, through material reality, that we or any religious people, can turn, in corporate worship, to the divinity, however that divinity is conceived.

BLOOD

From the sacrifice is obtained blood, symbol of life and death. To my mind, blood and water are two of the most powerful symbols in any religious system. Blood is the object of restrictions ("taboos") in every religion I know of. Among the Polynesians, blood and women are stringently restricted and both are feared lest the power of life [tapu] in them overcome the life [tapu] in others, or so I interpret it.[18] In Leviticus blood is declared holy because it is LIFE and life belongs to the Lord. The analogous understanding of blood follows it in its use of the sacrificial blood as the bond of the covenant. Thus for Christians it is the cup of the blood of Christ that seals the New Covenant. The horrific side of blood is made evident in the fear caused by blood spilled through death wounds and in the fear men have of the menstruating woman who is surrounded with restrictions and cleansing rituals among Polynesians as well as western Christians who used to "church" women after childbirth to purify them from the bloody messiness [read *powerful life fluids*] of the birth process. In the first Christian centuries, one of the reasons women were denied participation in the sacrament of ordination was *propter mensum*. In the middle ages, the cup was withdrawn from the laity for practical reasons, i.e., to prevent spills of the blood of

Christ But it was also a power-move on the part of the clergy who
alone had the right to handle and to drink the blood. The complex
theology of the Eucharist provided for the reception by all com-
municants of the whole Christ, but the symbolic statement of with-
holding the cup was not lost on Martin Luther or on those who
foster the modern liturgical movement. Blood signifies power and
life so profoundly that it causes an existential shudder when we
contact it really or symbolically and that power can be used or
usurped by those who control religious rites.

COMMUNION

Eating with or eating the divinity is also derived from the sacrifice and assures that the divine power and life are shared, first by
the celebrants, then by the people. In the Christian tradition, the
eating of the body and drinking of the blood of Christ have many
meanings: restoration of life through remission of sin, the making of
a new covenant, and within the covenant, a more intimate covenant,
the union of bodies which includes the analogy of the spousal union.
As bride and groom give each other their bodies, so the heavenly
bridegroom and the communicant offer themselves to one another
through communion, an exchange sealed by the communicant's
"Amen."[19] But behind this interpretation of generative life lies the
fundamental reality that in order to survive one must both offer to
and receive from the divinity. The relation of creature and creator
is here one of reciprocity, of immediacy, but there are also mediating realities that bind the body of Christ into one.

INTERMEDIARIES AS SACRAMENTS

Kauraka Kauraka[20] from the island of Manihiki, a Maori scholar
intent on bringing together his tribal traditions and the Christianity
brought to the Cook Islands by the London Missionary Society,
asked me whether there was anything in Christianity analogous to
the veneration of ancestors and to the heroes and divinities of the
Maoris. We spoke of kinds of intermediaries that Catholic Christianity recognizes, the first of whom is Christ, and those heroic
followers of Christ venerated as saints.

For Christians, Christ is the great intermediary, the sacrament
of God, the shaman who ascends the world tree at the navel of the
world to obtain life for his people. His journey is arduous, but
eagerly undertaken because without it, the connection between

heaven and earth would be lost. The cross stretches out the body of Christ to the four directions; it is planted deep in the earth, reaching to the sky and embracing the world in its outstretched arms. The tree bending with its holy fruit is the theme of a beautiful fifth-century hymn by Fortunatus still sung during Holy Week.

Early in Christianity, other intermediaries, the martyrs and saints, formed a heavenly ladder. Their relics gave bodily contact to worshipers. Heroes and ancestors were present to their relics and bound still closer the body of Christ reaching through time. Another aspect of the power of saints is their relation to the continuing life of Jesus as Eucharist, the most exalted "relic" of all and to which wonders and miracles are attached as they are also to the relics of saints whose bodies have not yet risen, but who are nevertheless in the unveiled presence of the risen Christ and can therefore intercede with him on behalf of their protegés on earth. Lastly, each member of the body is intermediary to every other as we experience the support of Christianity, Incorporated sustaining us in our own trials and as we pray for one another in the firm belief that such prayer does in fact strengthen the whole body and so each of its members.

CONCLUSION

Christianity is a religion among religions. It has ways of relating to earth and heaven, of mediating life and power, but its ways are not the only ways. The truth of Christianity is not whole until Christians have learned what it is to be *humanly* religious. Even those truths that Christianity has long revered as central are not fully understood except through the perspectives provided by other religions. Christians are enriched, deepened, and called to their own practices by understanding better the practices of other peoples of the world.

This respect for what Christians can learn from other peoples is the opposite of Christian triumphalism with its extraordinary insensitivity to the lives of those whom Christian missionaries encountered and often converted. Before they can hear well and share the wisdom of indigenous peoples, Christians must acknowledge the deep wrongs they have wrought and the permanent damage they have done by overpowering rather than impowering, by preaching and teaching without listening and learning. Most especially Christians must ask to be forgiven for so often distorting the Christian message by equating it with European culture imposed by conquest.

Healed by grace, Christianity incorporated can turn its face to the God it sees no longer in the image of Euro-Americans, but in the image of all peoples. From the many faces of the people of God, the face of God becomes clearer. In the many ways of being human, the face of Christ becomes at once more particular and more universal. Our sophisticated theologies will reflect better upon the nature of God when they see all peoples of the world as images of God in the fulness of their humanity. That fulness must include the cultural differences and ways of worship that make us who we are as human beings. Feminist theologies, African-American theologies, ecological theologies, and indigenous theologies have enriched and will continue to enrich our understanding of what it is to be Christian, to be the body of Christ, to be incorporated Christianity.

NOTES

1. Peter Brown, *The Body and Society: Men, Women, and Sexual Renunciation in Early Christianity* (New York: Columbia University Press, 1988), 28.

2. *Hawaii, an Uncommon History* (New York: W. W. Norton & Company, Inc., 1972), 76-77.

3. Valerio Valeri, *Kingship and Sacrifice: Ritual and Society in Ancient Hawaii.* trans. Paula Wissing (Chicago: University of Chicago Press, 1985), xxiii. Italics in original. The source is given by Valeri: *A residence of twenty one years in the Sandwich Islands; or the civil, religious, and political history of those islands*, 2nd edition (Hartford, Conn.: H. Huntington, 1848), 21. I have since obtained this volume and can confirm that Valeri has not misquoted Bingham.

4. *Forty Years' Mission Work in Polynesia and New Guinea from 1835-1875* (London: James Nisbet and Co., 1876).

5. *Ibid.* 10.

6. *Ibid.*

7. *Ibid.*, 39.

8. W. D. Alexander, *The Relations Between the Hawaiian Islands and Spanish America in Early Times* (Honolulu: Hawaiian Historical Society 1/28/92) Papers of, #1.

9. Jarves, 107.

10. *A Hawaiian Anthology*, edited by Garrit Judd (New York: The Macmillan Company, 1967), 67.

11. *Anthology*, 67-68.

12. (Christchurch: The University of the South Pacific, 1989), 82.

13. Because of a conversation following the presentation of this paper, it may be useful to delare my intentions. I am not engaged in a reductionist comparative study. Rather I value indigenous religions in themselves and for what I can learn, in their light, about Christianity and about other religions as well. The Department of Religious Studies at the University of Missouri, Columbia was built upon a tripod: western religions, Asian religions, and indigenous religions, a base that has proved durable and productive for all of us.

14. I do not want to say "theology" because the term tends to create a barrier between most Christians and learned specialists.

15. See M. Shirres' article *"Tapu"* in the *Journal of the Polynesian Society* 91 (1982), 29-51.

16. I owe this section to the many Maori scholars with whom I conferred in New Zealand and Rarotonga, but especially to Michael Shirres, O.P. and his kind sharing of his articles and insights with me during my stay in Auckland, New Zealand.

17. Lawrence E. Sullivan, *Icanchu's Drum: An Orientation to Meaning in South American Religions* (New York: Macmillan, 1988), 82-83, 631, 668, *et passim*.

18. Raitt, *"Tapu and Noa: Polynesian Women and Ritual,"* unpublished address before the Rocky Mountain, Great Plains Regional Meeting of the AAR, April 16, 1993.

19. I owe this metaphor to Bernard Cooke.

20. See Kauraka's book, *Oral Tradition in Manihiki* (Suva, Fiji: The University of the Southern Pacific, 1989). Kauraka had studied with Lévi-Strauss at the University of Hawaii, and applied Lévi-Strauss's structural method to his interpretation of the legend of Maui as it is told in Manihiki.

Inkblots and Authenticity:

A Response to Professor Raitt

William Loewe

"Christianity, Inc." indeed. Professor Raitt's title, read in its unadorned, abbreviated starkness on the convention brochure, was, I found, a tease. Christianity, Incorporated. Christianity as a corporation. Were we to hear a diatribe against ecclesiastical bureaucracy, patriarchal and Roman, perhaps, that reduces gospel to controllable routine? Would buying and selling be the target--a hundred dollars to walk down the aisle, honey, said the curate, or to be carted down it in your casket? In his lighter moments the bishop likes to sit at the piano and sing: the church's one foundation is b-i-n-g-o. Clerical humor. In the fifties it was reported with pride that the church had been rated among the world's best-managed corporations.

"Christianity, Inc.": This is a title full of possibilities, a veritable inkblot of a title.

The reflections Professor Raitt just shared with us are in no way so jejune as my initial speculations. Her paper has apparently simple structure: on the one hand, and on the other--*men*, and then *de*, as it used to go in Greek class. On the one hand Professor Raitt reminds us with graphic particulars of the many sins of corporate Christianity in its colonizing partnerships with European and American commerce and culture. On the other hand, she can yet commend a Christianity incorporation into which joins one to the power and life of the very body of Christ.

On the one hand, and on the other. Yet it is one and the same Christianity, or, to avoid abstractions, one and the same Christian church of which she speaks, and so to describe her address as composed of two juxtaposed, contrasting sections is too simple. It misses the movement, the journey, the "spiritual history," as Professor Raitt terms it, leading to the affirmation of that one concrete Christian church with and despite all its ambiguity. Far from a given, an obvious matter of fact, that affirmation is a hard-won achievement, even if one reckons such achievements, in the end, as gift.

Professor Raitt allows us at least a glimpse of the spiritual journey from which her paper issues. Serendipity placed her in Honolulu off and on for three years of scholarly conferences, in the course of which Polynesian spirituality grew fascinating to her. Polynesians, however, have experienced the attentions of Christian missionaries as a blight upon their culture and religion. Encountering their trauma was for Professor Raitt an experience "searing and salutary," "painful and instructive" (100). It plunged her into mourning, offered her a taste of being marginalized as an "outsider," a *ha'ole,* while at the same time distancing her, alienating her from her own tradition. Alienation is not, however, the last word, and she finds herself embarked on a gradual process of re-owning a tradition which, chastened, repentant, and transformed, still offers a story she finds appealing and sacraments that exert power, a tradition that can be persuasively presented and gracefully, beautifully lived.

For all its contingent, serendipitous elements, many of us may nonetheless recognize this narrative as a familiar one, similar, perhaps, to journeys of our own. Perhaps equally familiar are the categories into which someone like Paul Ricoeur would resolve this story's plot. Cultures clash when we begin from a traditional self-understanding of Christian faith, a self-understanding forged during the apostolic, patristic, medieval, reformation and post-reformation eras of Christian history. These were eras characterized by what Ricoeur labels the first naivete of an unproblematic relation to the world of the Bible, the mythic world ordering Western Christendom. But that naivete shatters upon a culture which, with its empirical natural sciences, its historical and now global consciousness, generates a hermeneutic of suspicion the existential correlate of which is alienation, distance from the tradition. Yet modern culture began with a brave new naivete of its own, and that naivete also crumbles as the Enlightenment shifts from an easy, rationistic optimism to face the crisis of objectivity, meaning, and value signalled by this modern culture's own masters of suspicion. Through all of this, however, the religious question--what is it all about, anyway?--persists, and upon the ineluctability of the dynamic from which this question of the whole arises rests the possibility of a hermeneutic of recovery and what Ricoeur terms, perhaps not too felicitously, a second or post-critical naivete.

Of course none of this occurs automatically, nor is it self-evident that it should. Rather than submit itself to an hermeneutic purge, traditional Christian self-understanding can harden into fundamentalisms. Or, the matter can end with an hermeneutic of suspicion--how many ex-theologians, to use a word Professor Raitt would rather avoid, have migrated to history and philosophy departments? Nor is it precisely clear just what a second naivete might entail. Might not the term mask a failure of nerve, a regression into illusion and fantasy as the sole solace available as we drift over the abyss on our frail linguistic rafts?

Bernard Lonergan can help focus our discussion on two fronts. First, he identifies as classicism the cultural embodiment of Christianity which constitutes the starting point of Ricoeur's, and Professor Raitt's, adventure. I can think of no better illustrations of classicism than the texts that Professor Raitt has chosen from her New England missionaries. Those texts bear eloquent, wholly unself-conscious witness to a stance which regards one's own culture as normative, as possessor of the literary and philosophical classics of the human spirit, as apex of human development. Upon this stance one's own religion is of course the one true religion, beside which all others stem from obdurate heresy, willful schism, or, in the case of cultures which can only be regarded as primitive, superstition. Many of us in this learned society are old enough to have been reared on a Catholic version of this classicist mentality.

Second, Lonergan stakes his proposal for theological method on authenticity. But, I would ask, might not the drive for authenticity, the three-fold conversion of which Lonergan writes--intellectual, moral, and religious--itself supply the dynamic of an hermeneutic of suspicion which dismantles the classicist embodiment of Christianity? For example, is not moral authenticity clearly discernible in the experience of revulsion Professor Raitt relates at classicist Christian imperialism? Again, is not religious authenticity the touchstone of her recognition of the beauty of Polynesian spirituality? Or again, does not intellectual authenticity commit us to what we know to be the case in place of what our nostalgia for childhood's security, for Ricoeur's first naivete, would like? And does not that commitment involve many of us in an effort to negotiate, not suppress, the problematic of Lessing's ditch? In each of these instances, I would suggest, it is the drive toward authenticity that generates the negative critique under which classicism dissolves.

To take it one step further: might not the same drive also carry one beyond these moments of suspicion? Might it not head towards the intellectually, morally, and religiously chastened reappropriation of the Christian tradition, a reappropriation enriched, to be sure, by awareness of Christianity's analogies and continuities with other traditions, of which Professor Raitt speaks and which Ricoeur points toward with his second naivete?

What might these ruminations on authenticity have to do with our theme of religion and the body? "The body" is of course a reification; there exist, not bodies, but embodied selves, not humanity in the abstract but the single concrete universal which is the human race. Embodiment is what we require for wholeness and self-definition, but as individuating it is also, as an older metaphysic had it, a principle of limitation. Now Christians form one body in Christ, a body which, we believe, carries nothing less than the meaning redemptive of the human race and, through it, the earth and entire cosmos. This redemptive mission, in turn, renders Christian faith something far more serious than the mere commodity available for servicing private needs for meaning to which modernity would reduce it. But if embodiment nonetheless makes whole precisely by limiting, does this not also mean that as Christ's body the Christian church is always individual, particular, specific and at least to that extent, as Professor Raitt has it, a religion among religions?

We have arrived, then, at the point at which a host of important issues erupt for our discussion. Once the Christian church has struggled free of classicism, once Christians have opened themselves to the genuine advances offered by a culture marked by empirical-scientific, historical, and global consciousness, even with the horrific ambiguities of that same culture, how, from this new standpoint, are Christian women and men to relate, in heart and mind, to members of other religions? At this point of burgeoning issues I would conclude with one final question: by encouraging us to reflect on "Christianity, Inc.," has Professor Raitt not also led us to an encounter with the issues posed by a recognition of what the British might call "Christianity, Ltd."?

Em-bodied Spirit/In-spired Matter:

Against Tech-Gnosticism

Gary A. Mann

Tech-Gnosticism Defined

One of the more profound and challenging phenomena in contemporary American culture is the impact electronic and information technologies are having on the question of reality: "What is truly real?" Everywhere we look we see the technological demateri-alization of reality as we encounter the cultural attempt to reshape our sense of reality. It is evident in the video arcades where virtual, or interactive, games allow the participants, most often adolescents, the thrill of "killing" an opponent without the messiness of blood--"virtual death." We engage in electronic communications in virtual communities in a vast network called Internet in which we neither hear nor see those with whom we communicate. We read electronic publications. Computer graphics literally create the perfect "virtual" models --"people" who only exist in electronic form--for the advertis-ing of products. The horrors of war are sterilized by "smart weap-ons" that distance us from the killing. More and more we live in the "virtual" world of our TV screens as we find we can now shop, bank and even worship without ever leaving the comfort of our remote control! This phenomenon touches us all--not just the com-puter jocks! I have come to call this phenomenon *tech-gnosticism*. The new technology of virtual reality is the best and most clear example of tech-gnosticism.

Virtual reality is a new way in which the human being interfaces with computer technology, by entering into an artificially created environment and interacting with that "virtual reality." Virtual reality already has many uses within our culture. It is being used in the

training of pilots, surgeons and architects. It is guiding radiologists
toward brain tumors. Virtual reality is allowing quadriplegics to have
a temporary sense of mobility in a "virtual" world in which they are
no longer handicapped but are able to move about freely by using
whatever movement they may have, be it eye or finger movement,
to propel them through an electronic world (Daviss 1990, 38). Given
the rate of development in this field that is already providing tactile
sensations of virtual objects, the technology could soon exist that
would allow persons to have sexual encounters with computer-con-
structed persons in virtual reality (the ultimate safe sex?), including
the actual physical sensations that go with the act.

One can begin to see some similarities between this new tech-
gnosticism and ancient gnostic movements.[1] Thomas Molnar argues
that most forms of gnosticism are reactions to extreme rationalism
in which the human reason is individually divinized and disembodied.
(Molnar 1983, 134) One could say, therefore, that contemporary
gnosticism is a result of a Western system of thinking which has significantly sacrificed a considerable amount of life's substance to a
rationalism subjectively centered on the self. Our age of technological science has had a profound impact on our culture by its
disembodying of knowledge and its disregard of the sensual knowledge presented through human affectivity and sensory experience
(Milhaven 1989, 341-343). We have relied more and more on positiv-
ist and absolutist truth claims of modern realism. We seem finally to
have decided to rely on disembodied reason--human or computer.
Tech-gnosticism is the exponential expansion of such a disembodying
technical reason that can create a virtual world without body.

A second similarity to ancient gnosticism is to be found in the
redemptive myths that equate salvation with the escape from the
imprisonment of the natural body/world.[2] The escape from this
reality can be seen to be one of the desires expressed by tech-gnosticism as it attempts to release its adherents from the stress and
strain of everyday life in America.

Third, both forms of gnosticism appear to be dependent on
revealed salvific knowledge shared with the devotee by an external
agent and neither derived nor formulated by the consciousness of
the gnostic. It was the priest of the ancient gnostic traditions, who
in sharing the various myths with the initiate, brought forth the
necessary revelation. In the late Middle Ages, it was the God-ori-
ented priest who was the revealer, with Scripture and Tradition
being the source of gnosis. Throughout most of modernity, it was the
politically oriented humanist who was the "priest" of revelation. In

the contemporary age it is the scientist, in conjunction with the artificial intelligence of the computer, who serves the priestly function of revealing this salvific knowledge. The scientist-computer organism is the gnostic demiurge, capable of formulating a new gnosis which in many ways is very much a "new" religion with a new twist on the old redemptive myth.

There are two elements of tech-gnosticism that I find to have particular theological significance: (1) the redemptive model of escape from the natural world through artificial means, and (2) the desacralization of God's creation. It has already been noted that tech-gnosticism stresses leaving behind one reality (natural) and entering into an alternate reality (electronic). This in itself is not a matter of great concern in that the posing of alternate realities and states of consciousness is a central element in many religious traditions, including Christianity and Judaism. Yet the implication of tech-gnosticism is that the alternate reality that serves in a salvific way is not a kingdom created by God, but is, rather, one of our own creating. Indeed, the participant in virtual reality, networked with a computer, becomes a new demiurge, creating a world in which one can be the determinative deity--omniscient, omnipotent, and eternal. But is virtual reality really "real?" Is it the case that virtual reality is a weapon in some electronic arsenal by which the human may finally strip God of the title of Creator and Redeemer?

> According to the neurocognitive entrainment theory of consciousness, multiple realities, and therefore, any reality, may be understood as constructs of the human neurocognitive system. The perception of reality as it arises within the sensorium is an integration of both cognitive and perceptual functions, provided with data by the various physical senses. Experiences of reality, therefore, are constructed and mediated by the nervous system and unfold during each moment of consciousness.[3]

Integral to this constructive process of reality are the social, paradigmatic elements which function in the integration. Societies typically define a set of possible states of consciousness for their members. Those members are then socialized to recognize the appropriate attributes that are definitive of their state of mind. Such a socialized recognition sets parameters around stages of consciousness typically experienced in a culture by the establishment of conditioned and internalized control of attention.

What this means is that the alternate perception of reality created by tech-gnosticism would indeed be considered "real" as it became a part of the cultural paradigmatic structure used in the social process of normative formation. The more virtual reality and similar electronic technology become ingrained in our cultural matrix, engaging our sensorium with such authentic artificiality and serving as a "portal to another world," the more it has the potential of replacing the natural world in which we live with a world that only lives in the deep recesses of our imaginations and consciousness. We will then have become Creators of a new heaven and a new earth, having successfully escaped from the "evils" of the material world.

But does this mean that tech-gnosticism is to be seen as another religious tradition? If we would understand "religion" in terms of its being a cultural paradigm by means of which a culture or community shapes its self-understanding in relationship to its environment, or as that vision that binds all experience together into an integral whole, we would have to say that tech-gnosticism fulfills those functions for a growing number of people. Therefore, it is at the very least a developing religious framework and one that stands in conflict with the understanding of the world as presented by Christianity.

This tech-gnostic concept of reality is contrary to a central affirmation of the Christian tradition that states that the physical and material world was created by God as "good" (Gen. 1:31). They are to be valued, respected and cared for in the fashion appropriate to what is valuable to God. This theme of goodness, indeed even of a sacredness of the material world, is reiterated in the Christian doctrine of the Incarnation in which God, the divine and infinite, "became flesh and dwelt among us." Biblically, the earth is spoken of as the home of God's spirit, the *shekinah*. The ongoing maintenance of the physical world is a part of the divine providence and God's continuing creation. The sacraments themselves express the faith assertion that God's presence comes in, with, and under the physical elements of bread and wine, that God encounters humankind through natural and material objects within our perceptual grasp.

This is the very same world that tech-gnosticism denies as it proclaims that this material world is one in which the human mind is restricted and limited by its physicality, its embodiment, imprisoned in the material world, and in need of release from its bondage. The sacredness of the world and the human body's very existence is set aside in favor of the freedom of the human imagination--an imagination without the limitations of matter nor the social paradigmatic elements that set the appropriate attributes and parameters for states of consciousness. Ironically, the imagination continues to be dependent on the material world as the brain must continue to be present to process the sensory stimuli even though it might not be cognizant of such dependency.

Once this world, the natural world, is relegated to a lesser position or totally disregarded, humankind's relationship with creation will no longer carry any value. The world will no longer be considered "home" but will be thought of as prison. The ecological consequences of such a paradigm shift in human cultural consciousness would be far more devastating than the utilitarian terracide we are witnessing now. As the alternate artificial reality becomes the more dominant paradigm for our concept of reality, the more we will retreat from any notion of this world as a gift of a gracious God (to be cared for as a sacred blessing and source of life) and into the dark recesses of our individual universes, our individual consciousness, our individual notions of "heaven." This would be the most radical of tribalizations. The more we long for an electronic savior leading us beyond the limitations of this world, the closer we come to having our tech-gnostic dream come true. The more the electronic myth is assimilated the greater will be the human disengagement as the world becomes mere object to be manipulated and toyed with for our own use. Once again, as in the ancient gnostic myths, we will claim that we are truly gods and the creators of "all that is."

EMBODIED SPIRIT/INSPIRED BODY:
AFFIRMATION OF A HOLISTIC CREATION

Given the challenges of the tech-gnostic religious myth, a major issue facing the contemporary Christian theological enterprise is the defining of the concept of the God-world relationship in a way that speaks meaningfully to the contemporary person and which continues to be faithful in its proclamation of the Christian story. Can we continue to affirm our creedal belief that God is active in the natural world/the body, given the increasing predominance of the tech-gnostic myth? Wherever we turn we discover this myth assimilated into our culture's cognitive framework, shaping our perception of world, self and God. In response to this, an approach is necessary by which we can interpret the Christian story using a framework that will allow our contemporary scientific culture to comprehend and accept it as relevant and formative.

THE CONTEMPORARY PARADIGM OF THE NATURAL WORLD

It has become increasingly clear in the past decades that a dramatic shift is taking place in the paradigms by which we understand the very nature of the world in which we live. The classical Newtonian model of mechanistic physics, which speaks of the world in materialistic and deterministic terms, has begun to crumble. The shift began with the ability of the scientist to examine microcosmic levels of reality--the fundamental elements of the universe. As these building blocks came more and more into the view of the human eye, the expected observations of the Newtonian paradigm were not seen. Such a model would expect to find particulate matter in unbroken continuity, existing as is through time and space, and clearly identifiable as stable in its location and velocity. What was observed did not fit this model. Instead of a stable materialistic model of reality, a new model began to be developed which portrayed reality differently. I would summarize this model as imaging three characteristics of reality:

1. Reality is foundationally staccatic.
2. Reality is thematic.
3. Reality is "alive."

Reality is foundationally staccatic.

At the microcosmic level, reality is not matter in continuous being but rather staccatic in becoming--broken, pulsating, and discontinuous. Microcosmic research led scientists to see the vibratory, fluctuating and indeterminate nature of matter. They observed matter as temporary manifestations of shifting patterns of waves that coalesce or concretize at particular points of observation, only to "deconcretize" when not observed. A new way of talking about matter was formulated as scientists struggled to speak of particles in flux, in and out of particulate material existence with a quantum jump occurring between one particular manifestation to the next.

Indeed this reality is a conceptually difficult thing to describe. Niels Bohr has spoken of it in language reminiscent of the Newtonian model--particles and waves. The difference in models is that the Newtonian model could only speak of an entity as being either one or the other. At the microcosmic level, Bohr argued, one must talk about matter in terms of two quite incompatible images: particles localized in time and space, and waves whose motion is extended through space but not localized. This led to the development of his principle of complementarity: the principal microcosmic world must be understood in terms of two conflicting yet simultaneous images--both particle and wave at the same time. Alfred North Whitehead chose to describe this phenomenon as neither wave nor particle but as "event" (from *evenire* = to come out) in which an entity actualizes but does not remain perceptibly in that state. (Whitehead 1978, 73) Relevant to our discussion of tech-gnosticism, this model suggests that there is more to reality than matter! If the foundation of reality is a series of events in which matter is actualized, we must say that reality is not "purely material" but "rather material" and that which exists "between" actualities/concrete events. We can call this *possibility* in Whiteheadian fashion or *potentiality* in Aristotelian metaphysics. It is as much a part of the process of reality as the actualized particles themselves, and will be seen to be quite significant in our enterprise.

Reality is thematic.

Theme denotes the principal subject that provides continuity and connectedness (relation) to composition. Even though the nature of reality may be expressed as fragmented particularity, discontinuous and indeterminate (staccatic), we still perceive continuity! Such continuity is also suggested by scientific theory and research. Indeed, we discover more and more that the world is not a collection of separate yet coupled entities, but a vast matrix of relationships.

The staccatic movement of reality which most certainly contains randomness and chance is not without theme or order. The movement of reality is not a random meandering but process. Henry Stapp argues that the universe is a "creative process that consists of . . . individual creative acts . . . Each event is a process in which all prior events are brought together, or prehended in a new pattern" (Stapp 1977, 322). In this way we can conceptualize reality as a matrix in which each event in its actualization establishes a new set of relations among the previously existing parts of the universe, the contemporaneously actualizing events, and with those possibilities that may not yet be actualized. Each microcosmic event is a novel synthesis of past actualized events prehended into its own actualized possibility. Given this process of prehension one might even speak of there being "decision" and "freedom" at the microcosmic level of natural reality, which brings us to the third characteristic of reality.

Reality is "Alive."

The unpredictability and indeterminancy of foundational reality resurrect the Aristotelian metaphysic of possibility-actuality and final causality. Such an interconnected matrix field in which events are actualized and "de-actualized" in indeterminancy could conjure up images of random chaotic disorder. Yet research continually discloses the vital, living character of reality with its own creativity (the ability to actualize its own possibilities for behavior) and sentience (subjective appropriation of external influences) (MacDaniel 1983, 300-301). The Newtonian notion of nature as a finite, determined mechanism that is static and dualistic in character has been challenged by a dynamic, holistic conception that highlights the unity of matter, possibility, life and energy. This new model conceptualizes nature as a complex, processional system of interconnected parts. Matter is understood as actualized, particular energy, being life-like, and having intrinsic value. It is understood in terms of an organism which has inclinations and goals. Even in their own randomness and uncertainty, it appears that material processes have direction (Polkinghorne 1991, 221-236). Ilya Prigogine's work with non-linear thermodynamics has shown many instances in which inanimate, self-organizing systems exhibit order emerging at higher levels out of the disorder at lower levels.[4]

Typically, the notion of causal emergence was understood as solely being upward emergence in that the complexities of higher levels emerge from and are dependent on the lower levels of creative simplicity. However, Polkinghorne and Sperry have challenged this one-directional causal emergence model (Polkinghorne 1991, 221-236; Sperry 1991, 237-258). They both argue that the higher levels of complexity also contribute to the emergence of the lower levels. This emergent characteristic of reality is evident in biochemistry where one encounters biofunction at the molecular level, apparently propelled by electronic forces that Holmes Rolston calls the "electronic character of life" (Rolston 1987, 85). This electronic characteristic can be spoken of as a "pulse of life" that inextricably connects life and matter into one process, an organism deciding actualities from the possibilities through biofunctioning at the molecular level.[5]

Therefore, instead of microelectronics predetermining the course of an organism's development as in the previously held materialist model, it is a two-way street. Vitality, or "life" itself can, therefore, be revisioned as both "particle and wave" simultaneously. It is particulate in that we find its biological identity associated with individual manifestations. It is "wave" in that there is a historical continuity in the pulse of life evidenced in the encoding and transmission of information and structures over millions of years--a prehension of all that went before. Life is like a corporate pulse in which a germ plasma with corporate and conformational biological identity flows on, and is prehended by later events even as individual actual events pass out of existence (Rolston 1987, 85-88).

Spirit Re-defined in Terms of Material Process

This scientific model of the world presents a number of criticisms to the dualistic paradigm of reality asserted by tech-gnosticism. Life and mind can no longer be seen in terms of their separateness from the physical world, the body. The recognition that life, mind, and matter are not disconnected but somehow inextricably intertwined no longer supports the kind of mind-body, spirit-matter dualisms upon which a gnostic myth depends.

The contemporary scientific model makes necessary a revisioning of the God-world relational concept, which in turn calls for a redefining of the concept of spirit. The traditional concept of spirit within Christianity as a third entity breaking into the natural world from beyond can be misleading and supportive of the tech-gnostic myth as it corroborates the dualistic vision, which in turn is not supported by contemporary scientific research of God's Creation. Any new model of spirit must be consistent with the model of reality that envisions life to be immanently and integrally present in the very material structures of the cosmos itself if it is to be consistent with how we see the world.

Oddly enough our work of redefining can begin with the revisiting of ancient concepts and metaphors. Here we discover the spirit of immanence and vitality enmeshed in all creation that stands prophetically critical to the tech-gnostic myth.

The biblical concept of Spirit has two ancestral trajectories from which it comes--the Hebrew *ruach* and the Greek *pneuma*. Both share common themes of vitality and presence, creativity and power. They both refer to the power of mobility, the force out of which motion comes. This is most clearly seen in their connection with "wind." *Pneuma* is derived from a verbal noun that defines the elemental natural and vital force which acts in the stream of air, as both matter and process, whether in the blowing of the wind or the respiration of the breath. Effective and directed power is the basic idea of dynamic contained in the term, as seen when *pneuma* is most often linked with *kinesis*--dynamic motion. *Ruach* is also used to speak of the tempest or the power of wind in a storm. It is what sets something moving over against that which is rigid and unmoving. It is important to note that both terms are used in conjunction with that which causes the air to move rather than with the air itself.

Yet there is more than motion involved in these ancient concepts. Not only do they denote the motion in air and respiration, but they also take on the mantle of animators of matter as they are connected with that which brings life to creation as in the Genesis cosmogonies and the story of Pentecost. Movement is a sign of life. It was the breath that animated the flesh, providing motion to the body with the pulsations of respiration.

The life-giving *pneuma* of the ancient world was neither anthropocentric nor biocentric. It came to denote the comprehensive life principle that integrated and overruled all things. This is exemplified in the Orphic cosmogony of the cosmic egg, when the wind brings life and motion to all the world as it animates the world becoming, "the breath of the world." The *pneuma* is understood both in relation to the human being and to the rest of the creation.

Another significant characteristic of the Spirit in the ancient world is that neither *ruach* nor *pneuma* was ever considered to be either totally transcendent and immaterial or totally immanent and material. They were understood as both. The *pneuma* was thought to be an element along with earth and fire out of which the human body was made. At the same time, it was also thought to stand, with the *psyche*, in contrast to the *soma*, with which it was inextricably bound in life. The spirit was never set in direct antithesis to matter as some supernatural, wonder-working spiritual part of a transcendent personal deity. It was, instead, a force of vitality in nature--immanent and impersonal. As the dynamic power in the movement of air, it continually dwelt in the cosmos and in all its parts, giving both existence and animation--authentic life. It was, to use the contemporary scientific model with which we are working, like "particle and wave" simultaneously.

The biblical notion of the spirit was not understood in some theistic way as being itself God. It was, rather, the efficacious event of God's presence in the very foundations of existence (Ps. 139:7, 23ff) (Moltmann 1992, 41-43). Spirit was the means by which the creative power of God was shared with and infused in all that God had made, animating it. This distinction between God the transcendent and the spirit led to the development of the incarnational concept of the *shekinah*, a term that originally meant tabernacle or tent. The *shekinah* came to denote the indwelling of God in time and space--at a particular time in a particular place--or to use Whitehead's terms, an "actual occasion." The *shekinah* was God's imminent presence in the particularities of creation (Moltmann 1992, 47).

The revisiting of the ancient concepts of spirit presents us with the opportunity to make the following assertions concerning the concept of spirit as a model of the God-world relation for the contemporary context.

The spirit as "divine" kinesis is the force within all process.

Whereas the natural sciences describe reality in terms of process, evolutionary and emergent, the spirit from the most ancient traditions was that power, or dynamic, which injected motion into all processes. As was earlier suggested, traditional trinitarian understandings of the spirit have given anthropocentric and anthropomorphic characteristics to the spirit. Any contemporary constructive concept of the spirit cannot be so narrow in its perspective. Our scientific paradigm no longer supports such a classical understanding of the human as being disconnected and separate from the rest of creation, on a pedestal above and beyond the natural world, perpetuating the modern utilitarian notion of the natural world as being for our sole benefit. Such anthropocentric concepts of spirit are disingenuous to the biblical notion that the God-world relation encompasses the whole world and not just that particular part of it that happens to have cognitive and creative abilities--the human creature. Many of the contemporary revisions of the spirit have been highly anthropocentric in their foci.

The spirit, which certainly is active in human development, is not to be exclusively defined in these terms. Spirit is all-encompassing, all-infusing, all-empowering *kinesis*--the divine power--which fuels the cosmic process on all levels of complexity and simplicity. It is the power in reality--but not of reality--in that it is greater than the reality of which it is a part. This transcendence of spirit is not, in terms of a deistic notion of the divine person, standing over against the process, manipulating mechanisms. It is more in terms of wave and field imagery in which possibility is a part. The possibilities that lie before every actualizing event in the process of reality, the novelty that provides newness of the present in its prehension, are not yet actualities and, therefore, although teleologically causal in their relation to the process, are not part of the process. Spirit is the divine power that passes through the cosmos as a wave bringing movement, empowering the process.

In this sense, spirit is not a separate and distinct person of the Triune God as understood in contemporary popular Christianity-- some vaporous, invisible entity with anthropomorphic attributes who moves around the universe, visiting particular locations at will, to perform specific deeds. Spirit is the *dynamis*, the power of God present in every actualizing event in the cosmos, from the micro- cosmic level to the universal level. God's presence is to be under- stood in the power of each particularization of cosmic possibility. In this way, the staccatic nature of the cosmos is seen as the pulsa- tion of divine power moving through the cosmos and empowering the process of becoming.

Spirit is the self-organizing dynamic in the creative process of emergence.

As the multilevel processes of nature move through the fields of becoming, we see both upward and downward causal emergence patterns which present self-organization, or self-shaping, as being a result of, if not a function of, the processes of Reality. This self- organizing emergence of vitality is founded upon the transmission of information from one particulate through to the next--be it genetic or extragenetic. This plasmic continuity of a whole through the particular is what Whitehead spoke of quite generally as "subjective" or "initial aim." It is similar to Aristotelian causation theory that recognized the impact of both material causes and final causes on any given entity. The upward and downward causal patterns suggest that the thematic continuity of the cosmic processes, the initial aim, shall we say, is a teleological power as well as an originating power, a dynamic from the future as well as a dynamic from the past. Quantum theory, which posits freedom, randomness, possibility and decision at the microcosmic level most certainly does not allow for this teleological or originating power to be deterministic. God's relation to the world is not a deterministic one. God's activity in spirit is not one of coercion. Instead it must be one of persuasion, encouragement and nurture. God empowers self-creativity at all levels of reality--not just the human level. At the same time, the process is not random chaos but a process of emergence--the creat- ing of that which is yet to be.

When understood in the ancient connection to the breath com- municating the logos/Word, the spirit is not an entity, a divine being which determines and organizes, which guides the process as an assembly line worker. Spirit is the dynamic principle of self-organization. It is the principle of emerging vitality that carries on the continuity, empowers the encoding and transmission of information, and invigorates decision in the prehension of possibility and novelty into the present moment, or the particular. Spirit dynamically presents "the ether of the spacetime fabric" within which particle and wave, matter and energy, body and mind, possibility and actuality intertwine and fluctuate in the dance of becoming (Mizer 1977, 86).

The material basis of spirit--the spiritual basis of the material

Suffice it for me to echo those voices of the past decades who have spoken against a spirit-matter, mind-body dichotomy in which the two are not understood to be inextricably inseparable. Let me also echo Philip Hefner in his observation that "If evolutionary theory is correct . . . Spirit and material nature must be considered within a single continuum rather than as two separate realms of being" (Hefner 1967, 138). However, often the dualism gives way to a strict materialism in which only material nature is of consequence; only that which is particularly actualized is significant in any meaningful way. This quite often appears ideologically within the scientific enterprise.

Theology can serve science prophetically with its re-definition of what is significant and "real" in the revisited notion of spirit. The processes of becoming are not a matter of material continuity as particle physics has so effectively pointed out. Our redefining of spirit as creative power and *kinesis* present an image of these processes as the fluctuation of spirit and matter, a pulsation of "spiritualized matter" and "materializing spirit," ongoing within the spacetime fabric with neither one being dominant or primary but both dependent upon the other.

CONCLUSION

The body-spirit, physical-spiritual dichotomy that has been so ingrained in our modern cultural paradigm has provided the basis upon which tech-gnosticism has constructed its myth of a world beyond this natural one, a world imagined yet real, a world under the control of the human consciousness and in which the human reigns supreme as god/goddess, a world that calls out to us in our "Babylonian captivity" in the body, encouraging us to be released from that which is around us and escape into "the new heaven and new earth of cyberspace" and the human-electronic consciousness. Such a religious myth carries grave consequences for the human community, and in fact, for the entire household (*oikos*), for the more separated we think our "true" selves (electronic selves) are from the world, the easier it is to ignore the needs of our world, the cries of the species as they fall into the holes of extinction dug by human hands, and the cries of the poor and suffering considered to be trapped in the world because of their lack of "true" value.

This article has not intended to indict science or its technology on charges of tech-gnosticism. Rather, it has defined tech-gnosticism as a cultural interpretation of the technology which science is providing for us--an interpretation that gives the technology religious dimensions that science as a whole does not claim for it. It is a valid critique of the theological enterprise in the US over the past decades to say that tech-gnosticism has developed because of a vacuum in theological and religious paradigms relevant for our culture and its scientific understanding of the world. In other words, as the various alternate visions of the world, central to the religious traditions in the US, were not publicly exhibited and put forward, the culture had no choice but to create its own eschatological vision from the conceptual resources at its disposal--that of technology. The cultural function of theology as the relevant interpretation and/or revision of the faith paradigm, which offers a holistic understanding of God-World-Self relation, must be restored, not for the sake of theology, but for the sake of the earth and our culture.

I have attempted to argue that the Christian concept of spirit revisioned in terms of contemporary science and the insights of the early theological tradition--as divine *kinesis* embodied in all cosmic processes, as the teleological dynamic in the creative process of emergence and as being unified with matter--can provide such an alternate paradigm of the God-world, God-body relationship and, therefore, an alternative model of reality. It is a relationship of incarnation in which God's energy, God's dynamic, is integrally embodied in every part of the natural world. Restoring such a sense of the divine presence immanent in the processes of the natural world would assist in renewing the social normative parameters of alternate states of consciousness and reality.

However, the theological enterprise in relation to science cannot rest with these insights. Theologians of the church and the academy must participate more seriously in the dialogue between theology and science so that (1) religious and theological assertions are expressed and understood as being relevantly connected with the natural world and (2) a prophetic and critical voice can be heard in science and technology. Continued sacramental study that focuses on the relationship of the divine presence and the natural world is integral to any attempt to restore the sense of sacredness and value of the whole creation. Such conceptual models of the divine desire for the salvation of the natural world as well as the "spiritual" can be a powerful criticism of the tech-gnostic myth and a didactic tool in the construction of new religious paradigms for our culture.

NOTES

1. There have been many attempts to define gnosticism. A recent work by Ioan P. Couliano, *The Tree of Gnosis: Gnostic Mythology from Early Christianity to Modern Nihilism* (San Francisco: Harper and Row, 1992) provides a survey of such attempts. The working definition used in this article is formulated by Eric Voegelin: ". . . the experience of the world as an alien place into which man [sic] has strayed and from which man must find a way back home to the other world of his origin" Voegelin, *Science, Politics, and Gnosticism*, (Chicago: Henry Regnery Co., 1968). This defintion is broad enough to avoid being restricted to a particular historic manifestation and yet narrow enough to provide the central element shared by those whose movements are labeled "gnostic."

2. Gnostic systems construct their redemptive myths around an escape-exodus motif in which the soul is directed through a maze of obstacles which imprison it in a material/natural world and into a promised land of non-material or transcendent origins. Voegelin perceives this redemptive myth of modern socio-political gnosticism in terms of (1) an absolute spirit which in the dialectic unfolding of consciousness proceeds from alienation to consciousness of itself; (2) a dialectical-material process of nature which in its course leads from the alienation resulting from private property and belief in God to the freedom of a fully human existence; and (3) a will of nature which transforms the human into a superhuman. Voegelin, *Science, Politics, and Gnosticism*, p. 11

3. George MacDonald, John L. Cove, Charles D. Laughlin, Jr. and John McManus, "Mirrors, Portals and Multiple Realities," *Zygon: A Journal of Religion and Science*, 24 (March, 1989): 39-64.

4. Ilya Prigogine and Isabelle Stengers, *Order Out of Chaos: Man's New Dialogue with Nature*, (London: Shambhala Publications, 1984); Ilya Prigogine, *From Being to Becoming: Time and Complexity in the Physical Sciences* (San Francisco: W.H. Freeman & Co., 1980).

5. "There is in simple chemical systems a kind of prebiological adaption mechanism; when in equilibrium matter appears to be 'blind.' However, when it enters a state of far-from-equilibrium matter begins to perceive, to take into account dif-

ference in the external world; e.g. weak gravitational or electromagnetic fields."
Prigogine, *Order Out of Chaos*, p. 74.

REFERENCES

Barbour, Ian. 1990. *Religion in an Age of Science*. San Francisco: Harper and Row.

Daviss, Bennett. 1990. "Grand Illusions." *Discover.* (June):36-41.

Hefner, Philip. 1968. "Towards a New Doctrine of Man: The Relationship of Man and Nature." *Zygon: Journal of Religion and Science* 2(Spring):127-151.

MacDaniel, Jay. 1983. "Physical Matter as Creative and Sentient." *Environmental Ethics* 5:291-317.

MacDonald, George F., John L. Cove, Charles D. Laughlin, Jr., and John McManus. 1989. "Mirrors, Portals and Multiple Realities." *Zygon:Journal of Religion and Science* 24 (March):39-64.

Milhaven, J. Giles. 1989. "A Medieval Lesson on Bodily Knowing: Women's Experience and Men's Thought." *Journal of the American Academy of Religion* 57(Winter):341-369.

Mizer, C.W. 1977. "Cosmology and Theology." in *Cosmology, History and Theology.* Wolfgang Yourgrau and Allen Brecke, eds. New York:Plenum.

Molnar, Thomas. 1983. "Science and New Gnosticism." *Modern Age* 27(Winter):132-138.

Moltmann, Jurgen. 1992. *Spirit of Life: A Universal Affirmation*. Minneapolis: Fortress Press.

Polkinghorne, John. 1991. "The Nature of Reality." *Zygon:Journal of Religion and Science* 26(June):221-236.

Prigogine, Ilya. 1980. *From Being to Becoming: Time and Complexity in the Physical Sciences*. San Francisco: W.H. Freeman and Co.

_____ and Isabelle Stengers. 1984. *Order Out of Chaos: Man's New Dialogue with Nature*. Boulder: Shambhala Publishers.

Rolston, Holmes III. 1987. *Science and Religion: A Critical Survey*. New York: Random House.

Sperry, Roger. 1991. "Search for Beliefs to Live by Consistent with Science." *Zygon: Journal of Religion and Science* 26(June): 237-258.

Stapp, Henry Pierce. 1977. "Theory of Reality." *Foundations of Physics* 7:318-331.

Voegelin, Eric. 1968. *Science, Politics, and Gnosticism*. Chicago: Henry Regnery Co.

Whitehead, Alfred North. 1978. *Process and Reality*. Revised Edition. David Ray Griffin and Donald W. Sherbourne, eds. New York:MacMillan Publishing House.

The World as God's Body:

Theological Ethics and Panentheism

William C. French

With quickening intensity over the last forty years, emerging data about our heavy impact on the natural biosphere has challenged humanity to rethink our fundamental understanding of our relationships to the nonhuman natural world. Jungles, the oceans, the atmospheric cycles, and myriad living species once seemed vast and stable, permanent and reliable backdrops to, and resource for, human life. But what was once experienced as a "given" is now viewed as increasingly fragile and threatened. This has caused a revolution in thought--namely humanity's emerging recognition that jungle and species, ecosystem and even climate pattern and temperate trends, are human responsibilities to maintain and protect.

One of the more challenging and impressive proposals being developed by Sallie McFague, Grace Jantzen, Jay McDaniel and others is that we need to construe the world as God's Body. Informed by process thought and ecological concerns, these thinkers argue that we need to emphasize that God is embodied in the material world. They attempt to overcome the presumptions of the dominant western Christian traditions which have sought to understand God as nonembodied, pure spirit, transcendent, above nature, unrelated to, and hence uncorrupted by, base matter.

In her recent book, *The Body of God*,[1] McFague develops criteria of relative adequacy for her proposed model of God as embodied. She is quite explicit that her theological proposal is metaphoric and heuristic, that it is not meant as an attempt to fully describe God. Rather it is a humble attempt to think through one account of God's ways in the world that does not exclude other proposals, each with their special strengths and weaknesses. Her criteria of theological adequacy are: 1) congruency with our common "embodied experience," 2) congruency with our "primary interpretive traditions," 3) "compatibility with the view of reality current in one's time," and 4) congruency with our assessment of its practical usefulness in guiding the conduct of life. Elsewhere she summarizes these as "commensurability with postmodern science as well as our own embodied experience and the well-being of our planet" (BG 149).

McFague follows the process theological critique of classical theism in that it understands God as a transcendent sovereign, "external to and distant from the world," unaffected by its suffering, and dominating it via divine will (BG 150, 176). Adding to this is a powerful feminist hermeneutic of suspicion regarding notions of hierarchy and transcendence which depict God in masculine terms of political kingship. Indeed, in her earlier book *Models of God*,[2] McFague rejects wholesale the dominant western theological understanding of God the monarch as necessarily triumphalistic and as reinforcing domination, alienation and sexism.

McFague develops a panentheist account of God as embodied in the world, and distinguishes it sharply against both the traditional theistic account and pantheism. Where traditional theism stresses the transcendence and disembodiment of God, panentheism complexly stresses God's radical embodiment and immanence in the world, yet also preserves an understanding of radical transcendence. God--though embodied--continues to transcend the world as a self transcends its body (MG 72-76). By not collapsing God totally into the material of the world panentheism breaks with flat out pantheism. Panentheism "suggests that God is embodied but not necessarily or totally" (BG 150). As McFague puts it: "Everything that is is *in* God and God is *in* all things and yet God is not identical with the universe, for the universe is dependent on God in a way that God is not dependent on the universe" (BG 149). She describes God as the spirit empowering the universe and holds that while the universe is "dependent upon the life-giving breath from the spirit, God, as the spirit, is not so dependent upon the universe" (BG 149). As Jay McDaniel describes, panentheism literally "means everything (*pan*) is in (*en*) the divine (*theos*). From a pan*en*theistic perspective, the universe is, in an important way, a part of God, as pantheism says, but God is also more than the universe, as supernaturalism contends."[3]

While her major theme is the radical immanence of God embodied in the material universe, she balances this with an emphasis on divine transcendence which means that none of our models, metaphors, or attempts at God-talk are finally adequate for fully accounting for the reality of God. As she repeats throughout her book, we see only God's back--never her face--which remains completely "unavailable" (BG 192-193).

The attempts by McFague, Jantzen and others to work out the implications of a construal of the world as the very Body of God are both provocative and compelling. In their broad outline and in their reading of the "signs of the times" I think they are right on the mark. As they well understand, such a construal of the world--all of its ecosystems and living species including the human--would greatly intensify one's sense of responsibility to protect and live in harmony with the rest of nature. If God is in each animal, each tree, each ecosystem, each person, then to damage that being or entity is to damage the being of God. By radicalizing the intimate connection between God and the world, McFague *et al.* radicalize our sense of participation in, and responsibility for, the rest of creation. By depicting God as embodied, McFague and the process school emphasize that God is intimately bound up with the suffering of the natural world and all of its creatures. If we continue to cause damage to the earth, its living species, its humans and its nonhumans, then we directly cause God to suffer.

This powerful vision of a God deeply related to the world and suffering with its demise generates potent ethical sensibilities and perspectives which can only empower ecologically responsible attitudes. By revisioning God in this way, we revision the meaning, shape, and scope of our ethical life.

Not surprisingly, McFague spends much more time laying out her theological reconstrual than in elaborating its ethical implications. She quite rightly notes that to transform patterns of attention and perception is to transform also patterns of decision and action. Thus she spends little time on the complex task of examining all the sorts of conflict cases that crop up in our dealings with other humans and nonhumans. She limits herself to a brief sketch of what an embodied theory of sin would look like corresponding to an embodied vision of God. She develops her "ecological view of sin" by emphasizing that "sin against any part of the body is against God." Sin is primarily "the refusal to accept our place." "*The* ecological sin is the refusal of the haves to share space and land with the have nots"--where the have nots are understood as the human poor, nonhuman animals, and all of the rest of nature (BG 114-117).

EVALUATION AND CRITIQUE

Panentheism's understanding of the world as God's body does much that is helpful and needed. I endorse much of the spirit and substance of McFague's project. However, as McFague herself has stressed, no theological project or metaphor can do everything. Metaphors highlight and focus attention here and simultaneously draw attention away from there. In what follows I will outline three areas of concern which I have about her constructive agenda.

The Need for an Embodied Notion of Sin: A Common, Global, Fall Story

McFague develops her panentheism in close conversation with the contemporary sciences' understanding of the evolutionary history of the universe and life on earth. This emerging scientific view provides us, she believes, with a compelling "common creation story," a "functional cosmology." However, she develops no corresponding "common fall account" to ground her reflections on the origins and scope of ecological sin. While she has a "thick" account of creation, she has a very "thin" account of sin. This occurs partly because, in *The Body of God*, she does not carry her emphasis on body and bodies into the social sphere to develop even a rudimentary social theory of corporate sin--the sin of groups, economic corporations, or nation/states. As is, her ethics remains one of response to a new vision. It is basically a conversion model. Without an explicit elaboration of the powerfully productive and powerfully destructive role of social bodies--not just individual bodies--we won't have a sense for the scope of the task ahead. It is not just that we are doing bad things to the earth, but once we find out people will convert to a more harmonious lifestyle. Rather there are powerful groups--bodies politic and corporations, incorporated companies united into one social and economic body--which have a powerful stake in continuing and accelerating our consumption and degradation of the earth.

I suggest that ecologists are not just presenting us with a "common creation story" but also a tragic and remarkable "common-global fall story." Barry Commoner, Paul Ehrlich, and many others argue that the ecological crisis first came to be discerned after World War II as technological and scientific changes began to change the patterns of industrial and agricultural production and growing populations began to greatly increase patterns of consumption. We have tripled our planetary human population and multiplied our economic production fifty-fold in this century. We now have over 5.5 billion people and 556 million motor vehicles together which vastly increase our global energy consumption, which with our rate of greenhouse gas emissions threaten to promote severe climate change in the next century.

Hans Jonas argues that while the nuclear threat is the most dramatic and vast threat of disaster we face, it is actually not as bad as the threat posed by ecological degradation. While a full scale nuclear war would be an utter disaster, Russia, the US, Ukraine, France, and England--the major nuclear powers know this. None have any incentives to launch. Yet in what Commoner rightly calls our "War against nature," corporations, individual consumers, and nations all have powerful, short-term incentives to continue high consumption and high energy usage life-styles. While no one wants nuclear war, every nation and corporation wants expanded economic growth. Thus while a nuclear war is most unlikely, accelerating ecological degradation is most probable. No national leader has so far called on his or her people not to seek increasing GNP. As we speak, Clinton's energy tax plan is being picked apart by corporate lobbyists--oil companies, the aluminum industry, GM.

Personal conversion to an ecological sensibility is needed certainly, but so is a careful analysis of the power and influence of social bodies--bodies politic and economic corporations--in the manufacturing of feelings of consumption need and wants. McFague distinguishes between the "haves" and the "have nots;" but we need a more nuanced social theory in order to begin to understand the *structures and engines of ecological violence.* Only with an explicit embodied social theory will we get an ecological ethic adequate to the prophetic and critical tasks at hand of protecting the cosmic body.

How, in panentheism, does God act?

Like many who develop creation-oriented theologies, McFague tends to emphasize metaphors of healing and nurture for the modes of divine presence. She retains an emphasis on divine agency and links it to an organic model of nature and an organic metaphor for God as body. She emphasizes certain terms in describing how God acts in the world--enlivening presence, creative spirit, healing power, nurturer, a sufferer who suffers with creation.

She rejects the traditional monarchical understanding of God and, not surprisingly, says in the *Body of God* nothing of God's judgment and anger against eco-sins. Interestingly, in *Models of God* she does elaborate here and there a strong image of divine judgment and anger. As "mother," God is the "giver of life and the judge who is angry when for any reason the fulfillment of the life given is thwarted." "The mother-God as creator is necessarily judge . . . condemning as the primary. . .sin the inequitable distribution of basic necessities for the continuation of life in its many forms." The goal of the judgement is "neither the condemnation nor the rescue of the guilty but the just ordering of the cosmic household in a fashion beneficial to all" (MG 114, 117). "Healers and liberators must be tireless in their battle against the forces that bring disorder to the body . . . . The military imagery here, repugnant as it may be to some, is necessary in order to express the anger that God as lover feels toward those who wound the body . . . . God as mother-creator feels the same anger and judges those harshly who deny life and nourishment to her children. Those who join the healing and liberating work of God are invited, then, into a fighting unit that does not easily accept defeat" (MG 149)

In *The Body of God*, McFague drops this language of divine anger and judgment. She puts the emphasis on God's suffering solidarity with a suffering creation. Like many creation-oriented theologians, McFague emphasizes the increasing power of humanity over the natural world so that nature is increasingly perceived as weak, vulnerable and fragile. With God intimately embodied in this increasingly fragile world, God is often depicted in metaphors which play down divine power and play up divine weakness. She clearly wants to avoid tapping into traditional categories of divine sovereignty for they, she suspects, buy into all of the paternalistic baggage of the monarchical model of God.

I'm not so sure that we can afford to give up all traditional emphases on divine sovereignty. Much of our ecological demise is organized and energized by the exaggerated and pretentious claims of political and economic bodies--claims rooted in appeals to national sovereignty and now the mobile authority of transnational corporations--sovereignty without borders. After all, claims of divine sovereignty, even though they are rooted in the monarchical imagery of a kingly God, have not always cashed out historically in support of oppression and injustice. Indeed, appeals to the sovereignty of God have been the dominant ground of prophetic indictment against the injustice and oppression of regimes and nations down through the centuries. Claims of divine sovereignty have been used to puncture the pretensions of claims about national or corporate sovereignty.

Panentheism's account of the world as God's body, I would suggest, needs to retain an explicit notion that even as God's enlivening spirit must be felt in each human, animal, plant and rock, so too may we see God's judgment and even anger directly impacting on us in embodied ways when we persist in degrading God's body. God may suffer with the groaning of creation. But what must we think of nature's kick-back in ozone depletion and rising skin cancer rates, or of global warming with increasingly intense storms, sea-rise, and species die-out? Might they be understood as God's direct and embodied judgment and anger for our eco-sins? I think so.

We should not kid ourselves too much that nature is so weak. In one sense, of course, nature is weaker and humanity is stronger. Yet in another sense, nature remains a most potent sovereign power, indeed a superpower, whose demise will do massive damage to the peoples and creatures of the earth. We must think dialectically. Where the cold war was structured as the hostile confrontation between two superpowers, so too the next period in human history will likewise be structured in a bipolar superpower confrontation. The global economy with its vast engines of production and consumption is attacking the global biosphere. Yet the biosphere remains the foundational superpower which itself sustains all the national human communities. If humans insist on continuing the attack--which of course we don't often describe as an attack (we prefer the language of development and economic growth), then we will experience in increasingly potent ways the retaliatory capacity of the biospheric superpower.

If we take seriously that the entire universe, not just the earth, is the body of God, then the God of panentheism remains an awesomely powerful superpower. This God may well suffer in solidarity with the earth, but let this emphasis not lead us to ignore the mighty and awesome strength of God. Traditional theism was clear about God's sovereignty and strength and I believe that traditional theism still holds out potent resources for developing helpful, ecologically informed theologies.

I suspect that the dominant discourses of our primary social bodies--nation/states and corporations--are biased greatly to respect power and ignore the weak. Christians have two options. First, we can dismiss these national and corporate discussions as so distorted that they are beyond hope of redemption and transformation. Second, we can try to engage them and persuade them of the gravity of our ecological problems. The stress on the biosphere as a superpower is meant to be heard by people who are used to thinking of the importance of defending national security. Even though much that is awful has been rationalized in the name of national security, there are a growing number of prominent ecologists, including our current vice-president, who wish to get the nations to understand that ecological demise is a major threat to national and global security. By stressing the powerful impact on humanity caused by nature's demise, it may be possible to gain a hearing from those who habitually marginalize ecological concerns.

I admire how an understanding of the world as God's body can radicalize our sense of the intimacy of God's presence and love directly embodied in our world--in this rainfall, this animal, today's oxygen cycle, my next sandwich. To be balanced, however, panentheism needs also to be more explicit about how God is also present to us in judgment and sometimes anger, in eco-demise. In pumping out CFCs we deplete the ozone shield--God's skin?--and thus damage God, the ecosystem, and ourselves. Is it too crude to see in rising skin cancer rates, in global warming fears, in species extinctions, in human diseases borne from pollution, in soil erosion--the negative judgment of God against our activities?

How is panentheism related to traditional theism? Is the panentheist critique of classical theism accurate?

McFague generally dismisses the monarchical model of God of traditional theism as necessarily paternalistic, oppressive, and sexist. I think its historical function has been far more complex. McFague likewise seems to accept the process school's general critique of traditional theism at face value, namely, that it depicts God as transcendent, external to the workings of the material world, and distant from its suffering. This unmoved mover, this transcendent immaterial spirit, they hold, is "alien to the world" (BG 150). This critique of classical theism has been earlier argued by Charles Hartshorne, Schubert Ogden, and John Cobb and has greatly influenced a wide range of theologians.

If they are correct in their harsh critique of traditional theism, then panentheism genuinely charts out a radical new theological path. But if they hold to a caricature of traditional theism, then they are distinguishing themselves sharply from a tradition which they should embrace fundamentally as an ally. The issue is: what is the relation of panentheists' attempt to balance divine transcendence with an explicit and "thick" theory of divine immanence and embodi-

ment with the dominant traditions of classical theism? Is classical
theism so lacking in stressing divine immanence and action in the
embodied world, as the panentheists say? Or did classical theism
stress too a critical balance between divine transcendence and divine
immanence?

A brief example. Hartshorne, Ogden, and Cobb take Thomas
Aquinas's position as a paradigm case of classical theism and interpret Aquinas as so stressing divine transcendence and immutability
that he understands God as not really related to the world. Much of
the debate rides on the interpretation of Thomas's statement in the
Summa 1a, q.13, art.7 where he states: "God is outside the whole
order of creation . . . [whereas] it is manifest that creatures are
really related to God . . . whereas in God there is no real relation
to creatures." I agree with David Burrell's view that this quote must
be understood in its context in Thomas's arguments about what we
may not properly ascribe to God. For Burrell, Thomas is concerned
here to deny that God is related to the world via any natural necessity. This clears the decks for Thomas's strong affirmation that God
freely wills to relate to the world. Not ontological necessity, but an
ongoing, intentional act of divine love joins God in solidarity with
the world.

If the process school is correct, then what are we to make of
the host of metaphors and terms employed by Thomas to describe
God's "interaction with" and "relationship to" creatures? Thomas,
for example, holds we can name God analogously from creatures, for
there exists some "mode of community," some "proportion" between
them (1a, q.13). As there is a likeness between effect and cause, so
too "all created things . . . are like God" (1a, q.4). God "is in all
things as causing the being of all things" (q.8). God is "in all things
as the object of operation is in the operator." Elsewhere Thomas
states: "God loves all things."

If process theology's critique of classical theism does not really
fit with Thomas Aquinas's views, then this would suggest that the
panentheist critique of traditional theism needs to be greatly qualified. Recall two of McFague's key criteria of adequacy of theological reconstruction--namely, 1) its congruency with the general testimony of one's religious tradition, and 2) its general usefulness in
helping us to address responsibly problems we face today.

If McFague's critique of traditional theism might be gravely
overstated, then it is quite possible that there may be far more
points of convergence between her project and many earlier projects
down through Christian history. Clearly she gives us a radical cor-

rective for much that has been distorted in our dominant theological traditions. However, it may well be that she actually has more allies in our theological traditions than she recognizes. This is of great practical importance because the reception of her panentheist stress on radical divine immanence will be much more widespread if people can be shown that the world viewed as God's Body isn't some "new age" aberrant fad, but rather is deeply compatible with certain core traditions in Christian theology.

NOTES

1. Philadelphia: Westminster Press, 1993; parenthetical references in the text (BG 93) are to this edition.

2. Sallie McFague, *Models of God: Theology for an Ecological, Nuclear Age* (Philadelphia: Fortress Press, 1987); parenthetical references in the text (MG xx) are to this edition.

3. Jay B. McDaniel, *Earth, Sky, Gods and Mortals: Developing an Ecological Spirituality* (Mystic, CT: Twenty-Third Publications, 1990), p. 51.

A Short Consideration of

Sallie McFague's *The Body of God*

John P. McCarthy

In 1928 Sigmund Freud wrote the following:

> For the principal task of civilization, its *raison d'etre*, is to defend
> us against nature. We all know that in many ways civilization
> does this fairly well already, and clearly as time goes by it will
> do much better. But no one is under the illusion that nature has
> already been vanquished; and few dare to hope that she will ever
> be entirely subject to man. There are the elements which seem
> to mock all human control: the earth which quakes and is torn
> apart and buries all human life and its works; water which
> deluges and drowns everything in a turmoil; storms which blow
> everything before them; there are diseases which we have only
> recently recognized as attacks by other organisms; and finally
> there is the painful riddle of death, against which no medicine
> has yet been found, nor probably will be. With these forces
> nature rises up against us, majestic, cruel and inexorable; she
> brings to our mind once more our weakness and helplessness,
> which we thought to escape through the work of civilization.
> One of the few gratifying and exalting impressions which man-
> kind can offer is when, in the face of an elemental catastrophe,
> it forgets in the discordance of civilization and all its internal
> difficulties and animosities, and recalls the great common task of
> preserving itself against the superior power of nature.[1]

An ecological theology would find much to be upset with in a
position like this. Probably most troublesome would be the underlying assumption that civilization not only is, but must be, at odds

with nature so that the stance toward nature must be some variation of war, conquest, and strategic domination. Troublesome also is the underlying conviction in a progressive technological reason, a scientific engineering, which, if it does not eradicate the enemy nature, will at least make it subservient to civilization's plans. An ecological theology will also find troublesome in a position like Freud's the dismissal of religious thought as poor science, unfounded knowledge, misplaced reflection on human wishes. The famous final lines of Freud's *The Future of an Illusion*--"No, our science is no illusion. But an illusion it would be to suppose that what science cannot give us we can get elsewhere"[2]--would clearly appear to an ecological theologian to be as destructively naive at the end of the twentieth century as religion appeared to be to many a positivistic scientist at the beginning of the same century.

A theological program like that proposed by Sallie McFague in *Models of God* and most recently in *The Body of God* provides an example of an informed and sophisticated academic theological proposal which clearly indicates the difficulties which an ecological theologian has with a position like Freud's as well as the corrective and constructive proposal which such a theology might provide. Like most academic theologies at the end of the twentieth century, McFague has made both an historical and a linguistic turn. The position advanced is well aware of the contextualization of scientific statements, epistemology, religious and cultural categories in the contemporary historical matrix. Likewise the position is well aware of the metaphors, models, in general, the poetics of constructions and deconstructions, in which science, politics, theology and religion all take place. Metaphysical claims, universal statements of fact or value, and totalizing communal narratives play little role in the formulation of this theology. What counts more than all else are four factors: 1) the recognition of the "crisis" situation which faces us as a whole human race, variously the nuclear and ecological threat; 2) the imaginative energy to respond to these situations with a vision based increasingly on the root metaphors of embodiment; 3) the caution to use the metaphors with the proper respect for what they purchase and what they do not; 4) the courage to engage in the task of Christian religion conceived as a task governed by the formalized criteria of the destabilizing, inclusive, and non-hierarchical vision of an incarnational Christ. This ecological theology is not primarily a propositional one but rather one which attempts to retrieve the rhetorical power of language to disclose and make truth, rather than rely solely on the declarative power of language to state truth. It is what McFague calls heuristic, a theology whose purpose is to suggest root metaphors by which a religious tradition may address constructively the traditional topic of "salvation" in a contemporary idiom.

"The World as God's Body" is offered as one such primary metaphor for four reasons. First, it offers a corrective to a tradition in which God and world designate separate realms ordered hierarchically. At a point in human history in which power is understood as domination, the world is understood as resource, and the human as technologist of pleasure and control, then models which place God, salvation and church in subtle and not-so-subtle opposition to earth seem to augment nuclear and ecological problems. Second, the metaphor of the world as God's body draws on an incarnational, sacramental tradition in a creative way to redirect this tradition from speculative explanation of God to practical theological vision for human life-threatening situations. Third, this metaphor suggests an intimacy with the world which reshapes the traditional issues of theodicy with the images of co-suffering and solidarity with an oppressed world. Fourth, like all good metaphors, it is meant to shock and puzzle. When the conventional metaphors of the relation between God and the world tend to be those which lend themselves to domination (king, creator, father, etc.) then this metaphor of body, properly nuanced, it is argued, can provoke a way of thinking which engenders care, solicitude, organic relationality, life and wholeness. Thus as a corrective, as hermeneutically appropriate, as liberating, and as rhetorically provocative, this model is offered as a primary candidate for a serious revisioning of God-language in an ecological theology.

Like a variety of late or postmodern theologies, this one is suspicious of a theism whose root metaphors seem less well suited to break the powers of the dominant images and social constructions which contribute to social and ecological oppression. "The world as God's body" is linked to the tradition of panentheism within Christianity as a way of theologically recognizing the creational and incarnational trajectories therein, while at the same time avoiding the accusation of pantheism. McFague's ecological theology recognizes the limits of any "ism" or any one metaphor either to respond adequately to the pressing world issues or to remain in harmony with the most profound contributions of the Christian tradition. Metaphors are as easily misused as used; there is no magic to the metaphor of the world as God's body in this position. Its primary value comes forward in the vision and direction it brings to the solution of fundamental problems in this world. Not a proposition seeking

assent about God, this metaphor acts adverbially to suggest a prag-
matic course: live in the world as God's body.

One of the most evident differences between a position like
Freud's and one like McFague's is that for Freud the human person
was not a threat to nature. Death came from the side of nature and
not from the side of the human. Whatever impeded the development of scientific knowledge was to be feared, for only with true
science could there be a truly informed cultural decision and the
wisest domination of nature. Religious ideas were not a candidate
for the type of knowledge needed; they were rather the deepest
symbolic wishes seemingly locked into a permanent childhood. If
understood as wishes they were harmless enough, but if they masked
as knowledge they were a veritable impediment to truth.

Much has occurred since this classic early twentieth-century
view was advanced. In a subsequent history which we all know too
well, death has become a human technology alongside all the technologies geared to save life and augment its quality. We live with
certain profound global ambivalences which simply were not at hand
in the time of Freud, ambivalences which make his view of scientific
knowledge seem a bit naive. Death still threatens in all the ways of
natural and social violence and finality which Freud reckoned with,
and yet Freud did not have to reckon with the hideous death of
human death in the oppressive and efficient ways in which we have
been able to deny the face of the other; not did he have to deal
with the human threat to worldly death in the death of the world.
Freud and McFague share a profound sense of threat, but the
character of the threat is quite different. And McFague's suggestion
is that "religious ideas" are in fact precisely what is needed to rescue nature and human culture from a pathologically unguided use of
scientific, turned technological, knowledge. Unless knowledge risks
in an informed way the ordering metaphors that orient the use of
scientific knowledge, then the threat of death does not in fact dimin-
ish but rather increases in proportion, even geometrically.

Probably few of us would have too much trouble accepting
some form of the aphorism, knowledge without vision is no knowledge at all. Indeed, McFague's position on embodied knowing and
embodied doing, her theological heuristic of the world as God's
body, and her concerns with postmodern science as organic vs.
mechanistic provide no simplified extension of this aphorism. And
likewise the caution against privileging any one metaphor to the
exclusion of others, even one as foundationally significant as "the
world as God's body" is for McFague, must not be put aside. Surely

there is no simple understanding of the semantic and practical purchase of the metaphor in this theology either. Thus it is not criticism that I offer to McFague's position but two questioning observations to the theological use of the embodiment metaphor in an ecological theology. First, ecological theologies generally share with McFague the conviction that some form of anthropocentric decentering needs to occur. If the center of the theological concern becomes the salvation of the human, or the incarnation in the human, or the history of the human, then the ecological always seems to be grafted on. Ecology is the condition for the possibility of human salvation, or the human holds hands with nature in a grand dance which is the salvation of all. In the first view an ecotheology seems something of an after-thought to salvation where what "needs saving" is a fractured, disfigured, misguided or contentious human, understood as will. In the second, the vision of eschatological harmony seeps through the cracks to temporality and finitude to disclose what is there already, the play of forces coming to ever greater consciousness of the very play that is already there.

But two things strike me about ecological theologies written as McFague writes. First, they are written in the genre of threat; and second, they are written. All theology is a human project and thus is inevitably "anthropocentric," although this anthropocentrism need not be male, western, middle class, twentieth-century, white, and so forth. It is still written. Even when, theologically, a strong link is made between a doctrine of creation and incarnation as McFague, or Rahner, or others make, creation seems to lead to the human, maybe not as domination, maybe as resurrection hope in accord with creation, but none the less the human *must* remain if the theology is to be written. But can a theology like this take its own threat even more seriously? To state it bluntly, must embodiment, particularly embodiment in a Christological tradition, always insure the *writing* of theology, that humanity always has a ticket to the show? If it were just "eco" and not "eco-logos theo-logos" would humanity have to be there, or could it not *from this perspective* (eco) be such that humanity like so many species before comes and goes, an experiment with consciousness where the links between violence, greed, power, and knowledge recurred so frequently as to destroy the conditions for the possibility of this species, but not "eco." Can the project ever be so decentered as to allow another "writer" to a "theology," or is embodiment still the human voice, speaking to be sure, more gently, more inclusively, more prophetically, more knowingly, but always for the world *as* human?

Second, the argument has been made by many literary theorists that tragedy is no longer a real option for composition in a modern world because of the significant change both in the sense of nature and the sense of the human as individual agent. In some sense tragedy depends on a pre-modern view of the world, aspects of which might be more present in post-modern decenterings of the subject than in modern versions of free agency. When McFague, as many ecological theologians, makes a case for holistic understanding and organic interrelationships as a corrective to the individuality and mechanistic tendencies of some forms of enlightenment science, I wonder if the position really allows for the tragic sense of a fate that is not in the control of the free actor alone, but is rather a kind of inertia of the whole of the organic. Wendy Farley states the gist of this forcefully when she writes:

> . . . Embodiment in a natural, material world may be the most basic feature of human life, but it subjects human beings to an assortment of dangers and sufferings. An exploding star is very beautiful as it passes out of existence, but when mortality is accompanied by nerve endings and self-consciousness, then physical pain, grief, fear, and anxiety will augment injury and sickness with deeper kinds of suffering. Since human beings are always social and cultural, frailty will extend itself to include culturally determined meanings and threats. A retarded or handicapped person may be excluded from society to an extent not warranted by the physical limitation itself. Bodies equipped to experience pain and pleasure can also be tortured, raped, or imprisoned. Embodiment makes it possible to experience all sorts of pleasures; mortality limits suffering with the final promise of death. But embodiment and mortality are also the causes of the most intense pain and deepest sense of foreboding. Certain goods are possible only in conjunction with certain evils.[3]

A tragic vision decenters the focus away from action under the control of a vision, however good one might understand such a vision to be, to a context in which fault and guilt, important as they may be, are inadequate to address the large problems of the human/nature relationship. Not nihilistic or deterministic, not an inevitable mechanics of nature, tragedy nevertheless suggests a holistic position which seriously questions the controlling power of either agency *or* vision (like the root metaphor of the world as God's body) to understand, and suffer with, the doings of humanity and nature. As much as an organic/holistic model may be a necessary corrective to a mechanistic/individualistic one, so the tragic/resistive model may be a proper corrective to the former. Or stated as an appreciative question, can there be an organic model without a more deeply articulated tragic vision, one in which the confidence in a change of models for God is stated not only as chastened hope, but also as resistance to the crushing, maybe inevitable, greed and violence which humanity has so finely tuned in the twentieth century.

NOTES

1. Sigmund Freud, *The Future of an Illusion*, Trans. James Strachey (New York: W. W. Norton, 1961), pp. 15-16.

2. Freud, p. 56.

3. Wendy Farley, *Tragic Vision and Divine Compassion* (Louisville: Westminster/ John Knox Press,1990), p. 33.

THE BODY OF GOD:

A FEMINIST RESPONSE

Susan A. Ross

Sallie McFague's new book, *The Body of God*, is an intriguing, well-written, and persuasive essay on the need to rethink radically our vision of ourselves, the world, and God. Taking the model of the world as God's body from her earlier book, *Models of God*, McFague considerably expands this model and makes a compelling argument for a much stronger version of this model--not only do we have *the world* as God's body, we now have a strong case for the *entire cosmos* as the body of God.

There is a great deal that can be said about this compelling new book from this most thoughtful author. I want to concentrate my own remarks here as a response from a feminist theologian--one concerned both with the sacramental and with ethics.

The central focus for this book and its predecessor is the human condition in the historical and ecological circumstances of the late twentieth century. Although the nuclear threat has subsided some-what, the threat to the ecological well-being of the world has only increased. Everything else is relative to this situation. This is a crisis that takes precedence over every other crisis, and is related to the other serious crises of the contemporary world, if not their root cause: poverty, injustice, hunger, etc. A feminist then asks whether the role of women is sufficiently addressed within this picture of the world so as to do justice to women's situation and history. Feminists know that we are always at risk of being left out of the picture as other, "more serious," issues take precedence. I do not see this as a *real* problem in McFague's work but her placing of feminist issues raises at least a few questions for me.

Surprisingly, there is little that is *explicitly* feminist in this book.

There is much that *assumes* feminism, but feminist principles are not in the foreground. One might call this post-feminist were there not connotations of this term that suggest exactly the opposite of what I mean. But some of the particular concerns of feminist thought, e.g., the social construction of reality, the wisdom of knowledge gained from women's experience, the importance of women's moral agency, are absent here. What one finds instead is a much (and I hesitate to use this word) *wider* context for thinking about what it means to be a human being in this cosmos than "simply" women's experience. This is a methodological issue and it brings me to my first question, which is whether we are at a point where we can assume that the insights of feminist thought have been sufficiently absorbed that we can move forward, to "bigger," comoslogical questions. Let me say that there is much in this book that is in strong sympathy with feminist thinking: her criticism of dualist and hierarchical categories, a concern for concreteness, a strong ethics of interconnection, a sensitivity for difference and multiplicity. But there are other things that, at the minimum, suggest that the very strong emphasis of feminism on the *social* construction of reality needs to be at least equally, if not more, attentive to the *scientific* understanding of reality. In other words, in order to be faithful to the integrity of the world *as it is*, there is a "givenness" to the biological order as McFague speaks about it, and about which feminism has for a long time had deep suspicions. There is more than a hint of "biology as destiny" here.

On the one hand, I find this a very helpful corrective to the assertions of many postmodern feminists that the body is entirely a social construction, and that little, if anything, in biology supports the notion of sexual difference as it is seen by most people. McFague would strongly differ. More than listening to the social scientists and the historians, she argues, we need to listen to the biologists, the physicists, and the natural scientists. But on the other hand, we need to be very sensitive to the social construction of science itself. There needs to be a dialectical relationship between natural and social science, and I wondered how feminist thought might both come to a deeper awareness of the natural and biological without being beholden to an androcentric understanding. Since so much of Roman Catholic ethics is based in "natural law," it seemed to me that McFague's reinterpretation of the "natural" might be a real resource for both ecofeminists seeking a greater appreciation of nature and the sacramental tradition of Roman Catholicism which tries to uphold a deep appreciation of the givenness of the natural. To restate my first question, does this understanding of the cosmos as the body of God, with all of the givenness that taking biology, chemistry, physics, cosmology, involve sufficiently take into account the revisions, corrections, and outright challenges of feminist thought, and their ethical implications--as feminism has challenged traditional understandings of "natural law"? This concern to be faithful to the scientific picture of reality *still* needs, I would argue, to be constantly balanced by an equal concern as to *whose* picture of reality this is.

My second question has to do with McFague's theological anthropology and its ethical implications, and it is related to my first question. Here I share some of John's questions about the *location* of the "writer" of theology. One of McFague's most valuable contributions is the de-centering of humans so that the good of the entire cosmos can be placed in the center. This emphasis on space is an advance over her discussion in *Models of God* where her understanding was much more temporal and historical. Indeed, it seems that there is a much greater sensitivity to what I would call (and in fact she does too) a traditional sacramentality. I like very much her appreciation for space and place and her understanding of "inverse dependence"--that human beings are "at the top" as guardians and caretakers of the planet but are dependent upon everything "beneath" us.

Along with this sacramental appreciation for the intrinsic goodness of the cosmos is a very Augustinian understanding of sin. As she puts it, "selfishness is the one-word definition of sin" (p. 115) McFague refers to Valerie Saiving's classic article on the particularly feminine slant on sin as *lack* of self and does argue that "righteousness is not selflessness" (p. 245 n. 12). But it seems to me here that there needs to be a more extensive discussion on the role of virtue in this vision of ourselves. McFague's vision is explicitly addressed to privileged first world people, and, as Saiving's argument goes, the virtue of selfless love, and the practice of relinquishment would be most appropriate here. But this leaves unanswered the practice of virtue by those not so privileged. My question here is not so much a criticism of what she is arguing for--that we who are privileged must develop a more accurate picture of our place in the cosmos and live with a whole lot less; I think she is right. My own race and class put me in a position of privilege with relation to the rest of the world that overrules the place of my gender--but rather a question about "the rest of the world." How might the world be reenvisioned from the perspective of the poor? Now McFague might argue that this is not the basic problem with which she is concerned. But I worry--as a feminist I worry--about solutions from the perspective of those with the voice. It seems to me that rather than simply leaving the solution to human--human injustice to the liberation theologians, which is what I think she does in her *very* brief treatment of this, that we need to develop a dialogical understanding of our situation. This book is a necessary first step--a wake-up call, so to speak, to those of us in the first world. McFague is careful to listen to the voices of the scientists who are attempting to speak "for the world," so to speak. But how might our own actions, our own visions of ourselves and the world, be adapted and challenged by conversation with those in the world who are at the other end? Now I know that Bill will suggest that we *will* hear a response from the world, and, therefore from God also, if we do not change our ways. But a theology of relinquishment, if I can call it that, for a first world person will not be the same theology for someone in the deforested equatorial areas of the world. Here I would suggest that again we need to listen not only to the scientists but also to the sociologists and economists, not to mention the feminists! And before we decide what we need to do, based on this very compelling vision of the world, we need to hear how others envision the world. The metaphor of the body of God needs to be subjected not only to the testing of our own western tradition but of others as well.

There are a number of other questions and observations that I would like to raise if we had more time: the role of hierarchy and McFague's dismissal, especially in *Models of God*, of any relationship remotely related to hierarchy; her development of a much enhanced sense of sacramentality from the earlier anti-sacramental position in *Metaphorical Theology* to the truly incarnational vision in *The Body of God*; the role of moral agency as feminism has come to see it, especially in relation to sexual ethics, and the way in which McFague sees it in *The Body of God*. As one concerned with the body, its role in women's lives and in the sacramental tradition, I find much to praise in McFague's work. But as a feminist I also know that a "return to the body" may not mean the same things for everyone: who is it that has lost a sense of the body? Who are those who must relinquish the riches they have? Whose understanding of the body are we drawing upon? While we must attend to the difference and multiplicity of the entire cosmos, as McFague so clearly puts it here, it also means that we must attend to the various voices and visions that make up this intricate complexity.

SPIRITUALITY

AND

THE BODY

CHRONIC PAIN AND CREATIVE POSSIBILITY:

A PSYCHOLOGICAL PHENOMENON CONFRONTS

THEOLOGIES OF SUFFERING

Pamela A. Smith, SS.C.M.

The pain inflicted by torture, war, unremitting oppression, battering, sexual abuse, and certain injuries and diseases can render people so inarticulate, isolated, and immobilized that the world around them "disintegrates," suggests Elaine Scarry, even as the voice and the sense of self undergo an "unmaking," a "deconstructing."[1] Considerable attention has been attracted by Scarry's study of the processes whereby torturous pain undoes the human personality and manages to "nullify the claims of the world."[2] But *The Body in Pain*, Scarry's work, has also raised intriguing questions about the dynamic which might be at work when pain does not produce psychic and emotional paralysis, does not deconstruct the sufferer's world. As Scarry has suggested, there are cases in which "pain and power" somehow end up "on the same side of the weapon."[3] When this happens, the world is in a sense "remade"--due, Scarry argues, to an uncanny psychic kinship between pain and imagination.[4]

Scarry's interest in the cases in which the experience of pain leads not to deconstruction but to "reconstruction,"[5] and her conviction that "belief," as an "act of imagining,"[6] can transcend and transform pain, has assisted at least two scholars in their considerations of pain and creative possibility. Maureen Tilley, first of all, has explored the question of how the "ascetic training" of the early Christian martyrs "allowed them to break the links between torture and psychic disintegration."[7] Phyllis Kaminski has employed Scarry's

insights in her foray into the question of how a new feminist understanding of "the passion of our bodies" might be formulated "in a
way which is transformative and creative of post-patriarchal Christian
life."[8] Both scholars have inquired into the psychodynamics and the
theological implications of situations in which exceeding pain has not
broken down or might not break down the voice, the sense of self,
and the world-relatedness of certain victims: martyrs subjected to
unimaginable torments; women subjected to domestic violence and
sexual abuse.

My own intent in this article is to extend the consideration of
pain that is "remade"--transformed by some "artifice" into a kind of
"artifact"[9]--to another category of people in pain: those with chronic
illnesses and considerable limits whose lives have been marked by
resolute creative activity. I propose first to show that the psychological profiles of a sampling of such individuals suggest an intimate
causal relationship between their pain and their productivity. I
believe that the creative chronically ill both relieve their pain and
reshape their lives by their creative production. Secondly, I propose
to point out the ambiguities which develop when one attempts to
apply the situation of the creative chronically ill to some of the
"tenets" often found in Christian theologizing on the question of
suffering. On the one hand, the phenomenon of creativity among
people in pain lends support to some notions of suffering as a
"vocation,"[10] as a call to "self-transcendence,"[11] as something "redemptive."[12] On the other hand, any endorsement of these notions
can be shown to be quite hazardous--not only to the self-understanding of the sufferer but also to the general conceptualization of the
kind of God encountered in suffering.

My own investment in setting forth these considerations should
be made clear at the outset. I, quite frankly, believe that I belong
to the category of persons whose chronic pain and realization of
creative possibility I am discussing. While I am not afflicted with
delusions of my kinship with geniuses (which many of the personalities mentioned here would seem to be), I am affected by health
problems which at least invite some identification on my part with
these figures. For nearly a quarter of a century I have been a "brittle" type-I diabetic. The extreme difficulties in arriving at a modicum
of control of this most unstable and unpredictable form of diabetes
have led me from one to two to three injections a day and finally to
reliance on an insulin pump. In the midst of living with diabetes, I
have encountered in mild form two of its complications: retinopathy
and neuropathy. I also have two ruptured discs and am a recently

diagnosed asthmatic. This combination of conditions has necessitated a regimen of medication, diet, exercise, steady attention, and delicate adjustments to the demands of a "normal" daily round. Careful compliance with that regimen has made for considerable quality of life, but it has not preserved me from making a close and frequent acquaintance with pain. The pain and botheration have not prevented me, however, from studying, ministering, and teaching full-time--with only one major disruption--during these years. My involvement in a variety of extracurricular activities and my compulsions to write and to make music remain unabated. Despite the fact that I dislike diabetes, back pain, and difficulty with breathing, I am inclined to muse that these have indeed stimulated much of my drive and have improved my ability to concentrate. Chronic illness and its attendant pain seem to have something direct to do with the books, articles, and poems I have produced and the musical adventures I have engaged in. And there is unquestionably a connection between my ailments and the promptings to reflect on them in a convention presentation and this consequent article. I have also lived and worked with a number of children, teens, young adults, mid-lifers, and seniors who have had to deal with a variety of chronic conditions and handicaps. That has afforded me the opportunity to observe that some keep on keeping on, taking up clowning or crafts or working at soup kitchens and remain upbeat and good-humored, while others settle down in front of television or on a porch swing and suspend most of their activities. What I offer here springs, then, from a "theology of experience" as well as from a consultation of some rich resources. My reflections on chronically ill personalities, the creative process, and some issues at stake in theologizing about their suffering thus ends on another personal note. Despite an inevitable tentativeness about my conclusions, I am inclined to believe that they second a key insight of Elaine Scarry: when imaginative work is undertaken, "the force of creation moves back onto the human site and remakes the makers."[13]

THE CREATIVE PERSON IN CHRONIC PAIN

Among the works which connect chronic illness and chronic pain to creativity are Paul Tournier's *Creative Suffering*,[14] Elisabeth Young-Bruehl's *Creative Characters*,[15] and two which will be relied on more heavily in this article, *The Witness of Edith Barfoot* (treated at greater length later) and George Pickering's *Creative Malady: Illness in the Lives and Minds of Charles Darwin, Florence Night-*

ingale, Mary Baker Eddy, Sigmund Freud, Marcel Proust, Elizabeth Barrett Browning. Pickering's study is especially useful because of his careful investigation and interpretation of the chronic illnesses of his six subjects.

In *Creative Malady,* Pickering recounts how productive the invalidism or semi-invalidism of each of these personalities proved to be, even as he notes how paradoxical their illnesses were. Pickering shows how physical limits helped to structure the creative projects of each of his subjects. The degree of isolation or marginalization which their regular bouts with "indisposition" entailed served to give them considerable freedom. All six were also well served by a circle of devotees or family members who protected them from strain and intrusion and made significant sacrifices to advance their projects and causes. Jacques Barzun, in his biographical, *A Stroll with William James*, indicates that a similar pattern is to be found in the life of the great psychologist and philosopher. His wife dedicated herself to his rounds of possibly neurotic illness, shielded him from undesired company, and doted on him, assuring the space and solitude he needed to prepare books and lectures.[16] Pickering admits himself that the genesis of his book occurred when his osteoarthritis became so severe that he became, for a time, bedfast. After he got metal prostheses for both hips, he resumed his customary schedule as a physician, was less waited on, and found himself rarely capable of writing. Illness for him proved to be, he says, "an asset and not an unmitigated disaster."[17] He suggests that such precisely was the case with the personalities he studied. Charles Darwin was well enough to walk four miles a day and to father ten children; he was, however, given to disabling days and thus could not see all potential guests or leave home for numerous public appearances. Florence Nightingale lived into her nineties, spending nearly all the years after her return from the Crimea as a semi-invalid, engineering nursing care and medical reform measures from her quarters and outliving all the key colleagues who ran her errands and assisted her during her intensely productive periods. Pickering observes that each of his six personalities seemed to have energy bursts and to be capable of remarkable concentration which, for a time at least, mitigated the manifestations of illness.

Norman Cousins, in his famed *Anatomy of an Illness*, attested that Pablo Casals at near-ninety became almost someone else once he began performing at piano or cello. Instead of being an old man, crippled by rheumatoid arthritis and labored of breathing, he became the absorbed, vibrant, and very whole genius-musician. "Creativity

for Pablo Casals was the source of his own cortisone," Cousins believes.[18] He explains the phenomenon by way of a comment by Ro-
manian endocrinologist Ana Aslan to the effect that "creativity--one
aspect of the will to live--produces the vital brain impulses that
stimulate the pituitary gland, triggering effects on the pineal gland
and the whole of the endocrine system."[19] This is not a wholly
agreed-upon interpretation, but it belongs to a growing school of
thought which links not only physical exercise to endorphin production (and thus a degree of mood-alteration) but also positive and
negative stress to multiple endocrine effects and significant changes
in the total sense of well-being in a human. Cousins notes Albert
Schweitzer's conviction that each person has a "doctor inside," a
doctor within who can, because of personal drive or a variety of
other aspects of belief systems, be given the "chance to go to
work."[20] Schweitzer believed, and Cousins' well-known healing
through comedy substantiates the idea, that "the best medicine for
any illness . . . was the knowledge that [one] had a job to do, plus
a good sense of humor."[21] Cousins' testimony considers how comedy
and creativity may heal or at least suspend the debilitating effects of
ailments. It does not consider, however, whether illness may actually
activate comic or creative energies and gifts.

Pickering, on the other hand, does posit a causal relationship
between ailment and creative response or reaction. He suggests that
for his subjects, and by inference for many others, "illness" may be
"an essential part of the creative process."[22] What Pickering cannot
resolve is quite how this cause-and-effect sequence operates. In some
instances (Darwin's, Nightingale's, for instance), the need to create
seems actually to generate an illness which provides the person with
both the limits and the freedom he or she must have to be able to
create. In other words, in certain people the drive to create is served
by an illness or condition which is not excruciating but is bother-
some, does require attention, imposes some limits, and demands a
mitigation of certain types of activities. Episodic pain and a composite of good and bad days allow for certain type of work--and even
the type of work which the person has been longing to do. In other
instances (Barrett Browning's and Proust's, for example), the creative
involvement seems rather to be the person's way of coping with, of
breaking free from, the oppression of physical limits and pain and
making them serve some purpose. In this latter case, the concentrated work is a kind of narcotic, an opportunity for extended moments of self-forgetfulness and pain-release.[23] In either instance--the
illness which is opportune for the work wanting to be done or the

work which is opportune for the pain wanting to be dulled--there seems, by Pickering's account, to be a cycle of illness, immersion in a creative project, completion of the project, and resurgence of the illness as more disabling until the next creative spurt.

Whatever else might be said about the ills of creative personalities such as those studied by Pickering, those ills were not experienced or imagined by their sufferers to be totally crippling. For a variety of reasons--their particular pain thresholds, personality types, and attitudes toward life projects--Pickering's creative sufferers of malady did not perceive those maladies as overruling everything in their worlds. They did not, therefore, experience the disintegration described by Scarry for some types of pain. Nor did they seem to view their bodies as "a field of combat" or "battleground," as Tilley asserts the pre-Constantinian Christian martyrs did.[24] They seem, instead, to have retained considerable self-indulgence and to have allowed no small amount of coddling during their less productive spells. In the midst of their creative productions, however, Pickering's subjects (and one can project the same of Pickering himself, William James, et al.) had the capacity for extraordinary single-mindedness and focus. While an idea was coming to fruition or a project was at hand, they seemed to have as little consciousness of their illnesses as athletes amid competition do of their individual muscles. Illness thus seems, in certain creative personalities, to have abetted their creative impulses in some causal way--and so to have been integral to their creativity. And yet an awareness of illness and pain seems not to have intruded upon the most intense phases of their creative processes.

THE CREATIVE PROCESS

The creative process itself defies analysis, though it is possible in part to characterize it. Susan Sontag has noted the occasional association of the process with malady in her small book, *Illness as Metaphor*. The British poet George Gordon, Lord Byron, wanted to have "consumption," she notes, because "the romantic treatment of death assert[ed] that people were made singular, made more interesting, by their illnesses."[25] What she proposes seems virtually undeniable: that being different from others, being set apart from them by illness, may contribute to the development of a creative or artistic persona. Furthermore, the drive to do, to say something, to create while there is still life and breath, may produce the urgency, intensity, and clarity that any scientific theory, artwork, revolutionary movement, or revelatory religious claim needs if it is to stand a chance of being judged a work of remarkable insight or virtuosity. The creative process, whether it is enacted by the healthiest or the most debilitated person, clearly involves several stages. First, there must be the underlying question--whether it is how the cosmos came to be, why objects fall, whether zero is divisible, what the effect would be if paint were applied to canvas in tiny, individual dots, how the fullness of passionate love can be expressed in four-teen rhymed and rhythmic lines, or why human beings suffer. The second phase, the response to the underlying question, may accompany it almost simultaneously in the form of a hunch, a vague notion, a seedling inspiration, a startling connection. For many creative possibilities, this intuitive stage is also the dead end. For one reason or another, the great idea is deflected, postponed, left unpursued or undeveloped. If it is pursued, however, the third stage ensues, and it is the most prolonged, most consuming, and most fat-iguing. It is the stage of enfleshment: testing, redefining, elaborating, trying, shaping, explaining, building, tearing, recasting, refining, and doing all the drab, mechanical, detailed work that brings a thing to being. As Paul Valéry has reminded readers, the final product, which may appear artless and effortless, as disarmingly simple as $E=mc^2$, arises from work, even from drudgery. The great creative work must nevertheless, he noted, be accompanied by this illusion of ease:

> Let us suppose . . . that the big effect comes off. Those persons who have felt it, those who have been, if you will, overwhelmed by its power and perfections, by the large number of lucky strokes, the piling up of happy surprises, cannot, and in fact must not imagine all the internal labor, the possibilities discard-ed, the long process of picking out suitable components, the delicate reasoning whose conclusions appear to be reached by magic, in a word, the amount of inner life treated by the chemist of the creative mind, or sorted out of mental chaos by some Maxwellian demon; and so those same persons are led to imag-ine a being of great powers, capable of working all these won-ders with no more effort than it takes to do anything at all.[26]

Anyone who has written a thesis, a dissertation, a scholarly article, or prepared a paper for a public presentation knows what concentration, tedium, time pressure, and physical strain precede the tidily organized, neatly arranged, and carefully articulated work. And anyone who has delivered such a work knows the paradoxical mixture of afterglow and exhaustion which accompanies it. For the creative chronically ill, the exhaustion factor makes the task of bringing any work to completion all the more challenging. There is animation in the idea phase and at the outset of the work phase. There is also the narcotic effect of engagement in the task. And there is the adrenalin push to see it through. But there is also the relentless reality of the havoc which intense work, ignored fatigue, postponed respite, and steady physiologic demand may wreak on a tenuously maintained constitution. Such pressing of limits and genuine risk to already dubious health can only be justified by a conviction that the project itself is consummately worthwhile, that it serves some fine purpose.

That the re-creation of the creative person's self is part of this worthwhile purpose is suggested by Elaine Scarry. She has remarked on the fact that human beings make things, create "artifacts" (including new theories) from the pressing schemata of the mind's imaginings. But then "the object is only a fulcrum or lever across which the force of creation moves back onto the human site and remakes the maker."[27] Any creative action, then, alters the reality of the one who undertakes it. The work of the chronically ill, chronically pained person, can be understood as restructuring a world, a life, and a personal identity fractured or impaired by disability. Such reality-alteration can truly be a lifeline: an assurance that the whole of reality is far better and far more manageable than the grim moments of suffering imply. The creative process itself is the route to the realization of a vision. It is also a means to the redefinition of the self. The process has a stimulation-sedation phenomenon about it which, for a time, consigns to oblivion the hurt, the ache, the vulnerability and the marginalization which pain or illness can insist on forcing to the center of one's world and consciousness. The self experienced while the artist, musician, poet, scientific theorist, social reformer, or prophetic religionist creates is skilled, accomplished, powerful. This self can perhaps afford to minimize the importance of the fact that he or she is also the same self who wakes up with fingers too numb to press a button or who finds it exceedingly difficult to climb stairs or who has learned to live with the steady blast of headaches. There is, in the process of creation, a kind of transformed embodiment. Scarry has suggested:

> [T]he human being who creates on behalf of the pain in her own body may remake herself to be one who creates on behalf of the pain originating in another's body; so, too, the human beings

who create out of pain (whether their own or others') may
remake themselves to be those who create out of pleasure
(whether their own or others').[28]

This "remaking," refashioning, of pain to pleasure may be a
further explanation of why the creative chronically ill risk setbacks
and personal demobilization to mobilize their projects. They somehow believe that the world, life, and they themselves are transformed
by what they dream and do. Meanwhile, they have enjoyed the
pleasure of being consumed in their work, wedded to it, made fruitful. The poet's "own work," Jung urges, "outgrows him as a child its
mother. The creative process has feminine quality, and the creative
work arises from unconscious depths--we might say, from the realm
of the mother."[29] In the creative process are found labor and birth-
pangs and the emergence of a new self beyond the self. Just as the
arrival of a child causes the mother to be mother, Jung urges, "It is
not Goethe who creates Faust, but Faust which creates Goethe."[30]

What sort of personality, then, might be more likely to make
a creative response to chronic pain? Internationally renowned cos-
mologist and theoretical physicist Stephen Hawking, the author of
the best-selling *A Brief History of Time*, might be invoked as a current illustration. Hawking's biographers have noted that he was
diagnosed in early 1963 as having ALS, "Lou Gehrig's disease." He
was twenty-one years old, at the beginning of his doctoral studies,
when he was told that he might expect to live two more years.[31]
After a period of depression, he decided to go back to his studies,
learn to walk with assistance (which he could then still do), pursue
a romance, and get on with life. Now, at over fifty years of age,
Hawking is wheelchair-bound, speechless, able to move only the two
fingers which control an array of computerized instruments which
operate his chair, speak for him, and transmit his brilliance to the
printed page. Michael White and John Gribbin, who have tracked
his career, assert that Hawking "simply has not allowed his illness to
hinder his scientific development."[32] As Pickering suggests was true
for many of his subjects, Hawking's biographers perceive benefit to
his creativity coming forth from his affliction:

> Naturally, Hawking's condition has freed him from many duties
> . . . . His various positions at [Cambridge] University have all
> come with reduced teaching and administration loads, and he has
> been allowed to spend a far greater proportion of his time
> thinking than ever the average professor can manage. Some have

attributed his great success in cosmology to this enhanced cerebral freedom, yet others have claimed that the turning-point in the application of his abilities was the onset of his condition, and that before that he was no more than an averagely bright student. Whatever the reason for his great insight and astonishing grasp of his subject, it may be true to say that he would not have progressed so quickly or soared to such heights if he had been expected to spend vast amounts of time organizing committees, attending faculty meetings and overseeing undergraduate applications.[33]

Hawking has testified himself that he drank too much and dissipated his energies before he was ill. Being severely limited has forced him to zero in on what he wants to do and what he can do.[34]

If Pickering's examples, Pickering himself, William James, and Stephen Hawking are regarded as representative of a "type" of the chronically ill, as I believe they ought to be, then it is possible to draw from them several conclusions about their creative personalities. First of all, the creative chronically ill have confidence that their physical limits or handicaps or chronic pain are not insuperable. Secondly, they are able to perceive that a bit of imagination can convert some restrictive aspects of their conditions into assets. Thirdly, they possess traits which help able-bodied creative personalities to succeed: a vision of how the question underlying their creative impulses might be answered; sufficient ego-strength to believe that the proposed creation can be brought into being--largely through their own efforts; the ability to give themselves over to their tasks and not only accept but also enjoy the pain-to-pleasure aspects. Like all creative personalities, those afflicted with chronic illness have to be types who are oriented toward bringing new things into being: oriented, that is, toward giving birth.

Such would seem to be some of the significant psychodynamic characteristics of personalities who bring forth creative productions from the "womb" of chronic pain. How their "creative suffering," as Paul Tournier terms it, relates to Christian theological reflection on human suffering in general remains to be considered.

THE CREATIVE CHRONICALLY ILL AND THEOLOGIES OF SUFFERING

Even while there are certain fixtures and recurrences in Christian reflection on the topic, one must speak of theologies of suffering in the plural. Their tone may vary as widely as C. S. Lewis's did between the rather detached intellectualism of *The Problem of Pain* and the raw emotionalism, nearly two decades later, of *A Grief Observed*. The treatment may be more abstract and speculative, as in Albert Harper's *The Theodicy of Suffering*, or more experiential, as in Gregory Baum's sermon, "Sickness and the Silence of God." Certain questions, however, seem constant: Why must human life entail suffering? What purpose, if any, does suffering serve? What relation does individual suffering bear to the crucifixion and resurrection of Christ, the paschal mystery? What might the experience and endurance of suffering call us to? How does it change us? And then there is the great question of theodicy: How can God be good and omnipotent and still permit the unrelieved suffering of innocents? A number of themes emerge in the Christian response to such questions. Among them are these claims: that there can truly be a vocation to suffering; that suffering is a catalyst to human self-transcendence; that suffering is redemptive; that suffering can be the occasion of an encounter with God. Each of these notions can be shown to have its assets and liabilities when applied to the plight of the chronically ill.

Responding to the first tenet of some theologies of suffering is sacramental theologian James Empereur. In his book, *Prophetic Anointing: God's Call to the Sick, the Elderly, and the Dying*, Empereur treats the sacrament of the Anointing of the Sick as a sacrament of vocation. His sense is that illness, particularly of the long-term and/or terminal variety, is something to which a person is, in some sense, ordained.[35] In a similar vein, Edith Barfoot, an Anglican who spent nearly seventy years severely crippled by rheumatoid arthritis and eventually went deaf and blind, speculated that her afflictions were the result of a radical self-offering to God in her youthful prayer. She referred to her own "vocation of pain-bearing and helplessness" as a call "to surrender" but also to "development in new directions," a prospective "fresh venture along the road [Christ] has travelled before."[36] She also spoke of the necessity for what she called an "active response" to the vocation of suffering, the willingness to embrace the "vast opportunities for work" presented by illness and disability.[37] In her case, "active response" meant many years of assisting with the Braille transcription of religious texts and, later in life, offering BBC radio interviews and producing a brief publication. This tangible work accompanied what she understood her "spiritual work" to be: intercessory prayer.[38] Essentially, this concept of a special vocation to suffering, which also appears in John Paul II, suggests that there is a direct, purposeful, divine intentionality in it, a "grace" which invites the sufferer to "maturity and spiritual greatness."[39] In other words, those who view serious illness or pain-bearing as a vocation see it as a call to deeper interiority and to the discovery of what one is truly meant to become. For the creative chronically ill, such a notion carries a degree of help with it, but it also bears potential for harm.

As already has been seen, the lives of a number of creative people present evidence that for certain individuals chronic illness, pain, physical burden, handicap and the like are the stimulus to their productivity. The conditions which these individuals endure may not only contribute to their life-projects but may also be their virtual cause. For the chronically ill person, it can be very consoling and character-affirming to believe that illness is the key to one's unique calling and is instrumental in activating an abundance of creativity. The hazard, however, is that the sufferer can become quite masochistic about the suffering and be inclined to cultivate an odd, and ultimately unchristian, asceticism about illness. Dorothee Soelle has pointed out that a "yes" to suffering is simply a "yes" to life,[40] but such a yes ought also to include a search for means to resist the devastating effects of illness, a will to change the grim realities of the situation, an effort to reclaim as much health as possible, an attempt to "organize to conquer suffering."[41] The temptation in ascribing one's pain to some special divine call is, as I read Soelle, that one might be inclined to remain quite "mute"[42] in the face of that suffering. There is a kind of "resignation" which, I would urge, renders a person heteronomous rather than autonomous and produces not a creative thinker but instead a melancholy, inert victim. Furthermore, an attitude of passive acceptance of illness can lead the sufferer to overlook, as Barfoot has importantly pointed out, that there is for everyone a more primary call to health, [43] a call to seek every reasonable remedy for the illness. It seems noteworthy that the creative sufferers of chronic illness noted in this article never interpreted their conditions as death sentence, irresistible fate, or self-definition. They sought comfort, help, and relief and seem to have, with the exception of Barfoot, eschewed thinking of their conditions as their "vocations." Instead they seem to have thought of themselves as scientists, artists, writers, medical practitioners, reformers who happened also to be sick.

A second tenet that may be encountered in a number of theologies of suffering is that, as John Paul II puts it, "Suffering seems to belong to man's [sic] transcendence: it is one of those points in which man is in a certain sense 'destined' to go beyond himself, and he is called to this in a mysterious way."[44] The idea that suffering proffers an invitation to self-transcendence is hardly a new one. It seems to be at the heart of Christian asceticism and a theology of the cross. Disciplines of renunciation, self-denial, even self-punishment seem to be and have been artificial means to causing the effect which involuntary but embraced suffering is traditionally considered to bear in potentia: release to another and better mode of spiritual living, transport to the realm of eternity and grace. There is in the creative process (whether undertaken by the well or the ill) a distinct asceticism, a discipline, of concentration and hard work. There is also a transcendent and self-transcending quality to the experience, it seems. As Mozart recounted (in a letter of disputed authenticity):

> Whence and how [my ideas] come, I know not; nor can I force them . . . [T]he whole, though it be long, stands almost complete and finished in my mind, so that I can survey it, like a fine picture or a beautiful statue, at a glance. Nor do I hear in my imagination the parts successively, but I hear them, as it were, all at once (gleich alles zusammen). What a delight this is I cannot tell! All this inventing, this producing, takes place in a pleasing lively dream . . . . What has been thus produced I do not easily forget, and this is perhaps the best gift I have my Divine Maker to thank for.[45]

There is a sense of gift, of connection with some other-worldliness, and of, as Mozart says, pure "delight" in this sort of creative experience. For the arthritic, the tubercular, the rheumatic, the diabetic, the multiple sclerotic, the palsied or dystrophied or anyone afflicted, this "delight" can carry with it not only great blessing and great gratitude but also great motivation for continuing. An undesired side-effect of such experiences of self-transcendence can, however, be the entrenchment of a kind of dualism. In giving over to that whatever-it-is which seizes the imagination and intellect and commands all the person's concentration and energy until there is a culmination in some "product," the afflicted creative agent may conceive of the process as bodiless. After all, while the person is creating, the fragility and the fluctuations of body chemistry and pain sensors seem relegated to some sort of oblivion. Or they seem irrelevant. Hawking's biographers occasionally speak of him as though his creative thinking amid ALS were rather disembodied: "[T]he disease has not touched the essence of his being, his mind, and so has not affected his work."[46] Intentionally or not, White and Gribbin present a Hawking in which creativity is "self-transcendent" in the vein colloquially referred to as "mind over matter." The temptation for the chronically ill creator--or his or her observer--can be to forget the tremendous bodiliness of the creative process. The senses, the nervous system, the circulating blood, the nutrients recently ingested, the bone structure and musculature all have been involved in the composition, the project, the original turn a thought has taken. Thus, while the body's pain may be transcended during intense creative activity, it would be greatly mistaken to communicate the idea that the body itself is transcended. "Self-transcendence" ought, in an incarnational and resurrectional Christian understanding, to include the whole being and thus not tempted to define the "essence" of being as the "mind," as Gribbin and White do, or as the "soul," as certain persistent brands of Christian spirituality seem to do.

What would seem to be far preferable to a dualistic theology of "self-transcendence" in suffering would be a dialectical one, one which encompasses dynamic oppositions, one which understands them as creatively coexistent. Such a dialectical theology would seem to be attempted by Schillebeeckx, for example, when, in his comments on suffering, he insists that "there are no two spheres of immanence and transcendence any more than there are dual truths of reason and revelation. There is one reality which is more than we know."[47] So too would seem to be the attempt of Johann Metz as he proposes the "dialectics of freedom in suffering and hope"[48] and urges that "dialogue" is the necessary vehicle for transforming the isolation of suffering to the "interpersonal."[49] It seems to me, then, that any developing understanding of the creativity of those who suffer will be theologically sound (and also psychologically healthy) only if it comes to terms with the vital interactions of certain dynamic oppositions. Body and mind, flesh and spirit, immanence and transcendence, self-concern and self-surrender, limitation and possibility, isolation and solidarity, inarticulateness and expression, idea and realization, pain and release, entrapment and freedom, powerlessness and power, silence and assertion, time-boundedness and all-at-once-ness, theologia crucis and theologia gloriae:[50] all of these are strands of the cat's cradle of the Christian understanding of suffering, and they are also strands of the creative process. It seems crucial to any theology of suffering, and critical to any theological interpretation of the creativity of those whose suffering is chronic, that the vital importance of these dynamic tensions be grasped. If "self-transcendence" conjures up images of disembodiment or etherealization, no theology of suffering will be served. And those who might be inclined to theologize about the creativity of those in chronic pain will be misled.

A constellation of questions is raised by Christian theological insistence on a third theme: the redemptive nature of suffering. For the creative chronically ill, this can all too readily be translated into a reliance on measurable productivity. The idea that a good end, a good product, can come forth from (or in the midst of) the evil of physical suffering becomes a "reality" when there is a tangible art-work, theory, social reform, or project to show for it. There is some "thing" which is very evident, some "artifact," as Scarry calls it, which may serve the general welfare, make the world better or richer or smarter, and thus can be interpreted as having "redemptive" value. The Elizabeth Barrett Brownings, Florence Nightingales, and Mary Baker Eddys of the world may be theologically gratified by the suggestion that the productions of their invalid hours are redemptive--that they are comparable to Paul's sense that "In my own flesh I fill up what is lacking in the sufferings of Christ for the sake of his body, the church" (Col 1:24). As with other mainstays of theologies of suffering already mentioned, this belief that suffering is redemptive may provide such consolation to the creative chronically ill, but is may also prove to be dubious on at least two counts. One is the problematic encountered if and when the time comes that the sufferer's creative action ceases. The other is the more universal difficulty with claims about the "mysterious" redemptive nature of suffering: the difficulty of using such a claim as a facile "explanation" or justification for much senseless suffering.

As alluded to earlier in this article, it is not unusual for the creative chronically ill to experience phases of increased physical pain and decreased creative activity. Sometimes there may be long stretches of silence and debilitation. Two authors, at least, have tried to put a positive cast on this sort of experience. Daniel Liderbach, for example, in this recent *Why Do We Suffer? New Ways of Understanding*, emphasizes and reemphasizes suffering's role as a "summons to hope," as a mythic, imaginative entry into the "supernatural existential."[51] He clearly believes that an immersion into a type of suffering that seems not to do anything can be rife with religious meaning and personal spiritual benefit--even, apparently, if this cannot be articulated. Edith Barfoot has recounted her sensation that in her moments of the most intense (and non-productive) pain she could only rest "in the everlasting arms" of God.[52] Barfoot did, however, have better days, and Liderbach anticipates a something

after misery, it seems, that makes some sense of it. The great di-
lemma that I see in proposing these positive interpretations of the
kind of pained hibernation that creative persons with chronic illnesses might have to endure is that they fail to deal with the fact
that these personalities might be altogether dependent on their
doing and may be altogether unable to cope, either psychologically
or theologically, if what I have called a "hibernation" period in
which they are quite ill or more severely disabled gradually is found
to be permanent, unimprovable. Is there a possibility that they will
come to view their suffering as no longer redemptive, as unredemptive and absurd, once the ability to produce eases? What happens if
Beethoven not only goes deaf but stops being able to produce a
piece of music? What happens if Elizabeth Barrett Browning not
only can no longer write the sonnet but, worse, cannot even count
the ways in which she loves? How do the creative chronically ill deal
with the trauma of having to reorient their whole stance before God
and the world if they suddenly stop being able to be creative and
simply have to live with being quite silent and stilled in their illness?
Thus one of the risks of propounding a belief in the redemptive
nature of suffering which is tied into visible, measurable creative
activity is that the suffering can be seen as meaningless as soon as
self-definition and "remaking" of the world through creative imaginings and creative productions become impossible.

What the creative personality would then enter into is perhaps
what I have identified as the more universal difficulty with notions
of the redemptive benefit of suffering. Despite the tomes, tracts,
theological texts and pious meditations that have appeared in response to the mystery of human suffering, I have yet to see one
which honestly and adequately addresses the problem of the pains
and losses which never reverse, never remit, never are relieved,
particularly when these sufferings leave the person inarticulate.
There is no satisfying theology of suffering for Alzheimer's or for
the permanently comatose. Worse, it seems to me, there is no attempt to address the suffering of the innocent pre-articulate (the
starving Somalian infant, the hemophiliac two-year-old who has
contracted AIDS, the crack-damaged newborn) which does not
flounder. One response inclines to assign this sort of suffering to
the realm of mystery, to the place of "an open question to be answered in the future," which seems to be the approach taken by
Jurgen Moltmann.[53] Another response is to interpret such sufferings
as the issuance of a call to others: to awaken humanity from apathy,
as Dorothee Soelle implies;[54] to summon people to compassion, as

John Paul II holds.[55] This whole larger question of redemptive suffering seems to me to be fraught with difficulty, not only because it becomes problematic for those with long-term illness whose condition drastically worsens but also because it fails to address the frequency with which human suffering and pain can provoke self-preoccupation, bitterness, and even despair in the sufferers and can evoke hostility and hard-heartedness from those around them. Add to this the possibility that creative types can, amid their sufferings, produce works of genius and yet remain insensitive to the sufferings of those around them.[56] Thus there are a number of counts on which a theology of redemptive suffering seems to fail. It cannot derive meaning from suffering when speech and art and theory and project and production cease. And it cannot seem to make sense of the anti-humane responses to suffering except perhaps by ascribing them to sin.[57]

Finally, there is, for the chronically ill as well as for all sufferers, the perennial problem of God. Sprung from the exclamation, "Now my eye has seen you," in Job (Job 42:5) and the recounting of the dying vision of Stephen (Acts 7:56), there has been a continuing tradition in Christian thought which teaches that suffering can be the occasion for an intimate encounter with God. Setting aside the fact that some of the creative sufferers mentioned in this article exhibit little or no belief in a God (Darwin, Freud, Hawking), we confront the problem that the kind of God envisioned by chronic sufferers can be quite baffling. Edith Barfoot's brief testimony signals the problem. Even while she enjoyed her moments of a kind of contemplative rest in God's arms, she also seems to have believed that God not only permitted her suffering but actually engineered it. As Dorothee Solle has urged, such a God seems not the benevolent parent of Jesus' teaching but rather a sadist, an "almighty Pharaoh."[58] An alternative to such a view is that of a companionable God who has not sent and cannot prevent the morass of human horrors and ills. Such is the God found in Harold Kushner's popular *When Bad Things Happen to Good People*. Sallie McFague's God, similarly, can be thought of metaphorically as friend, one who is "with us, Emmanuel, our companion, who steadfastly accompanies us in both joy and suffering."[59] This God is a caring God, but one whose omnipotence or almightiness is dubious.[60] Such a God may well seem, on first meeting at least, quite affable but distressingly ineffectual. The question of whether or not the God who is encountered in suffering ought to be thought of as omnipotent or non-omnipotent is a central issue for all sufferers. The quite varied approaches to this question suggest that a redefinition of the concept of omnipotence is imperative. Some of the new directions being taken seem to have particular relevance to creative sufferers.

Before considering the more helpful ways in which omnipotence might be reconsidered, I would like to note two unhelpful ways. One is the rather doctrinaire interpretation found is C. S. Lewis's classic, *The Problem of Pain*. For Lewis, God is the controlling Almighty whose incarnation in Jesus is theological and historical fact. In view of the mystery of Christ's death and resurrection, human suffering must be understood, however grudgingly or mystifyingly, as "remedial or corrective good," suggests Lewis.[61] If I may indulge in a bit of oversimplification, it might be said that the Lewis who wrote of pain long before his wife's illness and death[62] seems to have regarded suffering, even of the most agonizing type, as medicinal and instructive. The medicine might be bitter and the instruction stern, but it is of God. A taste of the passion of Christ is, for Lewis, the route to resurrection.

Quite opposite Lewis is Albert W. J. Harper, who, in *The Theodicy of Suffering*, proposes a God who is omnipotent but so far removed from earthly existence that he, she, or it could neither become incarnate nor relate to any human pleasure or pain. In a new deism, Harper presents a God whose omnipotence must be understood as "all creativity" and full Being.[63] The creative force which Harper identifies with God is tremendously powerful--so powerful that it has engaged in the complex struggles which have called the universe into being and continue to energize its development. That force is altogether Other, however, from the universe. In Harper's schema, pain and stress and wear and exertion are principles of existence, an existence wrought by God, but they are only of "intermediate value."[64] They are the twists and turns and roadblocks encountered on the route to something else, some new aspect of ongoing creation, which bear no direct relevance to an impersonal God. God, for Harper, transcends the realm of space or time so absolutely that any involvement or immersion in this realm is impossible. Jesus for Harper is not a deity or divinity, not a "person" of God, but rather an advanced human being, an "archetype of recreated humanity,"[65] a proleptic specimen of evolutionarily superior intelligence and insight. God's omnipotence is exhibited in the cosmic process which can arrive at such a human as Jesus of Nazareth, but it cannot intervene in any aspects of such a person's life.

Neither Lewis nor Harper present God's omnipotence in a way which would seem salutary to the creative sufferer. More helpful, it seems to me, are some hints in Kushner and some viewpoints expressed in works by Major Jones and Gregory Baum. It is quite well-known that Kushner, who wrote his much reprinted best-seller in the aftermath of his teenaged son's death from progeria (the rapid-aging syndrome), simply wishes to avoid attributing omnipotence to God.[66] He does, however, point to a power in God which might be better attended to. While Kushner believes that "having given [humans] freedom to choose, . . . there was nothing God could do to prevent" Auschwitz,[67] he also declares that God is the source of "strength and patience and hope,"[68] the source of endurance and sustenance, and also the origin of that inspiration which urges "people to help other people who have been hurt by life."[69] God encourages them to begin anew. This is not a power which provides miraculous cures or alters the course of flooding rivers, but it is a remarkable spiritual power. I would want to argue that an "omnipotence" understood as that which empowers persevering hope and compassionate, humanitarian response can be regarded as the force behind a Florence Nightingale--or an Itzhak Perlman, or the Bradys of anti-gun "Brady Bill" fame.

Major Jones, who does theology from the perspective of the African-American experience of slavery and prejudice, insists that belief in God's omnipotence has been essential to the faith of African-Americans. For the Black church tradition, he urges, conceiving of the Black God as "transcendent Omnipotent" has allowed believers to trust that God "cannot be assailed by the evil that has befallen us," and that over the long stretch of time there will be a triumph of "his omnipotent cosmic action on behalf of the righteousness of justice and love."[70] Jones notes the importance of Jesus for the African-American. There is an understanding that he is "fully identified with the sufferings of Black people because of his own sufferings in this world"[71] and that he is the "Christ of their liberation."[72] The very gospel of Jesus, Jones claims, stands in accusation against oppression and imposed suffering. And Jesus is believed by African-American Christians to be "effecting among them now" a definite "social, political, and this-worldly spiritual liberation."[73] The Christ is the enactor of "the perfection of divine omniscience" by extending God's own experience. Before the coming of Christ, Jones says, "God had known about human suffering, but he had not suffered."[74] God's omnipotence is seen by Jones, then, not in the quick remediation of unjust and intolerable situations but in God's creative responsiveness historically in Jesus and in the lasting inspiration and action of the Holy Spirit. Jones refers to the Spirit as "the preserver of Black personhood,"[75] who is "a Comforter of the oppressed, a counselor of liberation, and an Advocate of emancipation."[76] All the attributes of God, including omnipotence, are bound up in the sense of "Black theology," Jones asserts, that "our God is a God who gives persons the power to be and to become."[77] Jones's interpretation of God's omnipotence would seem applicable too to that unnameable force and energy which impels the creative being and becoming of many chronically ill people.

An even more precise connection between creativity and God's omnipotence can be found in the recent Duquoc and Floristan Concilium volume, *Where Is God? A Cry of Human Distress.* The edition reprints a sermon given by Gregory Baum after he had spent eight weeks of "total silence" with a stubborn viral infection which left him "completely demobilized."[78] There were times when his recovery looked uncertain, and Baum had to ponder what his response to severe chronic illness might be. His reflections led him to this perception of God: "God's omnipotence must be understood differently. Omnipotence refers . . . to God's limitless power to create, to redeem, to heal, to reconcile and restore. God here grounds and supports all of life and all of being."[79] For Baum, this means that God should not be expected to heal all ills or even to be able to. God instead should be expected to be a continuing life-force and freedom at work within, and sometimes in spite of, everything. For the chronically ill who create, it would seem to make great sense to believe that they have somehow encountered and even participated in God's omnipotence as they have found new routes to self-expression, new ways to make "artifacts," new means to propound a vision and to promote projects which serve human well-being. Jones, and Kushner, if he would permit the redefinition of "omnipotence," would seem to concur that God is encountered in impulses to altruism and liberation, which I believe, could be found at the heart of the motivation of many of the creative chronically ill mentioned in this article.

In summarizing this discussion of how theologies of suffering impact the creative chronically ill, I urge that these sufferers must recognize that ambiguities and unanswerables remain at large in theologies of suffering. Awkwardness and paradox will be confronted in any attempt to apply these theologies to their own situations. I propose that a degree of balance can be achieved if they would regard their illnesses as integrally bound up with their "vocations" but not as vocations in themselves. Along similar lines, I suggest that the creative chronically ill might recognize the call to "self-transcendence" as universal[80] and acknowledge that a variety of life experiences may catalyze the realization of that call: the demands of such numerous goods as love, parenthood, friendship, a profession, a ministry, any meaningful relationship or work; but also the challenge of such numerous evils as sickness, handicap, accident, death, divorce, unemployment, assault, any damage or trauma or relational breakdown. Thus, engagement in the creative process itself, as well as dealing with chronic illness, may in some sense move a person toward a greater capacity for self-transcendence. Suffering per se does not seem to be the one necessary factor.

Along with these observations about suffering as "vocation" or as invitation of "self-transcendence," I suggest that great care be exercised in any claim-making about the "redemptive suffering" of the chronically ill or anyone else. Suffering, it seems, is that which one ought to hope to be redeemed or liberated from, not redeemed or liberated by. Even the redemption enacted in Jesus of Nazareth can be seen as more a result of the unquenchable spirit of his attitudes, actions, message, and personhood than as the product of the suffocating and searing pain of crucifixion. The great drama of the Christian celebration of Passiontide and Easter need not be seen as a glorification of suffering. It can, rather, be seen as a demonstration that the "motif of glory," which John Paul II sees permeating the Pauline writings on the paschal mystery,[81] can override the motifs of crass injustice and gross suffering. For the creative person with a chronic illness, it seems most helpful to recall the message of the resurrection: that suffering may have to be endured for a variety of unfathomable reasons, but there is no call to concede its triumph. I agree, with the tradition, that there is "redemptive suffering," but I would hope that the "redemptiveness" of it would neither be identified with the suffering itself (as if it were a good) nor be interpreted as the "products" which creative personalities might generate amid their sufferings. Instead, I would like to see the redemptive nature of suffering understood as coming from that aspect of the human spirit and character which resists giving suffering final power. Not all people can experience suffering in this way-- inarticulate innocents, in particular. Thus, it seems to me that it has to be admitted honestly that some suffering is unredemptive.

Finally, it appears that the understanding of God's omnipotence advanced by Major Jones and Gregory Baum can be most beneficial in response to the question of what kind of God might be encountered by the creative person in chronic pain. What I wish to present in a closing personal reflection are three other attributes which might also be appropriately ascribed to the God met in such experience.

A Concluding Reflection

There is around Pittsburgh a bumper sticker which appears and reappears bearing, in rather inelegant language (slightly altered here), this message: Excrement Happens. I have also seen a counter-sign, offered in promotion of the Pittsburgh Symphony or WQED "Classical Underground," or some such, which proclaims this: Beauty Happens. My years of structuring much of my life around diabetes have convinced me of the former. My years of teaching, writing, singing, playing, and admiring great art, good liturgy, profound thought, and excellent people have displayed the truth of the latter.

While I am not sure that I understand the psychological-physiological interactions of my ailments and my creative moments, I can attest that an engaging project prevents my being too discouraged by a bad day or by the pain that the over-the-counter pain relievers barely seem to touch. I can also testify that the bad days slow me down and assure that I sit for a contemplative spell and that it is often in this enforced respite that my thoughts are reordered and I discover all the new things which I would like to do. I have never thought that God "chose" me to be diabetic or asthmatic. I will, however, admit that I regard many of life's goods and some individual talents as divine gifts. With Kushner, I believe that it is inaccurate to regard a disaster of health or weather as an "act of God." It seems fairer to regard it as an "act of nature."[82] And I will acknowledge that some few of those things which I count as "gifts from God" should also be regarded as "gifts of birth." In any case, the attempt to balance health, ministry, community living, and creative urges has led me to considerable musing about God's place in all of these.

One attribute of God which I find little reflection on is that of freedom. There are, of course, the Thomistic discussions about whether the creation of the world was a "necessary" or a "free" act. But what I miss in the tradition is much consideration of the idea that God is, has, and gives freedom. Even while we say that God is love and is wisdom, we rarely, if ever, go on to add that God is creativity or that God is creative freedom. It makes great sense to me as a diabetic to think of God as the one who has not only endowed human beings with freedom of choice but also has imbued all of creation with a kind of freedom. This means that viruses are free to provoke auto-immune responses in the islet cells of the pancreas which produce insulin; bacteria are free to grow, given an opportune setting; dust-mites and mildew are free to flourish, even if it means that members of another species find it hard to get their breath; volcanoes are free to erupt; rivers are free to overflow levees and banks; animals are free to follow instincts; earthquakes are free to set the earth and everything upon it trembling. Divine intervention would be only, if ever, by way of tremendous exception. For me, God's power or omnipotence is bound up with this type of freedom. Thus God's power is manifest in the persistence of beauty and goodness and the pleasure of human love and requires a deep reverence for the freedom of all creation which has allowed for the multiplicity and diversity of species and habitats. I feel that it is a great misconstrual to speak of God's power as if that meant the capability to do anything and everything.

The second attribute of God which I feel could stand much closer investigation and commentary is one more frequently acknowledged in the tradition. It is that of omnipresence. Lucien Richard gives the concept a kind of freshness of consideration. He notes that the Biblical treatment of God's role in suffering prompts further reflection on an ontology which "is not about being as such, but about being-with."[83] Such a God is the compassionate knower of pain and sharer of suffering. Major Jones has pointed out the centrality of belief in God's omnipresence in African-American theology.[84] Sallie McFague also avers, "The resurrection is a way of speaking about an awareness that the presence of God in Jesus is a permanent presence in our present."[85] A sense that God is ever at hand has empowered my own life journey and attuned me to the multiple "presences" of God, even in those moments when I have felt most alien and alone in illness.

Along with saying that the God I have encountered in creative undertakings and in illness is the God of freedom and of omnipresence, I want to say thirdly that God is the one who affirms and accepts the ventings of feelings and the visions of what might yet be. Such a God explains how the outcry which opens Psalm 22--"My God, my God, why have you forsaken me?" (v. 1)--can be transformed, by the end of the psalm, into the determined assertion, "And to him my soul shall live; my descendents shall serve him" (vv. 30-31). If Jung is right, as he seems to be, in his childbirth imagery, the creative things I have invested myself in might well be counted as my "descendents."

Job, for me, demonstrates superbly the manner in which God

allows for the human venting and visions and is part of that process which Scarry has called the "remaking" of the self and the world. Before the onset of his afflictions, Job was one of those who might have been deemed "gifted." He was more wealthy, successful, and fulfilled than most people of his time would have seemed to have been. He proved, amid the tests of suffering, to be more self-assured, persistent, and faith-filled than the average person. But Job was like anyone in his dismay at an onslaught of disasters which he had done nothing to bring on. And, like anyone in pain, he was understandably exasperated by his friends' pieties, platitudes, and belittling accusations. He protested, "Be silent, let me alone! that I may speak and give vent to my feelings!" (Job 13:13). In the end, after he had met God in the whirlwind, he conceded the incomprehensible splendor and complexity of the created world and the inscrutability of the mind of God. Yet he also acknowledged that, in the midst of his lamentations and questions and attempts to reorient his own vision, he had met God: "I have dealt with great things that I do not understand; things too wonderful for me, which I cannot know. I had heard of you by word of mouth, but now my eye has seen you" (Job 42:3,5). It seems worth noting that Job's story concludes with a massive restoration and creative "remaking" of his world.

I propose that for the notably creative among the chronically ill and chronically pained, the act of creation itself is a way of venting feelings while also forgetting, for a time, that each day entails difficulty and pain that would be happily jettisoned, if that were possible. The act of creating is a complex and paradoxical one: a way of dabbling "with great things that I do not understand" while trying to understand or even invent them. It is a way too, I believe, of attempting to see God, to partake of the Creator by participating in the work of creating, to come as close to touching the divine as the finger of Adam the earthling is to the finger of God in Michelangelo's agonized and ecstatic Sistine Chapel ceiling. Even the avowed atheist Stephen Hawking cannot resist characterizing the search for a "complete theory" of the universe as the human attempt to "know the mind of God."[86]

The question which continues to tantalize is, of course, what kind of God will be met by those who keep attempting to see. She may be a God, I am inclined to think, whose power is, a Lucien Richard says, after Rollo May, "neither power over, nor power against, nor power for, but power with."[87] She may be a very free and very responsive God who makes something up or makes something new when she winces with our pains or weeps our tears.

NOTES

1. Elaine Scarry, *The Body in Pain: The Making and Unmaking of the World* (New York: Oxford University Press, 1985), cf. 21, 35.

2. Ibid., 35.

3. Ibid., 218.

4. Scarry claims that "pain is like other forms of sentience but devoid of the self-extension that is ordinarily the counterpart of sentience," while "imagination is like other forms of the capacity for self-extension without the experienceable sentience on which it is premised." That is, one cannot really say what pain is or what pain is for. It is hard enough to say what it is like. It is virtually impossible to make pain real or concrete to others. One can, however, make up entire imaginary worlds, say what they are like, what they are or might be for, maybe even what they are. But one still cannot put real toads in imaginary gardens or imaginary toads really in real gardens (to borrow from poet Marianne Moore). It seems a natural impulse in pain to invent, to make something up. Perhaps that is because pain itself seems to blur the unreal and the real in our own consciousnesses. Both pain and imagination alter worlds--ours. Belief, Scarry says, "is what the act of imagining is called when the object created is credited with more reality . . . than oneself." (Scarry, 205).

5. Scarry, 161.

6. Ibid., 205.

7. Maureen A. Tilley, "The Ascetic Body and the (Un)Making of the World of the Martyr," *Journal of the American Academy of Religion*, 59 (1991): 467.

8. Phyllis Kaminski, "Embodied Passion: Reflections on the Meaning of the Cross and Pain and Pleasure in Feminist Theology," presented to Women and Religion section, Convention of the College Theology Society, 1992; typescript of the address, 2.

9. Scarry, 291.

10. Cf. Edith Barfoot, *The Witness of Edith Barfoot: The Joyful Vocation to Suffering*, ed. Basil Blackwell (Oxford: SLG Press, 1985), 3.

11. John Paul II, *On the Christian Meaning of Human Suffering: Salvifici Doloris* (Boston: Daughters of St. Paul, 1984), #2.

12. Lucien Richard identifies such varied voices as those of John Paul II and Carter Heyward with the claim that human suffering is, in light of the crucifixion and resurrection, redemptive. He also cites Schillebeeckx's counter-opinion that it is not suffering but the love "despite" suffering which is redemptive. Cf. Richard, *What Are*

They Saying About the Theology of Suffering? (New York: Paulist Press, 1992), 4, 7, 34.

13. Scarry, 307.

14. Cf. Paul Tournier, *Creative Suffering*, trans. Edwin Hudson (New York: Harper and Row, 1982). While Tournier begins with his own experience as an orphan, he broadens his psycho-spiritual considerations to those suffering from a variety of kinds of deprivation. Deprivation itself can be, he believes, the catalyst to creativity--as in the case of a number of handicapped authors (Tournier, 13). He does not believe that suffering in itself is the cause of creativity, but he insists that it can be "the occasion" which "gives rise" to it (58).

15. Elisabeth Young-Bruehl, *Creative Characters* (New York: Routledge, 1991). Young-Bruehl takes her psychoanalytic approach to "characterology." Among her subjects are such creative types as Sigmund Freud, William Butler Yeats, Simone Weil, Gertrude Stein, Virginia Woolf, Friedrich Nietzsche, and Marcel Proust. All of them are viewed as personalities whose psycho-emotional weaknesses shaped their creative pilgrimages. Her central theory is that "creative people . . . create whatever they create in the medium of, through the developmental lineaments and structures of, their characters. They have, consciously or unconsciously, an image of their characters, or, in other terms, of their general psychic (mind and body) organization, which they both aspire to--it is an idealized image--and project into whatever they create" (Young-Bruehl, x). Like Tournier, she seems to suggest that the afflictions of her subjects do not singly cause their creativity but do somehow impel it.

16. Jacques Barzun, *A Stroll with William James* (New York: Harper and Row, 1983), 29.

17. George Pickering, *Creative Malady: Illness in the Lives and Minds of Charles Darwin, Florence Nightingale, Mary Baker Eddy, Sigmund Freud, Marcel Proust, Elizabeth Barrett Browning* (New York: Oxford University Press, 1974), 8.

18. Norman Cousins, *Anatomy of an Illness as Perceived by the Patient: Reflections on Healing and Regeneration* (New York: Bantam Books, 1979), 74.

19. Ibid., 47-48.

20. Ibid., 68-69.

21. Ibid., 79.

22. Pickering, 183.

23. General observations concerning the narcotic or sedative effect of concentration are found in Jay B. Rohrlich, *Work and Love: The Crucial Balance* (New York: Summit Books, 1980).

24. Cf. Tilley, 467.

25. Susan Sontag, *Illness as Metaphor* (New York: Farrar, Straus and Giroux, 1978), 31.

26. Paul Valéry, "The Course in Poetics: First Lesson," in *The Creative Process: A Symposium*, ed. Brewster Ghiselin (New York: New American Library, 1952), 97.

27. Scarry, 307.

28. Ibid., 324.

29. Carl Gustav Jung, "Psychology and Literature," in Ghiselin, 222.

30. Ibid.

31. Michael White and John Gribbin, *Stephen Hawking: A Life in Science* (New York: Dutton, 1992), 61.

32. Ibid., viii.

33. Ibid., 165.

34. Interviews with Hawking by Dennis Overbye, Stephen Shames, Tony Osman, and by reporters for London's *Sunday Telegraph Magazine and Sunday Mirror* are quoted in White and Gribbin, 192.

35. Empereur elaborates on the notion that there is "a special vocation in the church of the sick and the aged." He also speaks of the Anointing of the Sick as a sacrament of initiation, a "liminal experience" preparatory for eternity. Cf. James L. Empereur, *Prophetic Anointing: God's Call to the Sick, the Elderly, and the Dying* (Wilmington: Michael Glazier, 1982), 141 ff.

36. Barfoot, in Blackwell, 3.

37. Ibid., 5.

38. Ibid., 6.

39. John Paul II, #26.

40. Dorothy Soelle, *Suffering*, trans. Everett R. Kalin (Philadelphia: Fortress Press, 1975), 107-108.

41. Ibid., 72.

42. Cf. Soelle's map of phases, 73

43. Barfoot, in Blackwell, 11.

44. John Paul II, #2.

45. Wolfgang Amadeus Mozart, "A Letter," in Ghiselin, 44-45.

46. White and Gribbin, 69.

47. Schillebeeckx is thus interpreted in Richard, 41.

48. Ibid., 64.

49. Ibid., 69.

50. Discussing Moltmann on theologia gloriae and theologia crucis, Richard observes: "These two theologies represent two different ways of knowing God: the

theology of glory knows God through his power as that is manifested in creation; the other knows God as hidden in the suffering and humiliation of the cross." Cf. Richard, 46.

51. Daniel Liderbach, *Why Do We Suffer? New Ways of Understanding* (New York: Paulist, 1992), 129-133.

52. Barfoot, in Blackwell, 8.

53. Richard, 45.

54. Soelle, 36-41.

55. John Paul II, #28-29.

56. Cf. Pickering on Florence Nightingale's manipulativeness and her heavy demands on those who served her, 122-127. One of Pickering's chapters about her is entitled "The Tyrannical Invalid."

57. Cf. for example, the commentary on Auschwitz and human inability "to take burning children seriously," in Kenneth Surin, *Theology and the Problem of Evil* (New York: Basil Blackwell, 1986), 144-151. Calling this "sin" is my own interpretation.

58. Soelle, 143.

59. Sallie McFague, *Models of God: Theology for an Ecological, Nuclear Age* (Philadelphia, Fortress Press, 1987), 169.

60. Ibid., 19.

61. C. S. Lewis, *The Problem of Pain* (New York: Macmillan, 1944), 76.

62. A striking undoing of Lewis's certainties about pain and suffering occurred as he dealt with his wife's death. *A Grief Observed* (New York: Seabury Press, 1961) narrates his inability to make sense of his wife's sufferings and his incapacity for applying some of his earlier published convictions to his situation.

63. Albert W. J. Harper, *The Theodicy of Suffering* (San Francisco: Mellen Research University Press, 1990), 10-16.

64. Ibid., 58.

65. Ibid., 83.

66. As he interprets the story of Job, for example, Kushner argues that the author of the sacred text "is prepared to give up his belief in [the] proposition . . . that God is all-powerful." Cf. Harold S. Kushner, *When Bad Things Happen to Good People* (New York: Avon Books, 1981), 42 ff.

67. Ibid., 84-85.

68. Ibid., 127.

69. Ibid., 139.

70. Major J. Jones, *The Color of God: The Concept of God in Afro-American Thought* (Macon: Mercer University Press, 1987), 53.

71. Ibid., 84.

72. Ibid., 86.

73. Ibid., 87.

74. Ibid., 95-96.

75. Ibid., 109.

76. Ibid., 110-111.

77. Ibid., 117.

78. Gregory Baum, "Sickness and the Silence of God," in *Where Is God? A Cry of Human Distress*, ed. Christian Duquoc and Casiano Floristan (London: SCM Press, 1992), 23.

79. Ibid., 25.

80. The whole of a book by Walter Conn is based on the premise that self-transcendence is the essence of human authenticity. Cf. Walter Conn, *Conscience and Self-Transcendence* (Birmingham: Religious Education Press, 1981).

81. John Paul II, #21.

82. Kushner, 59.

83. Richard, 125.

84. Jones, 63.

85. McFague, 59.

86. Stephen Hawking, *A Brief History of Time: From the Big Bang to Black Holes* (New York: Bantam Books, 1988), 175.

87. Richard, 128.

Rosemary Haughton on

Spirituality and Sexuality

Joy Milos, C.S.J.

To raise questions about 'the body and theology' will often times raise questions related to sexuality as well. In this essay I propose to focus on the insights of Rosemary Haughton as she relates sexuality and spirituality. Early in Haughton's writing career, Charles Davis' prophetic praise of her theology summarized three key elements which would, I believe, provide a framework for her writings on sexuality. These are her "brilliant and authentic use of the Pauline distinction between flesh and spirit, the enlightening way she develops and handles the concept of passion, and her understanding of the symbolic function of sex."[1] Variations of these themes appear and reappear in her work and they will provide a general direction for this essay. In order to establish Rosemary Haughton as a contemporary theologian and significant contributor to the discussion regarding a Christian appreciation of human sexuality and spirituality, a brief biographical sketch seems appropriate.

A Biographical Introduction

Probably Britain's best known woman theologian, Rosemary Haughton was born in 1927 of an American father, Peter Luling, and an English Jewish mother. Since her mother, Sylvia Thompson, was a novelist, Haughton grew up in and absorbed her literary environment, as is evident from the most casual survey of her writings. It was her own reading that brought her to convert from Anglicanism to Roman Catholicism at age sixteen.[2]

Haughton attended Queens College, London. She then met and married Algy Haughton in 1948. They soon began their first 'com-

munal' experiment with the founding of a family-style school in
Wales. When it proved too much for them, he took a teaching
position at Ampleforth and she began her writing career to supplement the family income. By the late 1960's, with ten children of
their own, the Haughtons responded to their community dream once
again. Eventually that dream became a reality in the foundation of
a year-round community, Lothlorien.

This was to be an educational venture whose impetus went
beyond their original educational zeal. As she recounted, there were
many factors contributing to their decision to sell their home and
belongings to purchase land in Galloway, Scotland, about seventy
miles south of Glasgow:

> The experience of a large family, the Christian values which we
> tried to live by and which so clearly could not be made to fit the
> values of a consumer society; the search of the young ones for
> different patterns of family and life-style; the universal need (be-
> coming yearly more apparent) for a simpler and less resource-
> wasteful way of life--all these began to come together.[3]

Borrowed from Tolkein's *Lord of the Rings*, Lothlorien was the
Elves' woodland kingdom where the worn and weary travelers found
refuge, refreshment, and new wisdom in their near-hopeless opposition to the Enemy who seemed everywhere victorious. As Haughton
described it, "It was not an escape, but a stronghold of sanity and
hope in a world under threat of death and worse. From it, the
pilgrims go out with fresh courage to fight the shadow."[4] Thus their
ideal of community proved a haven that would be for many an
intermediary step toward an integration of personal issues and values, one that enabled members to move out and on to their own
journeys once again.

What began with Haughton family members soon expanded to
include young people with various problems, individuals at different
points in life and personal pilgrimages, and other families. What they
created together was something of a 'wisdom community,' one which
drew upon resources from Christian tradition, from the spirituality
of the East, from the native lore of Findhorn, from fairy tales and
from Jewish tradition. In the midst of this foundation, Rosemary
Haughton continued her writing and ever-increasing lecture tours, all
of which helped underwrite their expenses.

Her lecturing brought Haughton more and more frequently to
the United States and by the 1970's she had shifted her center of

gravity here after extensive consultation on the matter. With full support from her husband and family, she began to spend most of the year in the States and only a few months in Britain, seeing her new call as the founding of a unique missionary movement aimed at inner city and rural poor. Her first attempts at creating this new community failed and led to both physical and emotional exhaustion. She later teamed with Nancy Schwoyer and together they established Wellspring House in Gloucester, Massachusetts. This 'house church' and its base community has offered housing and welcome to many, including abused women, teens in trouble, and the elderly.

Haughton's interest in alternate communal models of Christianity has continued and took the form of the Movement for North American Missions in 1982. In launching this movement, Schwoyer and Haughton did not see it as a missionary order in the traditional sense. Rather, their orientation sessions and extended formation period in a poverty area try to respond to new needs in new modes of religious commitment. As all of these new communal ventures have been evolving, Haughton has continued as a much sought after lecturer and a prolific writer.

HAUGHTON'S THEOLOGY AND WRITINGS

Since Rosemary Haughton has not shared a traditional or typical theological education and formation,[5] one might suspect that her approach to theologizing would be equally atypical. Such suspicions seem well grounded when one considers the corpus of her writings. Trying to systematize and analyze her works proves about as easy as grasping mercurial beads. But her presence has made a difference and has not gone unnoticed in the theological arena. Writers on topics ranging from imagination, saints and conversion to fairy tales and sexuality frequently refer to Rosemary Haughton. She is a woman who defies categorization, mainly due to the breadth of her interests and the uniqueness of her position as a contemporary theologian.

Haughton's 1966 book, *On Trying to Be Human*, is prophetic of the rest of her literary efforts. They all somehow touch on the human project, and all under the umbrella of the Christian story. In more than thirty books and numerous articles, she concentrates on such issues as scriptures and the people of the Bible; their descendants, the saints; family concerns; human relationships, marriage and sexuality; faith life and religious education; fairy tales and stories as media for the message of the Good News; conversion; the community life of Christians, both in the past and as possibilities for the future; the dailiness of Christian living; human experience as the basis for theology. Although she deals with concerns common to other Christian writers, she does so in an uncommon manner. She is a true eclectic in both interests and sources, always molding them with a genuine creativity. As theologian Charles Davis commented about her, "She is a writer of astonishing originality. Her thoughts are always her own, and she uses language in a fresh, personal way that avoids all the tired phrases common in most religious writing."[6]

In remarks about *The Passionate God*, Mary Collins provides perhaps the best categorical observation about Haughton when she refers to her work as wisdom literature, "the genre in which Rosemary Haughton excels."[7] True to the wisdom tradition of scripture, Rosemary Haughton manages to discover God in the commonplace, in the experience of daily life and in relationships. As she envisions Christian life, all of these are the ingredients of spirituality if one takes the Christian myth of the Incarnation seriously. If Yeats' insight is true, that there is one "myth for every person, which if we knew it would make us understand all that the person did and thought,"[8] I believe that for Haughton the mythic framework provided by the story of the Incarnation has offered that insight. It is from within her focus on the Incarnation that Haughton's interest in the relationship between sexuality and spirituality has emerged.

A cursory glance through the titles and topics of Rosemary Haughton's books and articles substantiates the claim that sexuality is a topic that has long fascinated her. Among her titles one finds *Acts of Love* (1968), *The Holiness of Sex* (1969), *Love* (1970), *The Theology of Marriage* (1971), *The Mystery of Sexuality* (1972).[9] Among other writings, where the concentration is not so obvious, sexuality is the vehicle used to convey significant insights regarding the human and Christian condition. Thus, in *The Transformation of Man*, her now classic study of conversion, Haughton uses a sexual encounter to illustrate the gradual movement from formation to transformation.[10] In *The Theology of Experience*, an intuitive understanding of sexuality is the foundation of a major section of the book.[11] *On Trying to Be Human* presents several chapters focusing on relationships, passion, and persons in community, ideas which are constant themes in her writing about sexuality.[12] Her series of articles on "Creation Sexuality" in the *National Catholic Reporter* is evidently the refinement of several themes which had been present in seed form in many earlier works.[13] This becomes more evident in her later book, *The Passionate God*, a work to which I will return.[14]

Within this wide range of books and reflections, Haughton pursues several recurring themes or areas of research involving sexuality. Her early study on marriage propelled her into the wide-ranging exploration of the historical evolution of marriage as an institution. In the process, she incorporated insights from theology, anthropology, literature, psychology and history. The period of the early middle ages ignited her fascination with the concept of Romantic love and, more specifically, 'passionate' love, both of which will appear frequently in her writings. From these areas of interest she shifted in several works into an investigation of the Catharist movement and other basically anti-body belief systems, all with the intent of offering positive alternatives to our past negativities regarding sexuality and bodiliness. This is particularly true of her writings about marriage.

Another undercurrent in her writing on the topic of sexuality is the relationship between the sexes, an area which is certainly of major interest in contemporary circles. Here she has built upon a basically Jungian foundation in a positive manner, but one that feminist readers might challenge in their critique of Jung's usage of stereotypical descriptions of masculine and feminine characteristics.

In light of this brief overview, it should be clear that the topic of sexuality is one which Rosemary Haughton has long explored from several perspectives and over a significant period of her writing career. In order to explore in greater depth her insights on the topic, I will now return to the three previously mentioned categories that Charles Davis had praised Haughton for: the spirit/flesh distinction; and her appreciation of sex and symbol; her use of the concept of passion.

SPIRIT AND FLESH

To appreciate Haughton's discussion of the relationship between spirit and flesh, one needs to start within her broader cosmic framework. Before turning to life in the particular, she believes it is necessary to think about the bigger picture--about creation, about the meaning of sin and redemption, and, ultimately, about the Incarnation. The rest of her thought makes little sense unless one realizes this Christian anthropological concern. It is logical to her, therefore, to raise several related questions before creating a theology of sexuality.

How can we make sense of being sexual creatures if we don't

have sensible ideas about being creatures? And how can we cope realistically with the appalling moral problems in the area of sexuality if we don't understand why human beings have moral problems? And how can we discover a Christian direction in all this if we don't have in our very guts, the sense of what it means to be 'in Christ'?[15]

To be fully alive is to move ever more deeply 'into Christ.' In her quest to "examine the experience of human life and see if and how Christianity illuminates the search for the fullness of being human,"[16] she finds the physical, the bodily, and the sexual aspects of life essential. These aspects are not extraneous matters if one takes the Incarnation seriously, for

Christianity is, far more than any other, a physical religion, which is one reason why many spiritually minded people find it gross and fleshly, and try to refine it and 'spiritualize' it. But it is inescapably 'fleshly,' being founded in the human flesh of . . . Christ.[17]

Christianity is not an 'extra' set of facts about the human condition. For Haughton it is the only way to take all the facts seriously and provide a meaningful explanation of the human condition.

We are indeed made in the image and likeness of God, a likeness most perfectly manifested in the humanity of Christ. Haughton proposes that this image is "expressed most of all in the many kinds and levels of exchange between the sexes."[18] She says this because of her overriding belief that sexuality is such an intrinsic and important aspect of being human and that human relationships are reflective of our human/divine relationship. Haughton finds this way of perceiving the person to be an integrating one, and one that is verified by human experience. She also believes it counters our frequent temptation to divide ourselves into compartments or categories, for example, mental, moral, biological, or emotional. This very tendency to divide rather than integrate leads to the living of that division, which "is one of the most powerful manifestations of sin, creating barriers within as well as between us."[19] Thus, there is a necessary connection between sin, redemption, and our bodiliness. Sexuality, then, like creation, sin, and redemption, has a mysterious, cosmic, yet familiar ring about it.

In spite of her advocacy for seeing sexualiity as part of this larger picture, there is a definite realism grounding her thought. As she observes, "Sex is 'usually found attached to a person of some sort,' which simply means that sexuality is *ordinary*."[20] Sexuality is about people, it's at the heart of our familiar selves, it's about being human and having human feelings. Sexual relationships cannot be separated from other types of human relationships. Neither can one, in a Freudian reductionistic sense, 'reduce' all other kinds of relationships to some kind of sexual category. As she observes in *The Mystery of Sexuality*, "Sexuality is the whole sexual nature of [a person], and it is his [or her] nature even if he [or she] never takes part in sexual activity at all and is (or thinks he [or she] is) quite uninterested in sex."[21] This 'mystery' is at the heart of our familiar selves, it is "ourselves as we live with other people we love . . . in individual relationships and in groups and communities."[22] As such it is not either necessarily good or bad, threatening, uncontrollable, or fearful. All these aspects are interconnected with the rest of life. The tenor of one's sexual relationships will simply reflect the overall direction of one's other choices and relationships and vice versa.

For Haughton, 'spirit' and 'flesh' in the Pauline sense, are directional choices one makes in living as a sexual person. One may opt for openness to God and others or for self-enclosure. As she characterizes sexuality, she describes it as mixed up with our loves and hopes, our jokes and worries. It is spiritual, earthy, crude, and sublime. "Our most exalted visions and our basest bits of self-indulgence are expressions of the same sexual nature."[23] Those choices that are life-giving, loving, other enriching are of the 'spirit.' Those that are selfish, uncreative and sterile are of the 'flesh.'

To probe the heart of the mystery of sexuality, rather than to romanticize or dread its reality, Haughton urges that "we have to be honest with ourselves and know ourselves to be capable of evil as well as good."[24] This basic honesty is needed to ward off the temptation of the past (and present) to dissociate our being sexual from our being equally spiritual. This spirit/flesh dualism, a pretense at being 'spiritually minded,' ultimately has a negative impact on both sexual and spiritual development. As Haughton presents it, the unfolding of human sexuality is also the unfolding of the human spirit, at least potentially. A stunting of growth happens when sexuality is kept separated from the rest of life. Using a picturesque analogy, Haughton describes this unbalanced effect. Individuals "may be highly intelligent, shrewd, capable, even kind and idealistic, but at best they grow crooked, like a tree that has been struck by lightning on one side, but the other continues to grow. The effect is interesting, but grotesque and pathetic."[25] This is true of the celibate or married person. Pretense achieves nothing for either the celibate pretending to be asexual or for the married person who views sexual activity as a matter of duty or 'legitimate' pleasure. Haughton suggests that in both cases it is the loving surrender to the necessities of one's state in life in relationship to one's sexuality "that brings about the repeated 'dying,' and leads ultimately to the total death, the complete liberation of the real self."[26] This is part of the ongoing rhythm and final end of Christian life. It is the ever-daily dying of fully living an incarnate life. Thus, rather than a Neo-platonic escapist attitude toward the body/soul dualism, Haughton advocates the necessity, omnipresence, and potential goodness of sexuality in any human life that is holy or spiritual. It is part of the mystery of being creature, sinner, and yet redeemed.

SEX AND SYMBOL

> "Shaping experience into meaningful patterns is the unceasing activity of the symbol-making animal."
>
> --John Shea, *Stories of God*

Since Haughton uses the category of 'mystery' when speaking of the relationship between sexuality and Christian spirituality, it is not surprising that she ultimately resorts to symbol and myth as a form for structuring her discussion. For that matter, this imaginative use of the Christian symbol and mythic system may prove to be her chief creative contribution to furthering a positive understanding of that relationship.

Haughton may not have the 'typical' theologian's credentials or background regarding degrees and education. What she does possess is a wealth of human experience, carefully reflected upon, and it is to this experience that she repeatedly turns with the conviction that a depth analysis of it is the chief source of any vital theology. Of course, part of the wealth of her human experience is the rich literary background which has nurtured her throughout her lifetime. It is primarily from this background that she draws the tools with which to communicate her own theologizing. These tools provide the necessary skills "shaping experience into meaningful patterns," for myth-making, an art which she uses skillfully to weave together the Christian story and contemporary human experience.

If one of Haughton's primary commitments as a theologian has been her use of human experience in theology, her appreciation of *intuition* has been a significant factor in her interpretation of that experience. By definition, she notes, "intuition is . . . a direct kind of knowledge" in contrast to the indirect knowing that the intellect must translate.[27] Intuitive knowledge is "partly an instant reaction *to* or *by* deeply absorbed symbols . . . and partly something of the nature of telepathy or 'second-sight'."[28] Among her early writings, especially in *The Theology of Human Experience*, Haughton pleads for and then defends her stance of taking more than a purely rational approach to the theological enterprise, especially in its interpretation of sexuality. She does so with spirited praise for the role of imagination and intuition in the knowing process. Along with this apologia, she takes pointed aim at the over-valued emphasis on scientific and systematic intellectualizing, an attack that may well provide some explanation for the lack of serious critical study of Haughton's work. Her plea on behalf of intuition rests on the belief that it is a direct and truer kind of knowing, whereas more rationally based study is indirect, goes through at least one translation in the process, and often many others before being communicated. Focusing on the intellect as the most valued human ability is, she proposes, the occupational hazard of the scientist and philosopher and the constant refrain of the mystic and poet.[29]

Taking a snipe at the systematic, overly-intellectualized approach to theology, Haughton suggests that an overemphasis on the human intellect may even be a "sort of evolutionary compensation for the loss (or non-achievement?) of a more perfect kind of knowledge."[30] Perhaps the intellect is the crutch rather than the crown, and intuition (inspired guess-work?) is the real channel of the Spirit. This way of knowing which the more 'tidy-minded' will find wholly unsatisfactory may ultimately prove more genuinely creative of theology that speaks meaningfully to people today. The questions she raises appear legitimate. Might not this approach uncover whole new ways of perceiving reality, of overcoming past dualisms, of connecting experiences in creative new ways? Might not this be part of what is needed in the creation of a positive, yet realistic Christian appreciation of sexuality?[31]

And yet, Haughton recognizes that there is an inherent problem in relying solely upon intuitive knowledge. By its very nature, a formulation of intuitive understanding is verified by the internal resonance of someone else who hears it, the classic *cor ad cor loquitur* experience. Of course, anyone by temperament or training suspicious of intuitive experience will probably find attempts at this type of theologizing inadequate. But then again, Haughton finds this reaction indicative of a kind of sickness, one far from uncommon, and "usually a matter of pride to those who suffer from it!"[32] Undaunted, she has held her own.

With this epistemological bent in mind, one might better understand Haughton's preoccupation with symbol, poetry and myth as her preferred media for communicating theological truth. These, rather than the more exacting, totally logical and clear methodologies of her theological peers are her natural habitat. Poetry, symbol and myth are essentials in her writings. As she indicates, poetry is not simply the illustration of prose, a simple adding of imagery. Rather, it is "the most accurate way in which some inkling of an incommunicable experience can be communicated."[33] Haughton believes that poetry is actually essential for an accurate description of any sphere of experience beyond the mundane and everyday. It is the only real medium for answering fundamental human questions. Thus, she views theology as nothing more than "a particular exacting kind of poetry."[34] Since, in her estimation, so many trained academicians presently miss the significance and importance of real human experience in their theological pursuits, her aim is to provide an alternate vision of reality and theology through the mediation of poetry, symbol and myth, the natural languages of mystery, and thus to arrive at true wisdom. To find her approach fleshed out in more detail, one has only to turn to *The Theology of Human Experience*. There, drawing primarily upon poetic resources, she seeks to discover the significance of sexuality in human experience.

In this work, Haughton investigates the intuitions of great poets throughout the ages as they have attempted to express their understanding of sexuality in human life. She turns to poets, since they are the ones who have reacted so creatively to the symbolic depths of daily living. Might they not, then, provide the great key to interpreting sexuality? Not necessarily. Even here in the poet's realm, she finds something missing in the over-all exposition and intuition. In her final analysis, even many of the Christian poets of the past have failed to arrive at a holistic understanding of sexuality. This is so because they lacked an adequate mythic construct which was all-encompassing enough to include both the passionate and procreative aspects of sexuality. Her personal project turned toward providing a creative alternative to other the intuitions that fell short in their promise of comprehensiveness and ultimacy as they related to the meaning of sexuality. In this earlier period Haughton used Christian symbols to start weaving her own tapestry of Christian myth. In a more recent work, one that has the potential for becoming another classic, she returns to a long held fascination with the concept of 'passion,' the third element for which Charles Davis long ago praised her. In the process she also further develops her own mythic construct.

THE PASSIONATE GOD

In her "Creation Sexuality" series, Haughton previewed the perspective that was to be evident in her major work, *The Passionate God*. Her article, "Divine Love Breaking through into Human Experience,"[35] provides a synopsis of the same. What has happened in these writings is a convergence of many themes, images, and symbols that have been remarkably consistent in Haughton's literary and theological efforts. What emerges is a mature vision of a more consistent (though no less creative) theological system, one that will not abandon her commitment to both human experience and poetry as parts of the theological endeavor. The final section of this essay will highlight several of these convergent streams of thoughts and imagery, with special note of how she deals with the question of the relationship between sexuality and spirituality.

Haughton's thesis in *The Passionate God* is her belief that

we can begin to make sense of the way God loves people if we look very carefully at the way people love people, and in particular at the way of love we can refer to as 'passionate' because that kind of love tells us things about how love operates which we could not otherwise know.[36]

By passion she is emphasizing not only the gentle, restful, kind experience of love, but also the strong, wanting, needy movement toward encounter which the image evokes. It is simultaneously a violent and passive image. It "implies a certain helplessness, a suffering and undergoing for the sake of what is desired and, implicitly, the possibility of a tragic outcome."[37] This, she believes, is true of both divine and human love. And the examination of both is the focus of this book.

The realm of spirituality will never be limited to the 'spiritual' dimensions of life in Rosemary Haughton's thought, if by that one means the isolated, disincarnated, ethereal aspects of human existence in relation to God. Her search for the meaning of Incarnation has been a life-long one, and here she views it specifically as a manifestation of the passionate love of God for creation. It is the breaking through of God into creation and history, a changing of both of the latter, and an elevating of both in the process. This image of 'breakthrough' is one of her myth-making components. As she has described it, a breakthrough event is an "impulse--of need, of love, of will-to-power--[which] manages to overcome some obstacle and pass through to a new and desired sphere of existence."[38] Breakthroughs occur in the physical world (e.g., a dam breaking), in the personal, in the mystical and in the scientific worlds. For Haughton, Incarnation is the great breakthrough, one which "involves every level of reality from the most basic particles to the ultimate Being of God."[39] Therefore, this manner of exchange conceptually offers a means of overcoming the past body/soul, spiritual/physical dualism that has plagued us. When it comes to the question of motivation of the divine-human or human-human breakthrough experience of love, passion provides the answer.

In her earlier writings, Haughton had explored the intricacies of medieval Romantic love and passion. Romantic love concentrated on the experiences of passion, "the release of spiritual power, in and between, a man and woman through their specifically sexual but not primarily genital, encounters. Passion . . . was the chief means whereby men and women might move into a different and more exalted sphere of experience."[40] Haughton proposes that the cultural 'breakthrough' of Romance came about in order to celebrate the fact of spiritual breakthrough between men and women, whole, bodily, and in love. It is something of an antidote to the sterile and legalistic medieval understanding of Christian marriage. This recovery of the bodily dimension of encounter and love is one which she believes is still necessary today. The doctrine of Romanticism, with its emphasis on passion, is essentially dynamic and transformative because of the power of the love involved. Its language and imagery are, therefore, apt theological language for expressing the sense of reality as Exchange[41] according to Haughton's reading.

In *The Passionate God* as in her reflections on 'spirit and flesh,' Haughton again begins her story with cosmic overtones. She starts with a Trinitarian theology that is cast in terms of the Exchange of Life within the Godhead and proceeds to the doctrine of creation as the overflow of this dynamic love. And yet, humanity as potentially most open and responsive to this Exchange, can and has refused exchange. "Human beings distort the nature of reality by stopping the 'flow' of exchanged love."[42] Here enters the reality of sin and the need for redemption and a new breakthrough experience in human history, namely, the Incarnation. As human and bodily,

Jesus is as much involved in the network of bodily exchanges in creation as any other human being. But at this point in the network there exploded the force of perfect love. It changed the sinful situation from within. The flow of exchanged life, dammed up by sin, was in him released into the exchanges of life in all creation, thus justifying forever the folly of all good lovers who are convinced that real love exists. This is redemption.[43]

Incarnation, therefore, makes the on-going process of exchange of life physical-yet-spiritual to the core.

Sexual exchanges become one particular way that we can image the mutual Exchange of Infinite Love. "The exchange of life in sexual relationship, in many kinds of living beings, displays in a symbolic fact of huge power the nature of exchange which gives life."[44] Haughton returns to the interconnectedness of creation, sin, incarnation and redemption with a frequent refrain: they are all bodily exchanges, bodily facts, no matter our temptation to 'spiritualize' them. In the context of "these tremendous and awesome exchanges, the bodiliness of sexual exchange begins to make sense."[45] Bodily beings are meant to be in exchange, as is the whole of creation. One of the facets of expressing this passionate breakthrough of loving exchange will be sexual experience. Without it one cannot enter into the flow of life in the world or respond to the divine exchange which is the ultimate source of holiness and spirituality.

Just as the passion of God broke through in Christ in an expression of the inner love of the Trinity, Haughton believes that it is breaking through once more. To try to explain how this occurs, she searches for and resorts to a meaningful myth which will enable the contemporary reader to breakthrough to the depth realization of this passion of God for humanity and their own for one another. She does so in the hope that it will evoke new breakthrough experiences, which she does not find happening within many other theological frameworks today.

CONCLUSIONS

In her dedication of *The Passionate God*, Rosemary Haughton provides, I believe, a summary statement of her contribution to Christian reflection on spirituality and its relationship to sexuality. Quoting T.S. Eliot, she dedicates the work to the Company of friends of Wisdom for whom the "hint half-guessed, the gift half understood is Incarnation. [H]ere the impossible union of the spheres of existence is actual."[46] From her earliest writings, she has herself been a friend and advocate of Wisdom, a Wisdom that she has defined as "simply the apprehension of God in human experience through its whole extent."[47] For her, intuition of the divine is only half-guessed, half understood until one discovers the 'breakthrough' experience of God in the mystery of the Incarnation. Then everything else falls into place within the Christian mythic framework.

If John Shea's insight into the role of myth is correct, Haughton appears to have made a distinctive contribution to the theological discussion of the relationship between sexuality and spirituality. In *Stories of God*, he suggests that human myth-making establishes the inner meaning and ultimate values of life situations while structuring consciousness, encouraging attitudes, and suggesting behavior. He further proposes that the "ultimate home of myths are the primordial situations of human existence," such as "experiences of birth and death, reverence and awe, the relationship with nature, the hope of an after-life, etc."[48] Myth's final ambition is to become the "structure of consciousness through which human situations will be appropriated."[49] These are the very occasions into whicht Rosemary Haughton has consistently delved in her search for an accurate contemporary expression of Christian theology and myth.

For Haughton, the root myth that gives unity and meaning to all of human existence is the Incarnation, with the whole gamut of events which that encompasses in the life of Christ and the Christian. Thus she constantly asks, in one form or another, "What happens if we take the Incarnation seriously?" What are the "radical implications of the poetic and scandalous statement that God became, and remains, human."[50] And her answer is always delivered with 'passion,' both stylistically and thematically. Her consuming passion seems to be the discovery of the motivation of divine-human and human-human love, the primordial reality of existence, as her previously stated thesis of *The Passionate God* declares. Since she is really exploring a "phenomenology of divine love for, in, through and between people, which means the entire, mysterious and infinitely complex system of inter-relationships which is creation, and the Creator in creation,"[51] the experience of sexuality is a dynamic force within this greater picture. It is an essential element since it is an intrinsic part of human nature, and anything that is truly human is embraced and blessed in the Incarnation.

Thus, one cannot appreciate Rosemary Haughton's understanding of the relationship between spirituality and sexuality without some appreciation of her larger project and story. Her quest for a contemporary mythic framework leads her from historical and theological research to the intuitive world of poetry as best expressive of reality which is always greater than the words that express it. From her first explorations of the poetic intuition of the experience of sexuality in *The Theology of Human Experience*, she has moved to an broader appreciation of Christian symbolism and myth in *The Passionate God*. She clearly senses that symbols capture the depth meaning of experience and reality, and she eventually moves toward an interweaving of various Christian symbols into a more coherent story form. In more recent writings on the topic of sexuality, she presents the fruit of her quest by incorporating by-now familiar images into a more comprehensive mythic formulation. She does so with an effectiveness which makes her work a distinctive contribution to the Christian discussion of spirituality and sexuality.

NOTES

1. Charles Davis, "Introduction," in *On Trying to Be Human* (Springfield, Ill.: Templegate, 1966), 9.

2. The following articles were sources for this sketch: Arthur Jones, "One Woman's Progress," *The Tablet* 238 (January 28, 1984): 79-80; Rosemary Haughton, "Lothlorien," *Sign* 53 (February 1974): 13; Rosemary Haughton, "Lothlorien: Where I Have to Be," *Sign* 56 (February 1977): 25-31.

3. Haughton, "Lothlorien," 13.

4. Ibid.

5. Haughton continued her own education through her love of reading and research into her many books, articles and lectures.

6. Charles Davis, *On Trying to Be Human* (Springfield, Ill.: Templegate, 1966), 9.

7. Mary Collins as cited on the dust cover of *The Passionate God* (New York: Paulist Press, 1981).

8. Cited by Dana Greene, *Evelyn Underhill: Artist of the Infinite Life* (New York: Crossroad, 1990), 6.

9. Rosemary Haughton, *Act of Love* (London: G. Chapman, 1968); *The Holiness of Sex* (St. Meinrad, Ind.: Abbey Press, 1969); *Love* (London: C.A. Watts & Co. Ltd., 1970); *The Mystery of Human Sexuality* (New York: Paulist Press, 1981); *The Theology of Marriage* (Cork: The Mercer Press, 1971).

10. Rosemary Haughton, *The Transformation of Man* (Springfield, Ill.: Templegate, 1967), Chapter 2.

11. Rosemary Haughton, *The Theology of Experience* (Paramus, N.J.: Newman Press, 1972), Chapter 6.

12. Haughton, *On Trying to Be Human*, Chapters 3,4,5.

13. Rosemary Haughton, "Creation Sexuality," a series of articles published in the *National Catholic Reporter 15* (June 1: 1+; June 15: 11; June 29: 16; July 13: 24; July 27: 24; August 10: 28, 1979).

14. Rosemary Haughton, *The Passionate God* (New York: Paulist Press, 1981).

15. Rosemary Haughton, "In Exchange with God," *National Catholic Reporter* 15 (June 1, 1979): 1.

16. Haughton, *On Trying to Be Human*, 14.

17. Rosemary Haughton, *Beginning Life in Christ* (Westminster, Md.: The Newman Press, 1969), 38.

18. Rosemary Haughton, "Creation Sexuality," *National Catholic Reporter* 15 (June 29, 1979): 16.

19. Ibid.

20. Haughton, *The Mystery of Sexuality*, 31.

21. Ibid., 10.

22. Ibid., 32.

23. Ibid., 31.

24. Ibid., 31-31.

25. Ibid., 37.

26. Haughton, *The Theology of Experience*, 138.

27. Ibid.,121.

28. Ibid., 122.

29. Ibid., 121.

30. Ibid., 122.

31. Haughton's insights seem prophetic of the growing body of writing on the various constructions of knowledge that has fascinated theologians, philosophers, and educators in recent years.

32. Ibid., 120.

33. Haughton, *The Passionate God*, 3.

34. Ibid., 5.

35. Rosemary Haughton, "Divine Love Breaking through into Human Experience," *International Review of Mission* 71 (January 1982): 20-28.

36. Haughton, *The Passionate God*, 6.

37. Ibid.

38. Ibid., 18.

39. Ibid.

40. Ibid., 45.

41. In using the Doctrine of the Exchange as part of her own mythic construct, Haughton is drawing on the literary image created by British novelist-poet-theologian-dramatist, Charles Williams. For further exploration of Williams' theology see W.R. Irwin, "Christian Doctrine and the Tactics of Romance," in *Shadows of Imagination* (Carbondale and Edwardsville: Southern Illinois University Press, 1969), 139-149; Glen Cavaliero, *Charles Williams, Poet of Theology* (Grand Rapids, Mi.: Wm. B. Eerdmans Publishing Company, 1983); and Charles Williams, *War in Heaven* (New York: Pellegrini and Cudahy, 1949).

42. Haughton, "Creation Sexuality," *National Catholic Reporter* 15 (June 9, 1979), 11.

43. Ibid.

44. Haughton, "In Exchange with God," 8.

45. Haughton, "Creation Sexuality," 11.

46. Cf. the dedication to *The Passionate God*.

47. Ibid., 4.

48. John Shea, *Stories of God* (New York: Paulist Press, 1978), 52.

49. Ibid.

50. *The Passionate God*, 6.

51. Ibid.

Spirituality as an Academic Discipline:

Reflections from Experience

Sandra M. Schneiders

Introduction

In articles published in the last few years I have written about the history of the study of spirituality and about the relationship of the field of spirituality to the theological disciplines. In those articles I cited most of the relevant literature on the subject. Walter Principe in his article entitled "Christian Spirituality," in *The New Dictionary of Catholic Spirituality* which appeared this year, has brought this discussion up to date. Since these materials are readily available I will not revisit them here but will reflect on the subject of "Spirituality as an Academic Discipline" out of my experience of founding and directing for the past sixteen years a Ph.D. program in Christian Spirituality at the Graduate Theological Union in Berkeley. With my students and colleagues I have struggled to define the field of spirituality, to clarify its material and formal objects, to relate it without separation or confusion to other sacred and secular disciplines, to develop an appropriate methodology, and to formulate an intelligible theory of the discipline which can be accepted by the broad range of scholars now working in the field of spirituality. The longer we have worked at the theoretical elaboration of this new field of study the more serious and complicated the questions have appeared.

During these years I have been challenged by theologians who think that spirituality, like brushing one's teeth, is absolutely necessary but should be done in private and definitely not for credit; by historians who think that spirituality, like happiness, is a term that should not be applied until its subject is quite dead; by psychologists who think that spirituality is the word pious types use for what normal people would call good mental health; and by scholars of religion who maintain that the competent study of any religion will include an objective account of whatever the term spirituality covers. While the attempt to gain recognition for the field has been frustrating at times, the opposition has forced me to reflect a good deal more on the subject of what the field of spirituality is, includes, aims at, and can contribute than would have been the case if the sailing through the academy's waters had been smoother. We probably have not yet earned the right to a permanent and licensed berth in the marina of academe but at least there is some recognition that what has sailed in with "spirituality" stenciled on its prow is indeed a ship of some sort, however unique it may appear in comparison with the stately disciplinary vessels already tied at the dock. I hope my reflections this morning on the results of our experience will stimulate some further discussion and clarification about this field that, in my opinion, is here to stay.

THE PROBLEMS IN DEFINING THE FIELD

Let me begin by trying to describe the problems we face in attempting to establish some theoretical clarity about the field of study of spirituality. After laying out the issues in each area I will indicate my own position. (Incidentally, unless I specifically state otherwise I am speaking now of Christian Spirituality as an academic field even though the term spirituality is increasingly being used for analogous non-Christian studies.) The problems concern principally three dimensions of the field: the appropriate purpose of the study of spirituality; the subject matter of the field; and methodology.

A. *The Purpose*: Spirituality as a field of study is analogous to art in one respect, namely, that one can legitimately study it for any of several quite distinct purposes. One can, for example, study the violin in order to learn to play it; in order to understand the theoretical aspects of music such as harmony and composition; in order to appreciate music even if one never actually plays an instrument; in order to understand the historical development of violin music including its chief figures, movements, etc.; or in order to become qualified to teach some aspect of music. In general, a person specializing in any of the five areas would know something of the other four. But how the areas are related, which if any has priority, how much of each one must know to be considered competent in the field of music in general and violin in particular, how talented and/or accomplished in the field one has to be to be considered educated, are very complicated questions. One thing is certain: there is such a field as music with a specialization in the violin and it is perfectly legitimate to study it.

Spirituality as a field is comparable in complexity. Some people want to study spirituality in order to learn how to live the spiritual life. Others want to understand it theoretically, its structure and function, its relation to theology or psychology or social context. Others are trying to appreciate spirituality as a powerful force in human affairs. Still others want to understand its development, know something about its most important movements and figures. And some people are primarily motivated by the desire to learn how to facilitate the spiritual life of others. Obviously, all of these purposes are interrelated and ideally a person in the field is concerned with all of them. But the question arises about how these aspects of spirituality are related to each other, which if any has priority, how much of each one must know in order to be considered competent in the field of spirituality, how gifted and/or accomplished in the spiritual life one must be to be considered educated in the field. For those of us in the field one thing is not open to question, namely, the existence of spirituality and the legitimacy of studying it.

There is no question about the fact that living the spiritual life has an ontological and existential priority over studying it, just as actually playing the violin has priority over studying music. But there is also no question about the fact that very, very few people will become accomplished in the spiritual life without studying it in some way, whether theoretical or practical, just as very few people become accomplished musicians without studying music. The question raised by these observations is how the study of spirituality, especially the academic study, is related to the living of spirituality. Is, or must, the primary purpose of the study of spirituality be the improved living of the spiritual life either by the student or by those whom the student will assist or guide in the spiritual life? Is experience of living the spiritual life necessary for its study? And how is it possible to judge this performative aspect? We will return to these questions at the end, but for the moment my purpose is to lay out the questions.

B. *The Subject Matter*: A second and closely related cluster of questions bears on the subject matter of the field of spirituality. In regard to its subject matter, the field of spirituality is analogous to the field of psychology. The primary application of the term psychology is to that dimension of the human subject in virtue of which

210   BROKEN AND WHOLE

the person is a relatively autonomous self, i.e., a center of personal consciousness and subjectivity. In this sense, everyone has a psychology or is a psychological entity. But the term psychology also applies to the experimental and theoretical academic study of human subjectivity and to the clinical disciplines aimed at the therapeutic fostering of healthy subjectivity.

Analogously, the primary application of the term spirituality is to that dimension of the human subject in virtue of which the person is capable of self-transcending integration in relation to the Ultimate, whatever that Ultimate is for the person in question. In this sense, every human being has a capacity for spirituality or is a spiritual being. But the term spirituality also applies to the experimental and theoretical study of human efforts at self-transcending integration and to the pastoral practices aimed at fostering the spirituality of individuals and groups.

This double application of the term spirituality, i.e., to a dimension of all human beings and the actualization of that capacity, and to the study of that dimension, raises two clusters of problems for those of us trying to define the field of study called spirituality. First, because spirituality is a dimension of the human subject as such many scholars doubt that the field of spirituality has or can delineate a specific subject matter. Is not spirituality simply an aspect of an experientially based theology or the application of good theology in daily living? Is not spirituality part and parcel of any adequately inclusive study of the history of Christianity? Is not attention to spirituality what differentiates transpersonal psychology from reductionistic, naturalistic, or mechanistic forms of psychology? Is not spirituality, in its multiform manifestations, part of what is studied and compared by the scientific scholar of religions? In other words, is spirituality not a dimension of or an approach to the subject matter of such established disciplines as theology, history of Christianity, transpersonal psychology, comparative religion? Is there a distinctive subject matter for this new field?

The second cluster of problems raised by the double application of the term spirituality is related to the previous section's concern with the multiple purposes for the study of spirituality. There are many people engaged in higher education, especially in seminaries and at the undergraduate and masters levels, who see the primary purpose of the inclusion of spirituality in the academic curriculum to be the development of the spiritual life of the students, particularly if these students are to become ministers in the Church. Furthermore, there are many students who want to enroll in courses and/or programs in spirituality primarily for the development of their own spiritual lives and/or to become competent facilitators of the spiritual lives of others. Again, the analogy with the field of psychology is evident. Many students go into the field of psychology first and foremost to understand themselves and to foster their own, and eventually others', personal development. We might call this approach to psychology or spirituality a primarily formative approach to the field of study.

Those whose focus is primarily on this formative study of spirituality tend to take a much more theologically focused and often denominational approach to the field. Their approach is closer to what used to be called "spiritual theology," i.e., the application of systematic and moral theology to the daily life and practice of the believer. Such scholars, both teachers and students, want to include in their courses in spirituality instruction in and practice of prayer within the tradition, liturgical celebration, group sharing of personal spiritual histories, journaling, social outreach, discernment, and so on. In these courses the religious tradition is normative and the primary purpose of studying it is to appropriate it personally. It is not difficult to understand the severe misgivings of most academics about the appropriateness of including such frankly formative studies in the curriculum of academic disciplines.

However, there is another type of scholar in the field of spirituality. These scholars are interested in the experimental and theoretical study of religious experience in its concrete and individual manifestations. In other words, they are research scholars whose object is to understand, theoretically and practically, the lived experience of God and to try to clarify this phenomenon in all its multiplicity and uniqueness and power. They are concerned with the conditions of possibility of such experience, its actual occurrence, the variety of religious experience, the structure and dynamics of such experience, the criteria of adequacy of such experiences, the effect of social context and theological milieu on religious experience, the expression of religious experience in literature, art, and social construction, and so on. Except for the fact that such researchers are studying the actual human experience of God rather than a purely "natural" phenomenon such as a social movement or a chemical reaction, there is no difference between the objective of the scholar of spirituality and that of the historian or natural scientist, namely, to understand the phenomenon in question. What makes mainline academics nervous about the research discipline of spirituality is the possibility of the "formative" approach leaking into the research project and, of course, the presuppositions about the existence and accessibility of God that are operative in the attempt to study the experience of God.

I think it can be said that there is real tension today in the field of spirituality between the "formative approach" and the "research approach." It often enough comes out in the language itself, with the former tending to prefer the terminology of "spiritual theology" and the latter that of "spirituality." In any case, a good deal of conversation is going to be needed to mediate these two clusters of concerns. Those concerned with formation fear that researchers in the field are "objectifying" and thus rendering irrelevant what is essentially personal and existential. Research scholars in the field tend to share fellow scholars' doubts about the appropriateness of formation programs in the academy. Research scholars tend to identify with the transformative potential of understanding rather than the formative objectives of guided practice.

As I will explain further in my conclusion to these reflections, my own tendency is to see the two projects, formation in spirituality and research-oriented study of spirituality as related but distinct. The formative approach, which is necessary and valuable, has its appropriate setting in the practical part of the seminary curriculum, as an optional and voluntary component of religious studies at the undergraduate level, and as central to practical masters degrees aimed at forming ministers in the field of spirituality. Spirituality as a research discipline is also absolutely necessary if we are to come to understand with theoretical depth and acuity the powerful dynamics of the human experience of God in its incredible complexity and mysterious simplicity. The appropriate place for this discipline is in higher education, specifically at the research masters and doctoral level. But just as we incorporate the best of technical biblical research into undergraduate and seminary courses on the Bible and the best of literary theory into lower level courses in literature, so the best research in spirituality should be incorporated into more practically and personally oriented courses in spirituality whose more direct aim may be the spiritual development of the students.

C. *Methodology*: These considerations lead directly into the third area of reflection about the field of spirituality, namely, the confusion in regard to methodology. Here I would like to raise two sets of issues, the first having to do with the disciplinary aspect and the second with procedures in the field.

Three distinct approaches to methodology seem to be emerging among scholars in the field of spirituality. For the moment they are being tagged the "theological approach," the "historical approach," and the "anthropological approach." The most traditional is the theological. Scholars who take a theological approach tend to be those most interested in the formative type of study of spirituality. They see spirituality as the living experience of that which theology sets forth conceptually and theoretically. In an older form, this led to a deductive approach to spirituality in which the conclusions of dogmatic and moral theology became the principles for both understanding and practicing the spiritual life.

Today, this deductive approach is greatly relativized by the recognized importance of experience. Theology is invoked today not to dictate or determine experience but to clarify, evaluate, validate or correct what is experienced, whether by a contemporary person or group or an historical figure or movement. The Trinitarian, ecclesial, sacramental, and moral presuppositions of spirituality are taken for granted. Questions concern not the importance or centrality of these features but how they are to be understood, incorporated, and utilized in prayer and life. A good example of this type of approach to the field of spirituality is the volume edited by Jones, Wainwright, and Yarnold called *The Study of Spirituality*, especially Part I or Kenneth Leech's *Experiencing God* which is significantly subtitled "Theology as Spirituality."

The historical approach to the field of spirituality is a somewhat more recent development. Its inception can be traced back to the beginning of this century when the burgeoning of interest in historical studies in general led to the writing of the first histories of Christian spirituality, and the beginning of encyclopedic historical projects such as the *Dictionnaire de Spiritualité*. Basic to the historical approach is the conviction that the only really reliable access to the lived experience of faith is the documents (in the broad sense of "historical artifacts") left by those who have had such experiences. In other words, spirituality can only be studied in actual instances and these are only available in historical sources.

However, as the field of history itself continues to develop there is increasing variety in historical approaches to spirituality. The attempts in the 1950's, such as that of Louis Bouyer and his colleagues, to write a comprehensive history of western Christian spirituality has been complemented by the "collection of expert essays" approach exemplified in the twenty-five volume Crossroad *Encyclopedia of World Spirituality* and the critical textual approach of the sixty volume Paulist Press Classics of Western Spirituality and Classics of American Spirituality series. Philip Sheldrake's *Spirituality and*

History raises theoretical questions about the very nature of history and how it functions in relation to spirituality. And Bernard McGinn, in his monumental *The Foundations of Mysticism*, exemplifies an analytical historical approach to a particular dimension of spirituality, namely mysticism. Increasingly, scholars interested in the historical approach are turning to particular topics such as the use of Scripture in spirituality, or particular periods such as the Middle Ages, or particular challenges to historical interpretation such as the role of women or attitudes toward the body in the spirituality of particular epochs.

There is no doubt at all that historical study is basic to any work in the field of spirituality in much the same way that field work is essential to cultural anthropology or scientific surveys are to sociology. History provides a large part of the positive data upon which theoretical reflection in the field of spirituality rests. The question that arises, however, is whether in fact the field of spirituality is reducible finally to the history of spirituality. In other words, is there anything to study other than the experience of people who preceded? Is there any legitimate way of studying spirituality except that of discovering, describing, analyzing, and criticizing what we find in historical records of one kind or another?

The third approach, which has been dubbed the anthropological approach, responds to the question raised by the historians with a firm "yes," there are indeed other questions to study than historically framed and answerable ones. As far as I know, Jean-Claude Breton of the Université de Montréal coined the term "anthropological approach" to describe his own approach to the study of spirituality in contrast to the deductive and dogmatic theological approach of Charles-Andre Bernard of the Gregorian University. Essentially, the anthropological approach takes as its starting point neither the theological tradition that informs or governs Christian spiritual experience nor the historical record of spiritual experience but the spirituality intrinsic to the human subject as such. In other words, it is the anthropological structures and functioning of the person as a subject called to self-transcending integration within an horizon of Ultimacy which raise and shape the questions and suggest the appropriate resources for the study of spirituality. Spirituality does not characterize us primarily as Christians but first of all as humans.

The immediate methodological implication of the anthropological approach is that spirituality is seen as a cross-cultural, inter-religious, and inter-disciplinary field of study that is essentially descriptive, analytical, critical, and constructive. Jill Raitt remarked in her paper that she recognized Christianity as the religion of "her tribe" but not as the exclusive, normative, or determinative religion for all people. Similarly, the anthropological approach to Christian spirituality recognizes Christian spirituality as one realization or actualization of the human capacity for the life-integrating experience of the Transcendent, which, in Christian terms, is God revealed in Jesus Christ and communicated to us by the Spirit in the Church. Christian spirituality then must be studied in the context of all the spiritualities of the world, some of which are not Christian or even religious, many of which are not western or literarily articulated or theologically explicated. The methodological approach to the study of some aspect of Christian spirituality is not determined beforehand as essentially biblical or theological even though these disciplines will play some role in any study of Christian spirituality, not because it is a spirituality but because it is Christian. Rather, the researcher must determine what methods--historical, sociological, psychological, artistic, scientific, biblical, comparative, theological, feminist, literary, etc.--are suitable and necessary in order to investigate the spirituality phenomenon which is under consideration. The researcher must then construct the methodology, i.e., the articulated combination of diverse methods, which will "do the job" as the researcher has defined it.

There is no doubt that the anthropological approach with its necessarily inter-disciplinary methodology is much more complex and difficult to handle than the strictly theological or historical approaches which are determined by the methodologies of a single discipline. But the advantage of the anthropological approach is that it puts the scholar of spirituality in the very center of the wider scholarly discussion of the human enterprise as a whole rather than in a religious or theological enclave.

The final question in this third cluster of issues, namely the methodological cluster, bears upon the role of practices or personal involvement in the academic study of spirituality. Should the student of spirituality be a practicing religious person? Should that practice be operative in his or her research? If so, to what extent and how? And how can such involvement be controlled so that it does not contaminate research with subjectivistic biases or skew it to inappropriate personal agendas?

Obviously, those who espouse a formative approach to the study of spirituality vigorously promote the actual practice of the spirituality which the student is being encouraged to appropriate. But what of those who take a research approach? In my experience all students of spirituality are, in fact, spiritually involved people. I have yet to meet a student in our program, or a scholar in the field of spirituality, who had a purely theoretical interest in spirituality. In other words, all of the students I have encountered are using personal experience of the spiritual life as a source of questions, as analogical data, as comparative resource, as an indicator for validation or falsification. Furthermore, we require all doctoral students in spirituality in our program to engage in a year-long practicum, which is not an internship aimed at developing their skills in leading or fostering spirituality in others, but is an engagement with the actual spirituality of some other people. The purpose of the practicum is to bring the student into contact with living spiritual experience other than her or his own. So, from two directions, namely, personal introspection and involvement with the spirituality of actual others, the research student is making use of lived spirituality as a resource for the study of spirituality.

However, as a research-oriented scholar I would not make extensive use of students' personal spiritual journeys in the classroom or assign ongoing spiritual practice or require subjective reporting of personal practice. Nor would I attempt to evaluate, much less grade, a student's personal spirituality or insinuate myself, in the context of academic advising, into the spiritual life of a student. In my opinion, personal involvement in spirituality on the part of research scholars in spirituality is quite analogous to the personal involvement of psychologists in their own psychological growth. Obviously, the spirituality student or scholar is going to be engaged in a continuous dialogue between her or his own spiritual experience and whatever she or he is studying. Furthermore, introspection will be a primary source of data and criticism as the student encounters new material in the field. The more the student learns about spirituality the more deeply he or she will interiorize what is being learned. But the academic study of spirituality as a research discipline cannot, in my opinion, involve a specifically catechetical or formative practice without contaminating the properly (not positivistic) objective character of the research.

CONCLUSION

By way of conclusion I would like to summarize for you my own position in regard to each of the clusters of issues I have raised, not because my position is necessarily better than other positions but in order to give you a concrete example of what consciously articulating choices in each of these areas results in.

First, I recognize that there are many purposes for studying spirituality but I do not think all of them are appropriately pursued in the academy. Specifically, I believe that, although learning to live the spiritual life and to foster the spiritual life of others are important purposes for the study of spirituality they are more appropriately pursued in other settings such as formation programs, practically oriented masters programs, internships and the like. This is not to say that the academic study of spirituality will not foster a student's own development nor that growth in the spiritual life will not deepen and enrich the student's research but only that personal spiritual development is not the primary direct objective of spirituality as an academic discipline.

Secondly, in regard to the subject matter of the field of spirituality, I would maintain that spirituality is a distinct field of study. I think that spirituality as a field is in roughly the same position that sociology was about fifty years ago or psychology seventy years ago. At those times there were scholars who were interested in studying phenomena they intuitively knew existed but which were not the precise object of any recognized discipline, namely, relationships as such, and the human psychic structure and function. Today there are scholars who want to study religious experience as such, not just the subject of such experience, or the ritual and credal and moral expressions of such experience, or the history of such experience, but the experience itself. It is going to take some time to delineate precisely the subject matter of this new field and to distinguish it adequately from that of other fields but we know that we are interested in studying something that exists and that does not fit precisely into any of the existing fields of study. The birth last year of the Society for the Study of Christian Spirituality and the appearance last month of the first issue of its official organ, The Christian Spirituality Bulletin, indicates a growing consensus and confidence among scholars in this new field.

Obviously, from what I have already said, I would situate myself among those students of spirituality who are concerned with research in the field of spirituality rather than with the spiritual formation of students. I believe that excellent research, especially as it is published, will serve the purposes of formation at the undergraduate and practical masters levels and in the seminary as well as resourcing the efforts of believers in their own spiritual quests. But I think that this service is an indirect result of first rate research, not the direct objective of the field of spirituality itself.

Finally, I situate myself among those taking an "anthropological approach" to spirituality and thus espousing an inter-disciplinary, cross- cultural, and inter-religious methodology for the study of Christian spirituality. I think that this is necessary if spirituality is to be a full and credible participant in the scholarly enterprise of humanistic study. The world is too small and the stakes are too high to privatize religion or ghettoize spirituality. The religious wars in places from Bosnia to Ireland, the tragedies of Waco and Jonestown, the aimlessness of our young people and the despair of our elderly as well as the power of a Cesar Chavez or a Dorothy Day and the eloquent testimony of mystics and martyrs of past and present are sufficient evidence of the incredible power of lived religion, i.e., of spirituality, for good and for ill. This phenomenon, the human phenomenon of the God-quest, is eminently worth our intense study and that study has to engage the best efforts of people from every location, religious tradition, gender, race, and personal interest.

Finally, my self-location in the research area of the field governs my approach to practice in relation to spirituality. I seriously doubt that anyone who is not involved in her or his own spiritual life will have the insight and sensitivity to the subject matter necessary for first-rate research in the field of spirituality. And I also doubt that anyone who seriously works in this field will fail to experience the transformative effects of deeper understanding in her or his own spiritual life. But just as I do not think that formation in the spirit-ual life is an appropriate direct objective of the academic study of spirituality I do not think that personal practice should be an explicit factor in most research projects. There is certainly a place, even in the academic setting, for practical programs in spirituality whose aim is the spiritual development of the participants or their training for ministry in the area of spirituality. And within such programs the incorporation of the results of research scholarship in the field of spirituality is of critical importance. But the two agendas are distinct and in my opinion should not be confused or conflated.

In short, I would define the academic field of Christian spiritual-ity as the inter-disciplinary study of Christian religious experience as Christian, as religious, and as experience for the purpose of under-standing it theoretically and allowing that understanding to serve as an intellectual resource for the living of the spiritual life and a basis for productive interchange among the spiritual traditions of the world.

About the Contributors

WILLIAM C. FRENCH is Associate Professor in the Theology Department of Loyola University, Chicago. His research focuses on ecological ethics, theology, and peace and conflict studies.

JAMES GAFFNEY is Professor of Ethics in the Department of Religious Studies of Loyola University, New Orleans. The author of seven books and the editor of two, he has contributed portions of ten other books and published many articles in more than thirty different journals.

MORNY JOY is Associate Professor in the Department of Religious Studies, University of Calgary. She has published articles on women and religion, and contemporary continental philosophy. She is currently President of the Canadian Society for the Study of Religion.

WILLIAM LOEWE is Associate Professor in the Department of Religion and Religious Education at the Catholic University of America. His teaching and research focus on Christology, soteriology, and Lonergan studies.

WILLIAM MADGES is Associate Professor in the Theology Department of Xavier University, Cincinnati, Ohio. He is the author or co-author of three books and has published articles dealing with nineteenth-century theology in journals such as *The Journal of Religion* and the *Heythrop Journal*.

GARY MANN teaches systematic and constructive theology at Augustana College in Rock Island, Illinois. He received an M. Div. from Wartburg Theological Seminary, Dubuque (1980) and a Ph. D. in Theology and Religious Studies from Drew University in Madison, New Jersey (1988). He previously served Lutheran parishes in New Jersey and taught part-time at the Lutheran Theological Seminary in Philadelphiaa and at Stockton State College in New Jersey.

FREDERICK G. MCLEOD is a member of the Society of Jesus of the New England Province. Since receiving a doctorate in Ecclesiastical

Oriental Studies at Rome in 1973, he has taught at St. Louis University. His major work is a critical text and translation of the homilies of Narsai, a fifth-century East Syrian theologian, which were published in the *Patrologia Orientalis* in 1979.

JOHN P. MCCARTHY received his Ph.D. from the University of Chicago in 1986. He is currently Associate Professor in the Department of Theology, Loyola University Chicago.

MARGARET R. MILES is Bussey Professor of Historical Theology at the Harvard University Divinity School. Her books include *Desire and Delight, A New Reading of Augustine's Confessions* (Crossroad, 1992), *Carnal Knowing: Female Nakedness and Religious Meaning in the Christian West* (Vintage, 1991), and *Image as Insight* (Beacon, 1985). Her interests focus on religious and cultural constructions of body, desire and gender.

JOY MILOS, C.S.J. received her Ph.D. in Christian Spirituality from the Catholic University of America. She is presently a member of the Religious Studies Faculty of Gonzaga University in Spokane, Washington. One of her major areas of interest is women's experience of God, with special focus on women in the Anglican Tradition.

JILL RAITT is Professor in the Religious Studies Department of the University of Missouri, Columbia. She has published extensively on the history of Christianity in Europe. Her most recent works include *Christian Spirituality in the High Middle Ages*(Crossroad, 1987) and *The Colloquy of Montbeiard: Religion and Politics in the Sixteenth Century*(Oxford, 1993).

SUSAN A. ROSS is Associate professor in the Theology Department and Director of the Women's Studies Program at Loyola University Chicago. She is working on a book on women, the body, and the sacraments.

SANDRA M. SCHNEIDERS is Professor of New Testament Studies and Christian Spirituality at the Jesuit School of Theology and the Graduate Theological Union in Berkeley, California. She founded the doctoral program in Christian Spirituality at the Graduate Theological Union, is co-editor of the *Christian Spirituality Bulletin*, and is a member of the steering committee of the Society for the Study of Christian Spirituality.

PAMELA A. SMITH, SS.C.M. is a doctoral candidate at Duquesne University and teaches in the theology departments of both Duquesne and Carlow College in Pittsburgh. She is the author of four books: *Waymakers: Eyewitnesses to the Christ* (Ave Maria, 1982); *WomanStory: Biblical Models for Our Time* (Twenty-Third, 1992); *Life After Easter: Mystagogia for Everyone* (Paulist, 1993); *Woman-Gifts: Biblical Models for Forming Church* (Twenty-Third, 1994).

MAUREEN A. TILLEY is Assistant Professor in the Department of Religion at The Florida State University in Tallahassee where she teaches classes in the history of Christianity. Her articles on martyrdom and Donatism have appeared in *Studia Patristica*, the *Journal of the American Academy of Religion*, the *Harvard Theological Review*, and *Church History*.